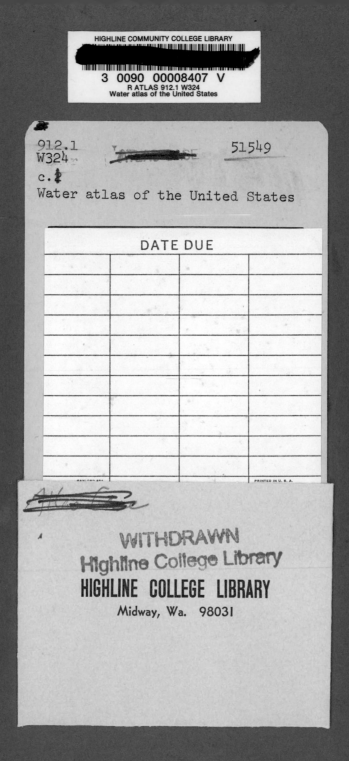

DATE DUE			

PRINTED IN U. S. A.

WATER ATLAS *of the* UNITED STATES

AUTHORS

> JAMES J. GERAGHTY
> DAVID W. MILLER
> FRITS VAN DER LEEDEN
> FRED L. TROISE

CARTOGRAPHERS

> MIKLOS PINTHER
> ROBERT S. COLLINS

JAMES J. GERAGHTY and **DAVID W. MILLER** are officers of Geraghty & Miller Inc., a consulting firm specializing in ground-water studies. Both men are recognized specialists in the field of water resources and serve as advisors to a wide variety of public and private organizations in the United States and abroad. **FRITS VAN DER LEEDEN** is a senior member of the professional staff of Geraghty & Miller and has had extensive experience in the compilation and evaluation of worldwide basic water information. He is also the author of *Ground Water—a Selected Bibliography,* published by the Water Information Center in 1971. This greatly expanded edition of the Water Atlas was assembled under his supervision. **FRED L. TROISE** is Director of Publications of the Water Information Center. In this capacity he actively participated in the preparation and publication of this new edition of the Atlas.

MIKLOS PINTHER is Chief Cartographer of the American Geographical Society. He served as a private consultant and prepared and scribed the major part of the Atlas maps. **ROBERT S. COLLINS,** geographer, designed the maps and layout of the two former editions. **TED SIECZKOWSKI** assisted in the conversion of the statistics into graphic form.

LORETTA JOHNSON and **MARIE EDMONDS** of the Geraghty & Miller staff prepared manuscripts and completed the working drafts of the text. **DOUGLAS MacCALLUM** contributed a number of the text descriptions.

WATER ATLAS *of the* UNITED STATES

GERAGHTY • MILLER • VAN DER LEEDEN • TROISE

A WATER INFORMATION CENTER PUBLICATION — 44 Sintsink Drive East, Port Washington, N.Y. 11050

Third Edition

Library of Congress Catalog Card Number: 73-76649

ISBN: 0-912394-03-X

Printed in the United States of America

Text Composed by Trotta Composition, Inc.
Printed by Williams & Heintz Map Corporation
Bound by The Optic Bindery, Inc.

Preface

The Water Atlas of the United States is the only available, comprehensive, visual guide to the water situation in the United States. The first edition was published in 1962, and consisted of 40 maps covering subjects related to water resources and water use. This new up-dated edition has a total of 122 maps with subject matter that has been expanded to include water pollution and water quality, water conservation, water law, and water-based recreation. Also new in this edition are 36 maps covering Alaska and Hawaii.

The basic purpose of the Atlas is to present complex national water data in a readily understandable form. Some of the maps used in the book were acquired from governmental and private sources, whereas others were developed by the authors and have not been seen before. All the maps have been modified and drawn on a similar base so that the reader can compare data from map to map. The text description accompanying each map contains facts and statistics that could not be expressed on the map itself. All time-dependent information has been identified by date so that the reader can judge its relation to the current situation.

It is hoped that this new expanded edition of the Water Atlas of the United States will prove more useful and receive even wider acceptance than the very popular original edition. The authors and the publisher would like to regard this book as a contribution to help the International Hydrological Decade program fulfill its expressed need for practical water resources publications.

The many comments and suggestions received from readers of the original version have been taken into account in the preparation of the new edition. The authors will welcome and appreciate similar comments and advice on how to make this new Atlas even better.

THE AUTHORS

Port Washington
May 28, 1973

Contents

Contents (Continued)

LIST OF PLATES

WATER ATLAS *of the* UNITED STATES

PLATE 1 – PHYSIOGRAPHY

The conterminous United States extends from the Pacific Ocean on the west to the Atlantic Ocean on the east and from Canada on the north to Mexico and the Gulf of Mexico on the south and is located more or less centrally in the temperate zone of the northern hemisphere. Its total area is 3,022,387 square miles and its principal geographic features are: a mountainous region covering approximately the western third of the country, a central area of plains and relatively flat lands covering 45 percent of the country, and an eastern region consisting of a coastal plain along the ocean and an inland chain of mountains and hills extending from the northern tip of Maine southward to Georgia.

Topography determines the drainage patterns of surface-water resources. From a broad viewpoint, for example, rain or snow falling on the nation is diverted toward either the Pacific Ocean or the Atlantic Ocean and the Gulf of Mexico. The Continental Divide runs more or less north-south along the crest of the Rocky Mountains and constitutes the boundary between these two major drainage systems.

PLATE 1   WATER ATLAS

Physiography

By Erwin Raisz, 1954

PLATE 2 – DISTRIBUTION OF PRECIPITATION

Precipitation is the water that falls on the surface of the land as rain, snow, and sleet. The map shows lines, called contours or isohyets, that connect points of equal precipitation. The numbers on the contours represent the average number of inches of water falling on the land in a year.

The amount of precipitation in any particular locality usually varies from year to year, but over a long period, its average is more or less constant. The average annual precipitation in the United States is different from place to place owing to the great size of the continental land mass, the long mountain chains that partly block the flow of moist air, the presence of open seas on three sides, and the directions of flow of air masses.

Precipitation is the basic source of the nation's water supply. The total amount received in an average year is 1,570 trillion gallons, which is equivalent to a layer of water about 30 inches thick over the entire country.

Among the heaviest rainfalls ever observed in the United States were 1.23 inches in one minute in Unionville, Maryland; 12 inches in 42 minutes in Holt, Missouri; and 19 inches in 70 minutes in Rockport, West Virginia.

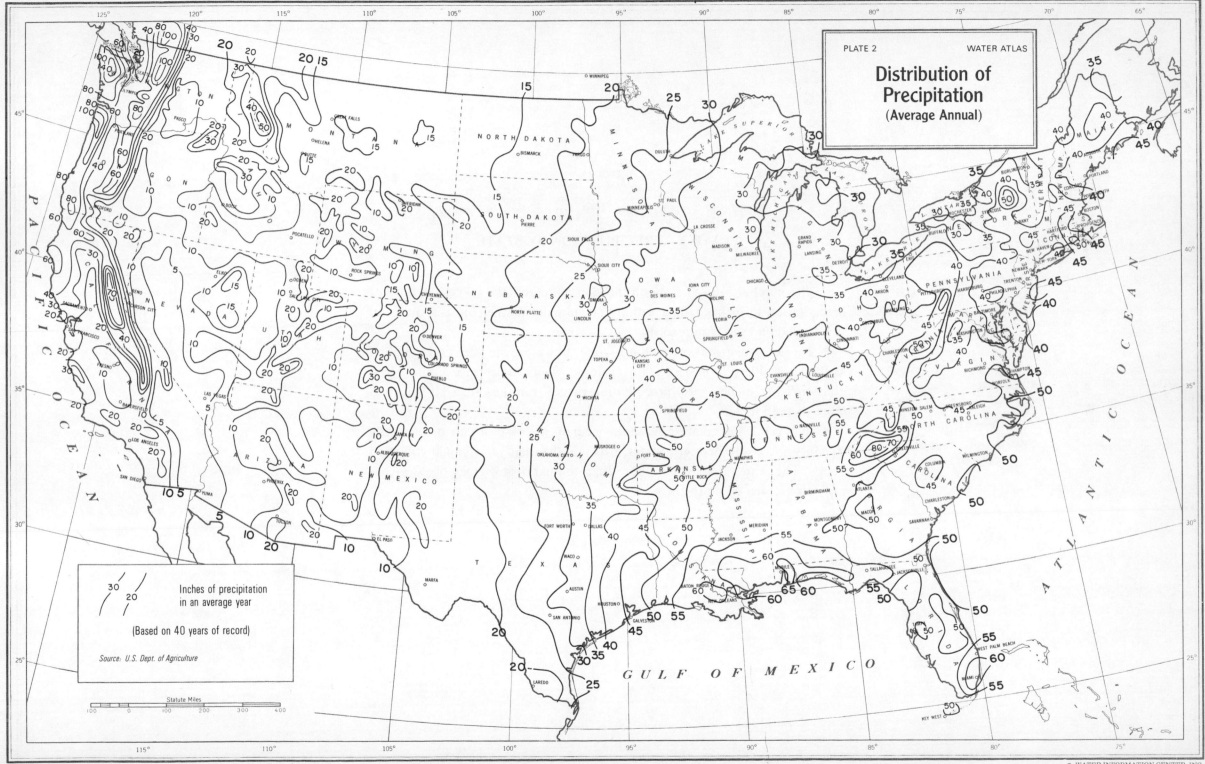

PLATE 2   WATER ATLAS

Distribution of Precipitation
(Average Annual)

Inches of precipitation
in an average year

(Based on 40 years of record)

Source: U.S. Dept. of Agriculture

Statute Miles

Base Map by U.S.C.&G.S.

© WATER INFORMATION CENTER, INC.

PLATE 3 – PRECIPITATION BY STATE

The number in each state on the map represents the average amount of precipitation in inches falling within that state during the course of a typical year, based on long-term records.

The local distribution within a state, however, can vary considerably, as shown on Plate 2. In Texas, for example, where the average annual precipitation is 31 inches, local precipitation ranges from less than 10 inches to more than 50 inches.

In general, the greatest amounts occur in the eastern part of the country. In some of the Western States, it is less than half that in many Eastern States. The states that receive more than the national average of 30 inches per year are shaded on the map.

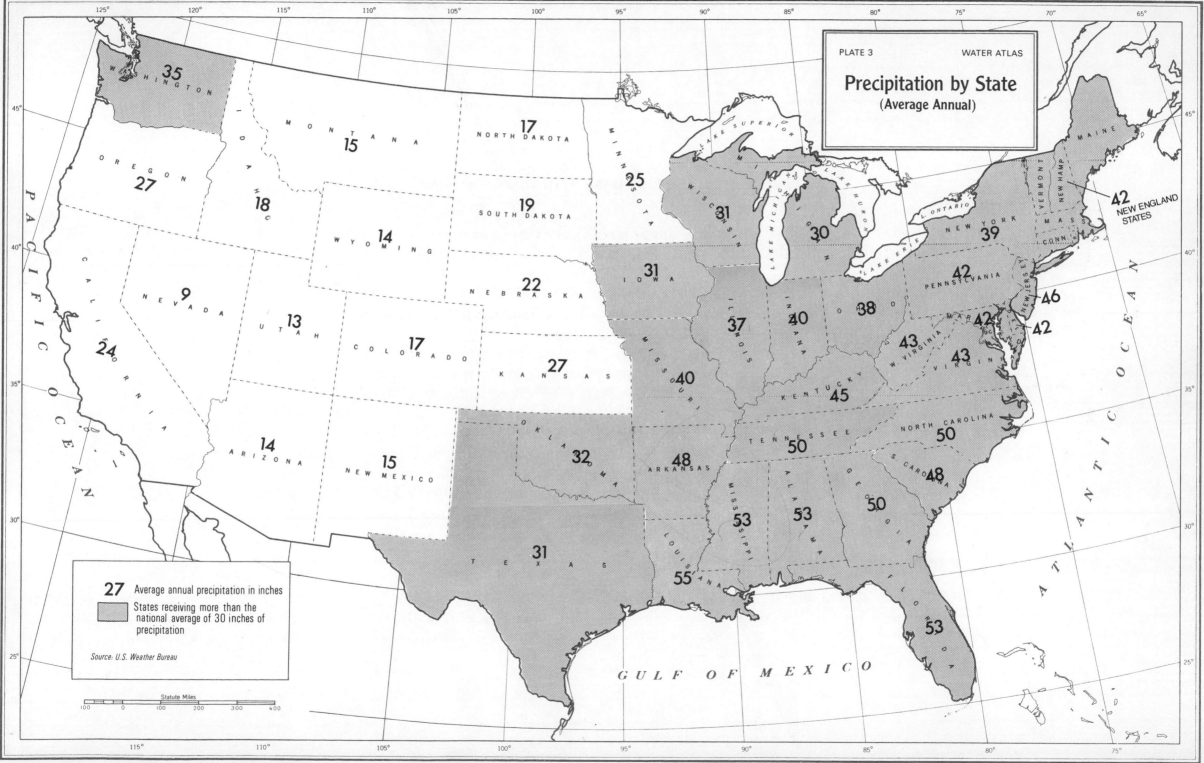

Precipitation by State
(Average Annual)

PLATE 3   WATER ATLAS

27 Average annual precipitation in inches

States receiving more than the national average of 30 inches of precipitation

Source: U.S. Weather Bureau

Statute Miles
100   0   100   200   300   400

Base Map by U.S.C.&G.S.

© WATER INFORMATION CENTER, INC.

PLATE 4 – NUMBER OF DAYS WITH THUNDERSTORMS

Thunderstorms generally occur only during the summer, when the heating of moist air at the land surface results in strong updrafts, turbulence, and heavy rain. Updrafts caused by rapidly moving cold fronts or by mountains also may produce thunderstorms. Although local in occurrence, thunderstorms are often responsible for the major portion of a region's precipitation. This is especially true of desert locations.

Because precipitation during a thunderstorm tends to be very intense over a short period of time, sudden floods of short duration may occur in rivers and streams. Unless reservoirs have been built to capture these flows, the water will pass on downstream and be lost for future use.

The main source of warm humid air is the Gulf of Mexico. In the region directly north and east of the Gulf, thunderstorms occur on an average of from 50 to 80 days a year. Small areas of high thunderstorm frequency exist along the Rocky Mountains and the Appalachian Mountains. The West Coast of the United States averages less than five days a year with thunderstorms because the relative humidity there in summertime is too low for their formation.

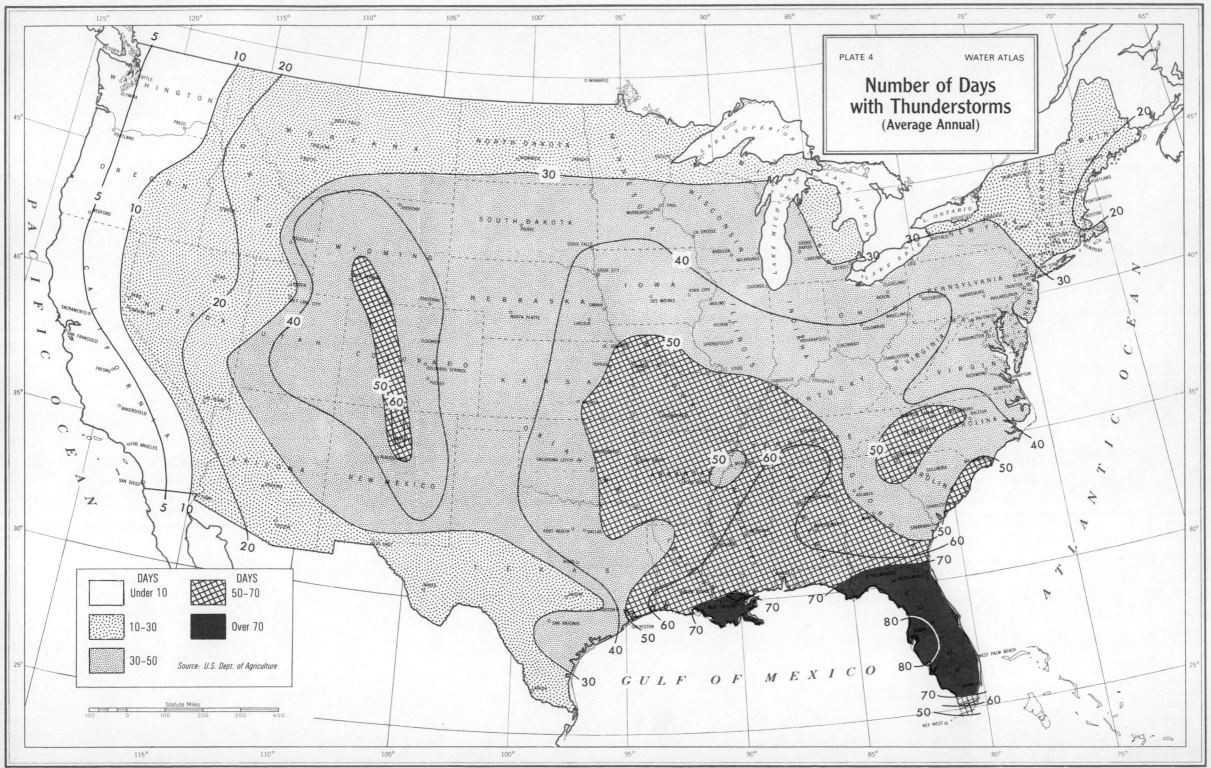

PLATE 4   WATER ATLAS

Number of Days with Thunderstorms
(Average Annual)

DAYS — Under 10

DAYS — 50–70

10–30

Over 70

30–50

Source: U.S. Dept. of Agriculture

Statute Miles
100 0 100 200 300 400

PLATE 5 – NUMBER OF DAYS WITH HAIL

A hailstorm can develop from a thunderstorm if there are strong vertical updrafts, large quantities of liquid water, and suitable temperature conditions in the thunderhead. Updraft velocities of 60 to 100 feet per second will force a water droplet upward again and again until it grows large enough to overcome the uplift. Research has shown that if maximum updraft velocity occurs at a point in the cloud where temperatures are above 23 degrees F., only rain will fall. Between 23 degrees F. and minus 4 degrees F., large hailstones are formed, because some of the cloud droplets freeze to produce a few large stones. Below minus 4 degrees F., a large number of cloud droplets freeze, creating many small hailstones, snow, or snow pellets. Frequently, the size of the hailstones is enormous. One hailstone, collected in Kansas in September 1970, measured 17.5 inches in circumference and weighed 1.67 pounds.

Hailstorms cause an estimated $200 to $300 million damage a year in the United States, more than the damage from tornadoes. The loss is about equally divided between crops and property. Studies are under way to suppress or reduce hail by seeding clouds with crystals of silver iodide.

Most of the hail falls in the interior part of the nation. The highest incidence is in the so-called "Hail Alley", an area centered roughly where Colorado, Wyoming, and Nebraska meet and extending north into South Dakota and south into Kansas. Cheyenne, Wyoming, near the center of "Hail Alley", has the highest incidence of hail in the nation. Kansas, which grows more wheat than any other state, ranks first among all states in hail damage.

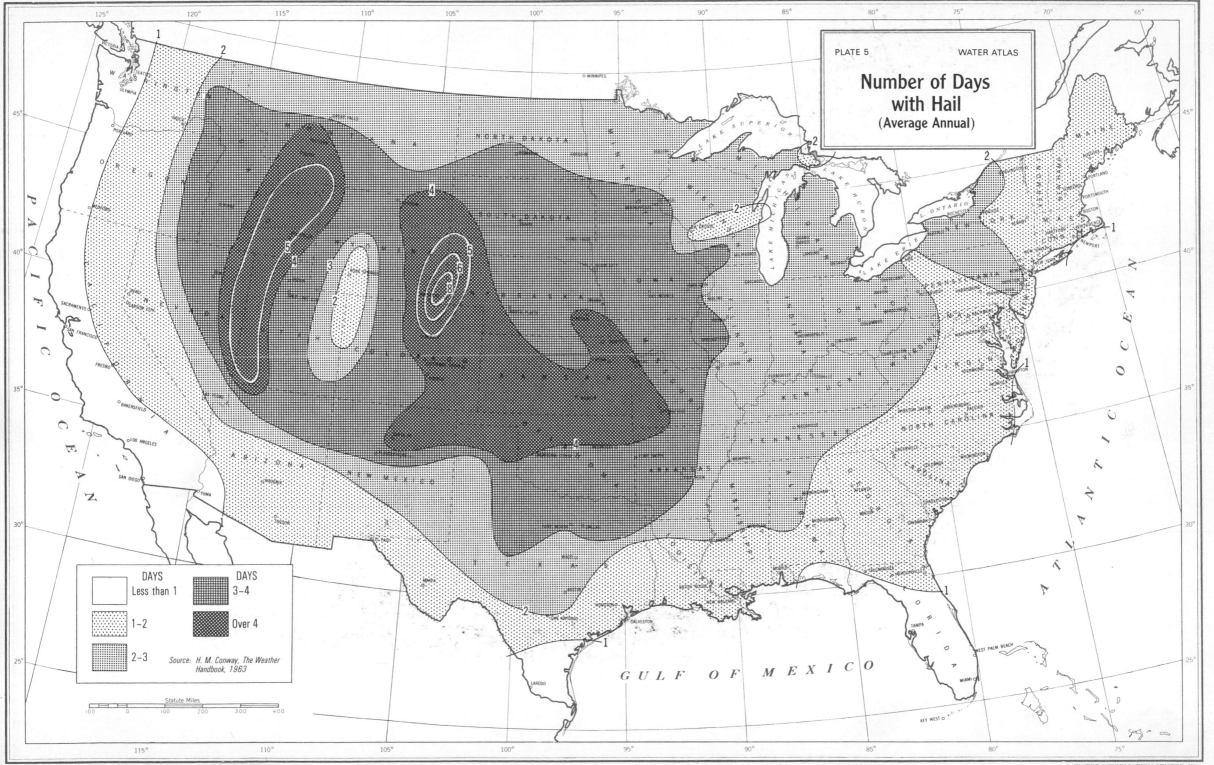

PLATE 5   WATER ATLAS

Number of Days with Hail
(Average Annual)

DAYS
Less than 1

DAYS
3–4

1–2

Over 4

2–3

Source: H. M. Conway, The Weather
Handbook, 1963

Statute Miles

Base Map by U.S.C.&G.S.

© WATER INFORMATION CENTER, INC.

PLATE 6 – NUMBER OF DAYS WITH FOG

Of all the major climatic elements, fog is the most variable with regard to areal distribution. As may be seen from the map, fog occurs most often in the central Appalachian region and along the New England and Pacific Coasts.

Fog consists of very small water droplets suspended in air. These droplets are so small that they do not settle on horizontal surfaces and therefore do not register on a rain gage. Unlike rainfall and snowfall, fog is usually not considered important as a source of water, and yet it is vitally important to certain forms of vegetation.

Along the northern coast of California, for example, redwood trees flourish in a narrow belt influenced by sea fog. In other areas with equal amounts of precipitation but without fog, tree growth is poorer.

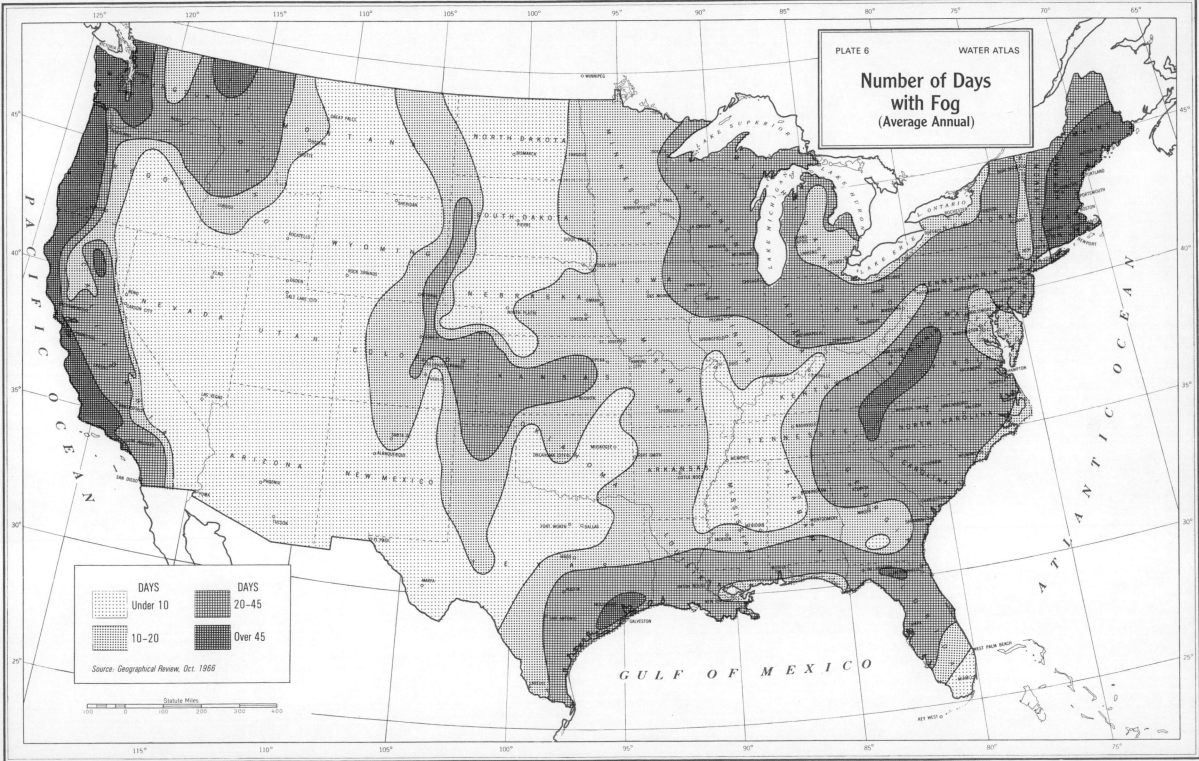

PLATE 6   WATER ATLAS

Number of Days
with Fog
(Average Annual)

DAYS
Under 10

DAYS
20-45

10-20

Over 45

Source: Geographical Review, Oct. 1966

Statute Miles

Base Map by U.S.C.&G.S.

© WATER INFORMATION CENTER, INC.

PLATE 7 – DISTRIBUTION OF SNOWFALL

Snowfalls have been recorded in most parts of the United States at one time or another, although they are a rare occurrence in the extreme South. Locations around the Gulf of Mexico seldom experience snow; this is also true of the coastal area of southern California. Extremely heavy snowfalls take place in the Rocky Mountains and also along the eastern shores of the Great Lakes where westerly winds pick up moisture from those large bodies of open water. In the western half of the country, the annual snowfall pattern is uneven because of the irregular topography.

Snow is an important form of precipitation in the West. Snow that accumulates on the ground during the winter constitutes a "moisture bank", ready to supply water to the semi-arid valleys and plains of the region when it melts during the spring. In order to estimate how much water will be derived from the snowmelt, surveys are conducted throughout the winter and spring to measure the thickness and water content of the accumulated snow.

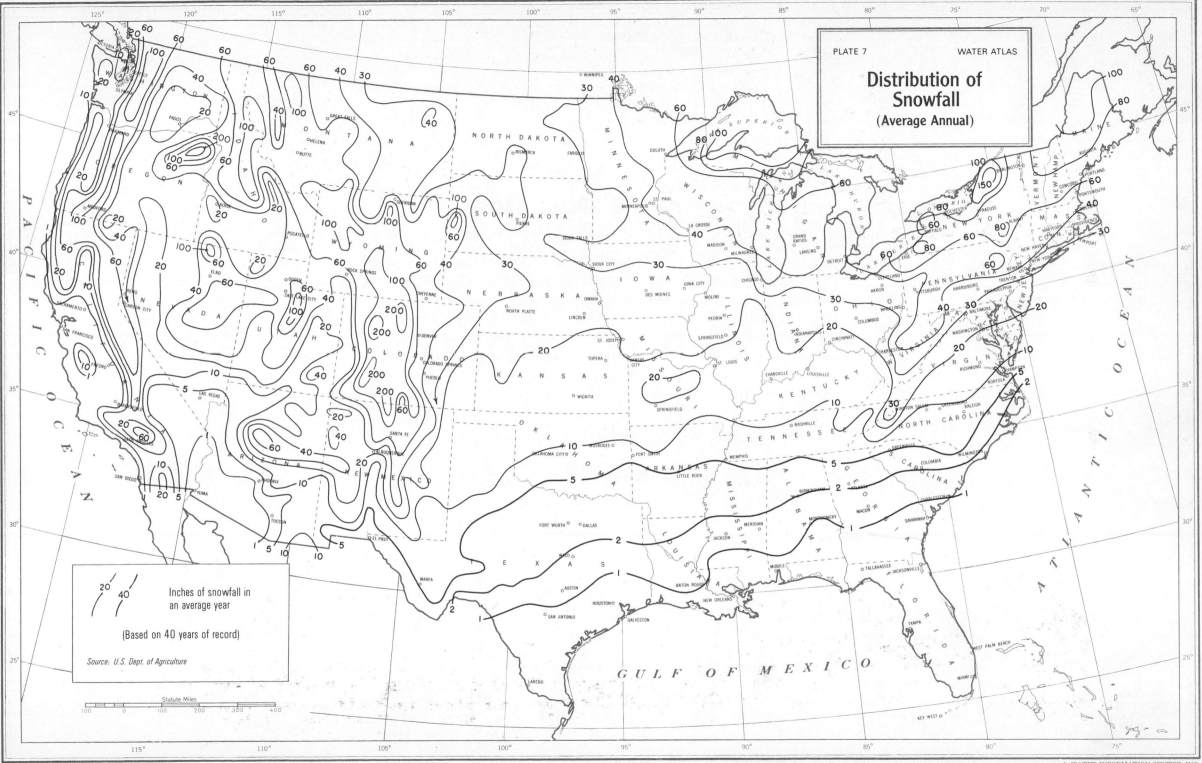

PLATE 7   WATER ATLAS

Distribution of Snowfall
(Average Annual)

20   40   Inches of snowfall in
an average year

(Based on 40 years of record)

Source: U.S. Dept. of Agriculture

Statute Miles
100   0   100   200   300   400

Base Map by U.S.C.&G.S.

© WATER INFORMATION CENTER, INC.

PLATE 8 – DISTRIBUTION OF GLACIERS

The only glaciers now found in the conterminous United States are masses of slowly moving ice formed by the compaction of snow in mountainous regions. In past geological periods, huge regional glaciers, referred to as continental glaciers or ice sheets, covered 30 percent of the land area of the world, but today, they cover only 11 percent. The ancient continental glaciers once extended across all of Canada and a large part of the northern United States. The map shows the greatest extent of ancient continental glaciation in the United States and also the areas where mountain glaciers still exist.

Although the individual glaciers are small and are not tapped directly as sources of water supply, they are an important source of streamflow in summer months. In the State of Washington, for example, as much water is stored in glacier ice as in all of the reservoirs, lakes, and rivers in the state. During July and August in a typical year, the 1,117 melting glaciers in the conterminous United States release some 557 billion gallons of water.

PLATE 8   WATER ATLAS

Distribution of Glaciers

Extent of continental glaciation

★ Existing glaciers

Source: Am. Geographical Society, 1956

Statute Miles

Base Map by U.S.C.&G.S.   © WATER INFORMATION CENTER, INC.

PLATE 9 – DEPTH OF FROST PENETRATION

The depth to which frost penetrates in the soil in the Central and Eastern States is determined mainly by latitude. In the mountainous Western States, it is mainly controlled by altitude. On the map, contours showing depth of frost penetration in inches have been drawn where possible; elsewhere, figures are given indicating measurements made at specific stations. The depth of frost penetration determines how deep water and sewer mains must be buried for protection against freezing.

Where thick layers of soil are frozen for long periods of time each year, water from rainfall or from melting snow rapidly runs off over the surface of the ground. This prevents infiltration into the soil where the water could have helped to sustain plant growth or replenish ground water.

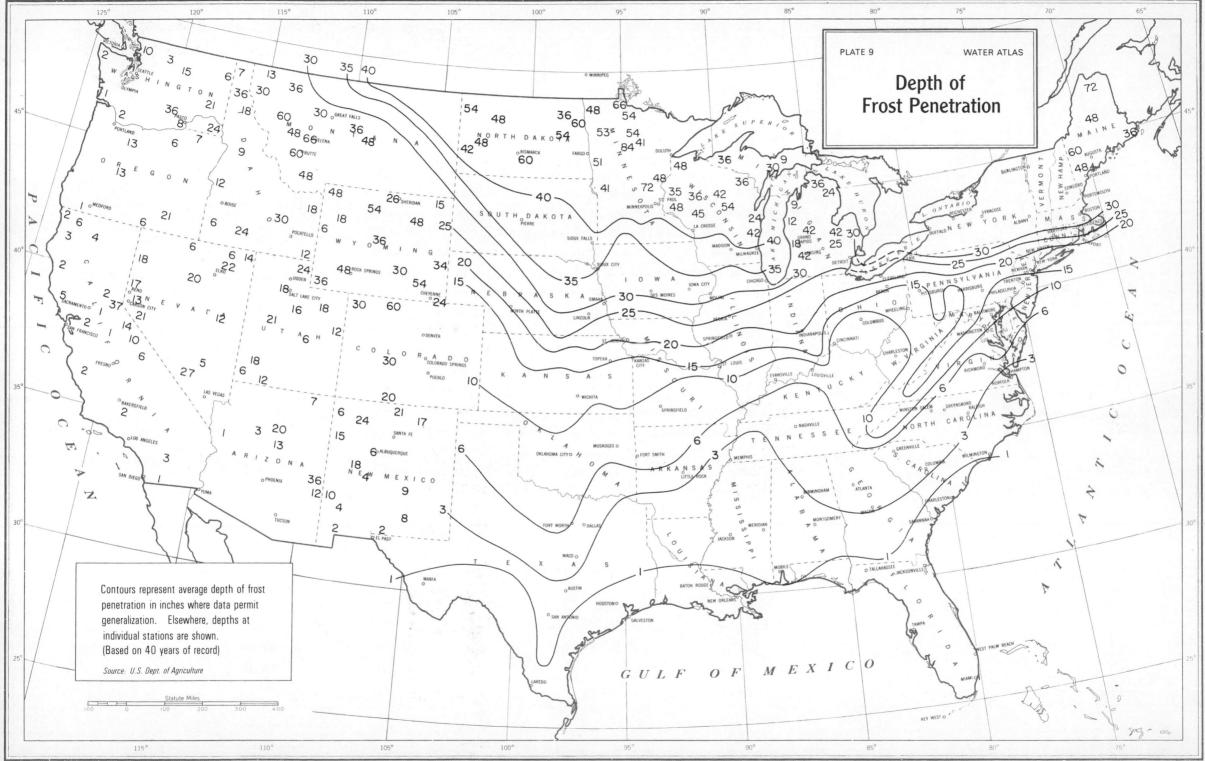

PLATE 9   WATER ATLAS

Depth of
Frost Penetration

Contours represent average depth of frost
penetration in inches where data permit
generalization.   Elsewhere, depths at
individual stations are shown.
(Based on 40 years of record)

Source: U.S. Dept. of Agriculture

Statute Miles

PLATE 10 – TEMPERATURE OF SURFACE WATER
(JULY AND AUGUST)

Variations in the temperatures of water in rivers and lakes in the United States are determined mainly by seasonal changes in air temperatures. The map shows the average surface-water temperature during the months of July and August, which is normally the warmest period of the year.

In the central part of the country, where the topography is relatively flat, temperatures show a gradual increase proceeding southward. The highest summertime water temperatures are in parts of southern California, Arizona, and Texas, where average readings of 85 degrees F. and above are recorded. The coldest summertime temperatures, less than 60 degrees F., are in the Rocky Mountains of Wyoming and Colorado and along the West Coast. The marked irregularity in temperature patterns in the West reflects the rugged topography of that region. Some deflections of contours are apparent along the Appalachian Mountains in the East, but these mountains are not very high and have only a moderate cooling effect on water temperatures.

The summertime temperature of surface water is of great concern to industry, because approximately ninety-five percent of all industrial water taken from these sources is used for cooling purposes. The efficiency of a cooling system goes down as the water temperature increases, and for that reason, cooler ground waters are often a better source of supply (see Plate 30).

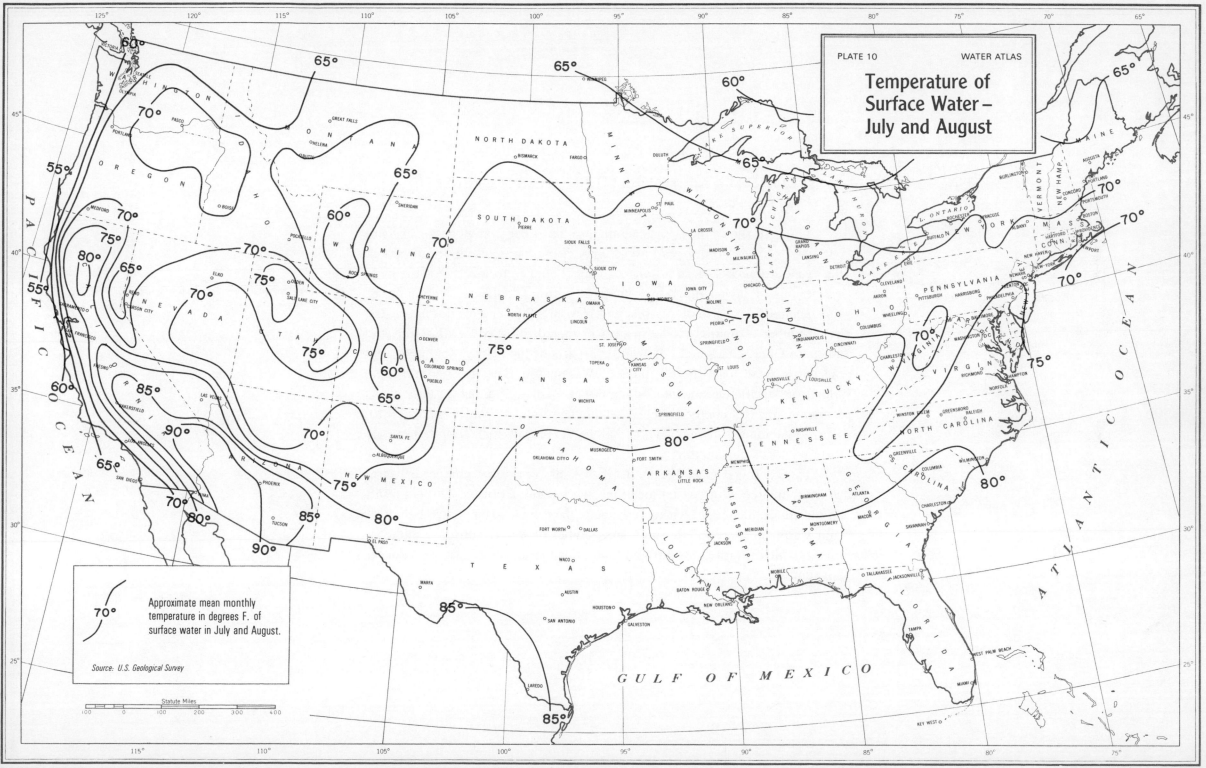

PLATE 10   WATER ATLAS

Temperature of Surface Water – July and August

Approximate mean monthly temperature in degrees F. of surface water in July and August.

Source: U.S. Geological Survey

Statute Miles

PLATE 11 – AIR TEMPERATURES OVER 80 DEGREES F.

The map shows the average number of hours per year when the air temperature is above 80 degrees F. Air temperature plays an important part in the evaporation of surface water (see Plate 12). The region having the longest periods of high temperature includes central Oklahoma, central Texas, and the southern parts of Arizona and New Mexico. The regions having the least number of hours over 80 degrees F. include most of New England, the northern Great Lakes area, the northern parts of the Rocky Mountains, and the entire west coast of the states of Washington, Oregon, and California. Along the Pacific Ocean, the cooling effect of the prevailing westerly winds accounts for the comparatively low temperatures. A similar tendency toward low temperature may be noted along the Appalachian Mountains in the eastern part of the country.

The central part of the nation has an above-average number of warm hours compared with coastal locations at the same latitudes. This is a result of the different heating characteristics of land and water. Large bodies of land warm up more rapidly than large bodies of water. Thus, the mid-continent, which is far removed from moderating marine influences, experiences hot summers.

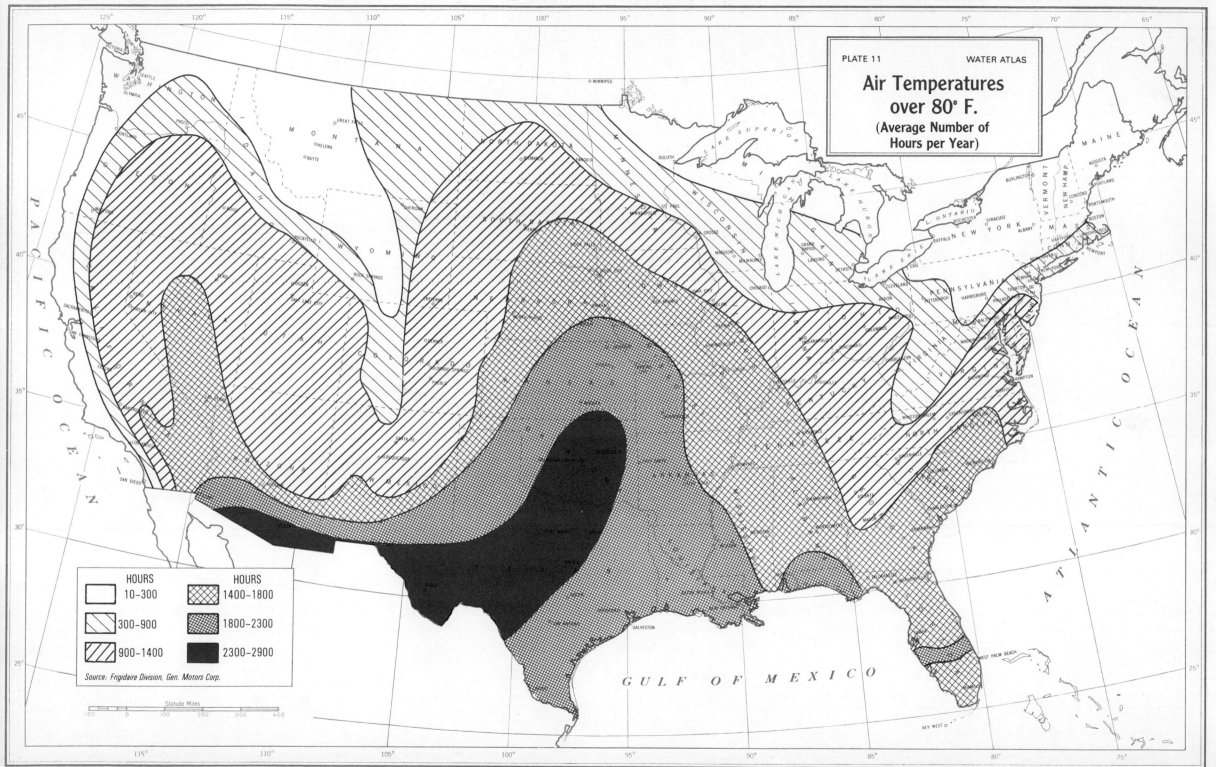

PLATE 11   WATER ATLAS

Air Temperatures
over 80° F.
(Average Number of
Hours per Year)

HOURS   HOURS
10–300   1400–1800
300–900   1800–2300
900–1400   2300–2900

Source: Frigidaire Division, Gen. Motors Corp.

Statute Miles

Base Map by U.S.C.&G.S.

© WATER INFORMATION CENTER, INC.

PLATE 12 – EVAPORATION FROM OPEN-WATER SURFACES

One of the most important ways in which water from precipitation is lost after it has reached the land surface is through evaporation back to the atmosphere. The map shows by contours the average amount of water in a typical year that would be evaporated from an open lake or river surface. This quantity is surprisingly high in the warmer regions of the country. It is as much as 86 inches in southern California and 80 inches in parts of southwestern Texas. The lowest annual rates of evaporation are in the extreme northern parts of Maine and along the coast of the State of Washington.

In many parts of the nation, the number of inches of water evaporated each year from an open body of water is greater than the inches of local precipitation. This discrepancy is explained by the fact that a lake usually receives, from streams and from seepage of ground water, far more water than falls on the lake surface itself. Thus, loss of water by evaporation can be a serious water-supply problem in places where water is stored in lakes or reservoirs. Evaporation consumes a major portion of the available fresh-water supply of the entire nation, and its annual rate of eight trillion gallons in the Western States could supply 20 cities the size of New York. Evaporation from open-water surfaces is often combined with the use of water by vegetation, in order to arrive at estimates of the total water loss (see Plate 13).

A great deal of research is being conducted in many parts of the world on ways of retarding evaporation. Experiments thus far seem to indicate that a substantial reduction can be accomplished by spreading thin chemical films over the surface of the water.

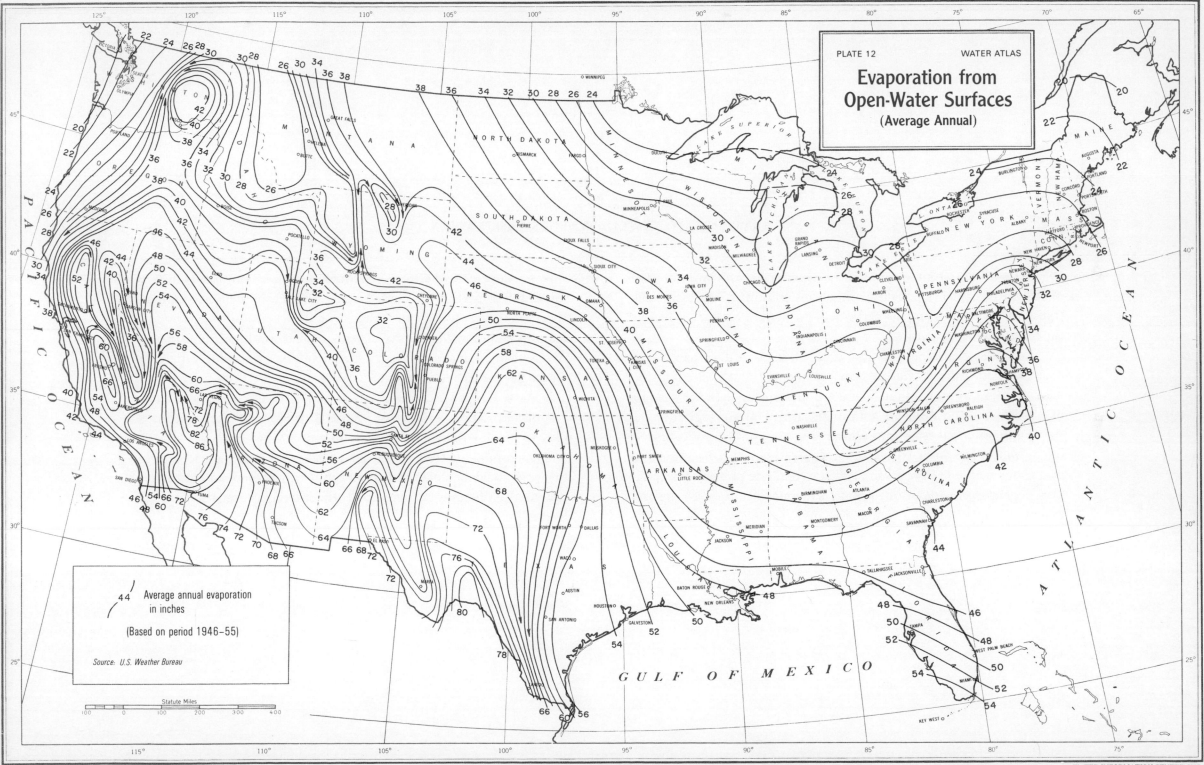

PLATE 12   WATER ATLAS

Evaporation from Open-Water Surfaces
(Average Annual)

44 Average annual evaporation
in inches

(Based on period 1946–55)

Source: U.S. Weather Bureau

Statute Miles

GULF OF MEXICO

PACIFIC OCEAN

ATLANTIC OCEAN

PLATE 13 – POTENTIAL EVAPOTRANSPIRATION

Evaporation from water and soil combined with transpiration of water from plants is called evapotranspiration. It represents the transport of water from the earth back to the atmosphere, which is the reverse of precipitation.

Potential evapotranspiration is the loss of water that would occur if there were sufficient water in the soil at all times for the maximum use by vegetation. It is generally greater than the amount of water lost to the atmosphere through actual evapotranspiration.

Since potential evapotranspiration represents a theoretical transfer of water, it cannot be measured directly, but may be estimated by various mathematical formulas. The actual rate of evapotranspiration depends principally on climate, soil-moisture supply, type and extent of plant cover, and land-management techniques.

As shown by the map, potential evapotranspiration is high in the southern part of the United States and low in the northern part. It ranges from less than 10 inches in the Rocky Mountains to more than 60 inches in the deserts of Arizona and southern California. It is less than 21 inches along the Canadian border and more than 48 inches in Florida and southern Texas.

As would be expected, the combined water loss from actual evapotranspiration is immense. Seventy percent of the water that falls as precipitation on the conterminous United States is lost by evapotranspiration from non-irrigated lands. If only one percent of this loss could be converted to streamflow, it would satisfy the entire metropolitan water needs of the present population of the United States.

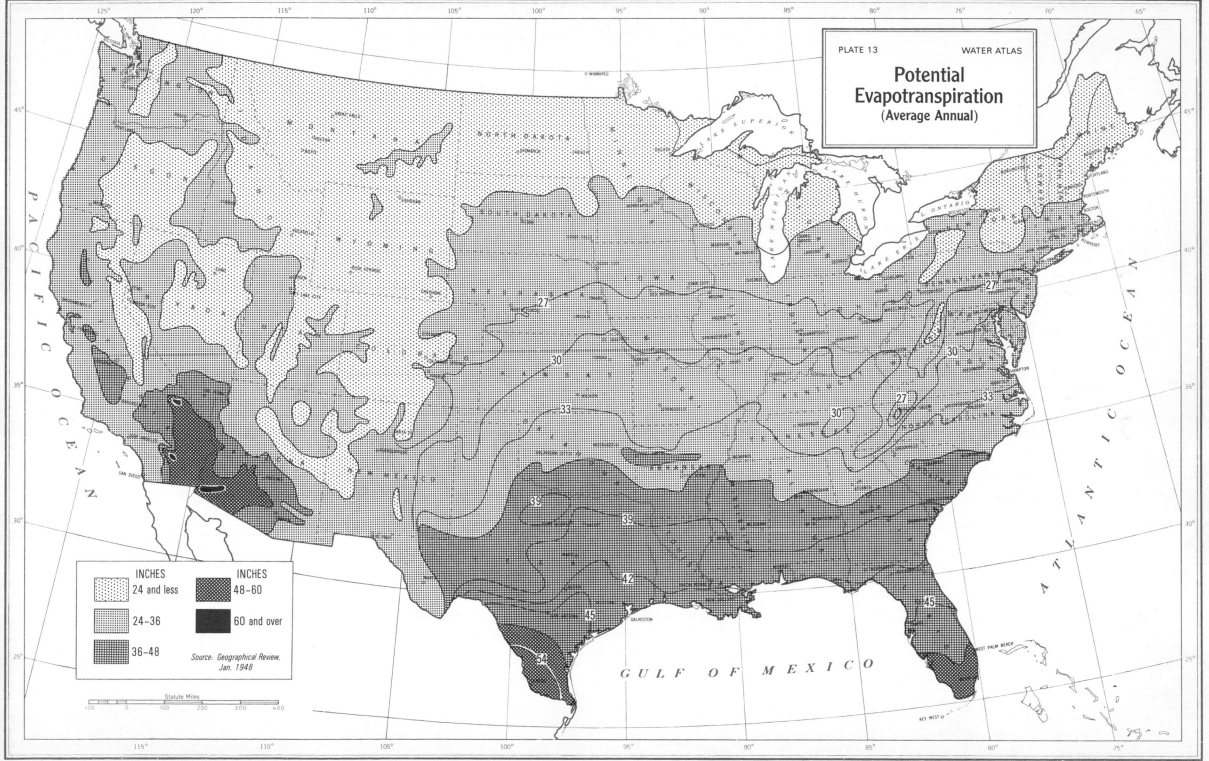

PLATE 13   WATER ATLAS

Potential Evapotranspiration
(Average Annual)

INCHES
24 and less

INCHES
48–60

24–36

60 and over

36–48

Source: Geographical Review, Jan. 1948

Statute Miles

Base Map by U.S.C.&G.S.

© WATER INFORMATION CENTER, INC.

PLATE 14 – AREAS OF CLOUD-SEEDING OPERATIONS

Cloud seeding involves the artificial introduction of tiny particles of such substances as silver iodide, water, or carbon black into clouds so that moisture can condense around the nuclei to form raindrops heavy enough to fall to earth. To date, the greatest number of cloud-seeding attempts have been made by releasing particles from generators operated on the ground. However, hundreds of seeding operations using aircraft have demonstrated that this technique may be more effective.

The purpose of cloud seeding is to artificially increase the amount of precipitation over a specific area. The most favorable conditions for artificially producing rain are in regions where warm moist winds blow more or less constantly up the slopes of mountains. If the mountains are high enough, clouds will form in abundance on the windward slopes, and will tend to be at temperatures low enough for successful cloud seeding.

Although cloud seeding has been tried in many places in the United States and elsewhere, few of these experiments have been clearcut successes. In most instances, it is impossible to tell whether the rain was artificially induced or would have fallen anyhow as a result of natural causes. However, there is some statistical evidence that seeding of winter storm clouds in mountainous parts of the West has resulted in an average increase in precipitation of 10 to 15 percent.

The map shows only the general areas in which operations have recently taken place, because the mapping of the actual extent and delineation of treated localities is not possible. One reason for this, as shown by tracer studies, is that seeding releases often have dispersed into areas different from those intended, or else have never reached cloud altitude at all.

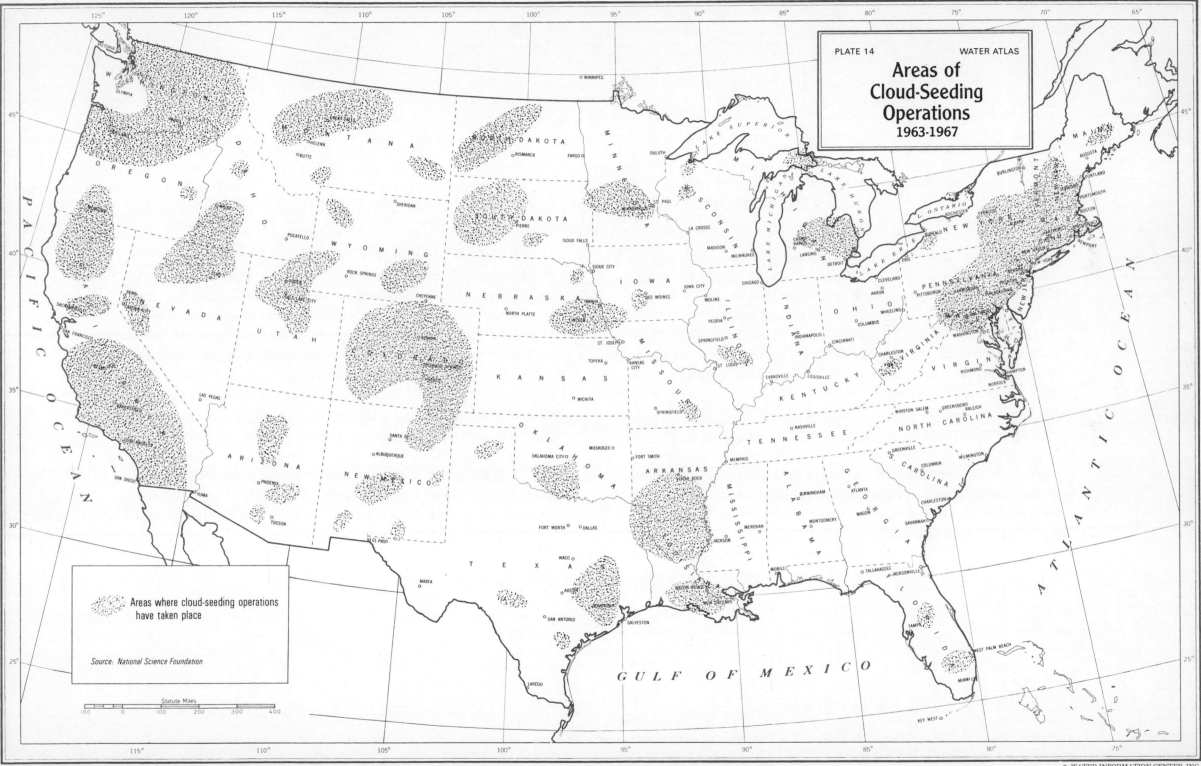

PLATE 14 · · · · · · · WATER ATLAS

Areas of Cloud-Seeding Operations
1963-1967

Areas where cloud-seeding operations have taken place

Source: National Science Foundation

Statute Miles

100 0 100 200 300 400

Base Map by U.S.C.&G.S.

© WATER INFORMATION CENTER, INC.

PLATE 15 — WATER TRANSFERS BETWEEN RIVER BASINS

The moist climate of the eastern United States and the dry climate of the West can be separated by a line extending from western Minnesota southward to the Gulf of Mexico. This is a very important line, for it also divides regions of water surplus from those of water deficiency. Although dry climates predominate in the western United States, there are exceptions, like the belt of moist climate along the Pacific Coast as far south as the San Francisco Peninsula in California. Scattered moist areas are also present in the western mountains.

Interbasin transfers of surplus water to areas of water deficiency are being made in all but two of the Western States. However, most of the transfers occur in California, Colorado, Texas, and Washington. The importance of water transfers is made evident by the fact that one out of every five persons in the Western States is served by a water supply system that imports from a source 100 miles or more away. Of the total quantity of water diverted, approximately half is for municipalities and industries and the other half for irrigation. The total of more than 18 million acre-feet of water diverted annually across river-basin divides represents only a small proportion (13 percent) of all water withdrawn from streamflow in the West.

The map shows water transfers across boundaries of major basins. Notice that the Colorado basin is a well tapped source. The Columbia and North Pacific basins are largely self-sufficient, water-abundant regions. Also note that at the present time none of the transfers crosses a state boundary, although the first interstate transfer, from the Colorado River system into New Mexico, is under construction. No significant interbasin transfers take place in the eastern part of the nation, with the exception of Delaware River water that is diverted to New York City and Connecticut River water diverted to the City of Boston.

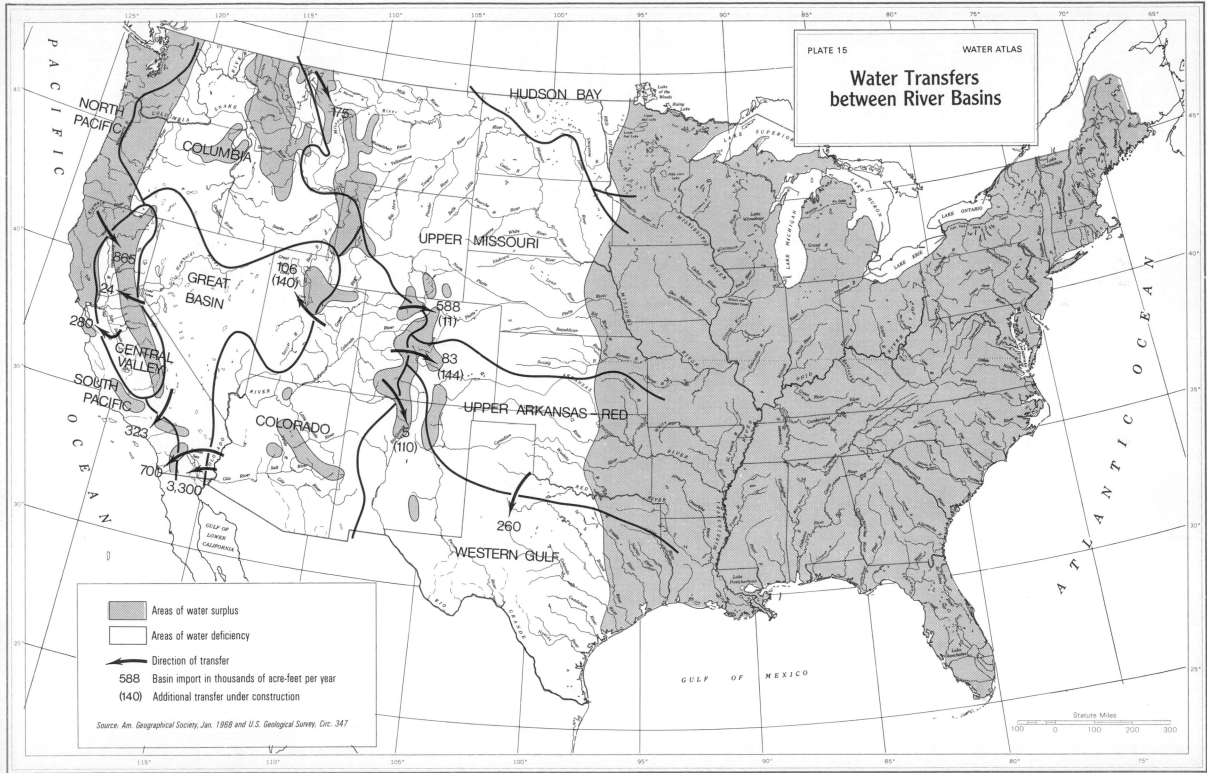

PLATE 15   WATER ATLAS

Water Transfers
between River Basins

Legend:

- Areas of water surplus
- Areas of water deficiency
- → Direction of transfer
- 588 Basin import in thousands of acre-feet per year
- (140) Additional transfer under construction

Source: Am. Geographical Society, Jan. 1968 and U.S. Geological Survey, Circ. 347

Statute Miles
100   0   100   200   300

© WATER INFORMATION CENTER, INC.

PLATE 16 – INTERREGIONAL WATER TRANSFER PROPOSALS

Some of the more imaginative plans to satisfy present and future water demands involve the physical transfer of water over great distances from areas of water surplus to areas of water deficiency. Eleven of the more ambitious interregional transfer proposals made since 1963 are shown on the map.

Four of these schemes would tap surplus water of the Snake and Columbia Rivers for conveyance to Lake Mead, and three (including one by undersea aqueduct) would take excess water from the rivers of northern California and Oregon for use in the Central Valley and the southern coastal plain of California. One plan calls for the diversion of Yellowstone River and Snake River water into the Green and Colorado River Basins. In the Great Plains, one plan proposes to pump water up the Niobrara River and across Nebraska, Colorado, Oklahoma, and Texas to the Pecos River in New Mexico. The Texas Water Plan, now under intensive study, involves distribution of excess water from the rivers of east Texas by means of a coastal canal and the Trans-Texas distribution system; it is also designed for the eventual transport of Mississippi River water to New Mexico.

The only interregional transfer system under construction is the first phase of the $2 billion California Water Plan, which will divert waters from the Sacramento-San Joaquin delta southward along a 444-mile-long aqueduct.

On a much larger scale, NAWAPA (The North American Water and Power Alliance) would use Alaskan and Canadian water and store it in the Rocky Mountain trench, a natural gorge extending into northern Montana. Canals, tunnels, and waterways would distribute water to Lake Superior, the Upper Mississippi and Missouri Rivers, the Southwest, and Mexico. The plan has been strongly opposed by Canadian officials.

None of the interregional transfer proposals gives priority to municipal or industrial water supply. Under the California Water Plan, for instance, irrigation is to receive five times as much water as urban uses.

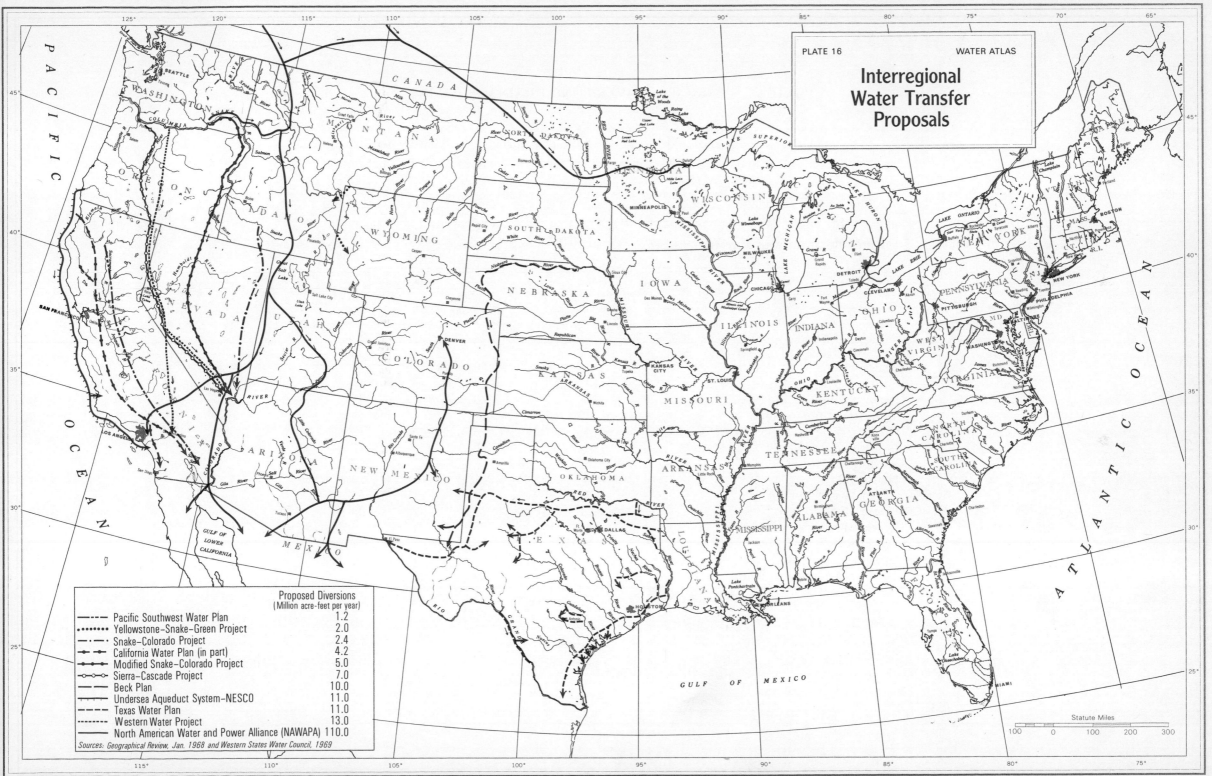

PLATE 16   WATER ATLAS

Interregional Water Transfer Proposals

Proposed Diversions
(Million acre-feet per year)

Plan	
–·–·– Pacific Southwest Water Plan	1.2
●●●●●● Yellowstone–Snake–Green Project	2.0
–··–··– Snake–Colorado Project	2.4
●—●—● California Water Plan (in part)	4.2
●—●—● Modified Snake–Colorado Project	5.0
○—○—○ Sierra–Cascade Project	7.0
——— Beck Plan	10.0
┼┼┼┼┼ Undersea Aqueduct System–NESCO	11.0
┬┬┬┬┬ Texas Water Plan	11.0
- - - - Western Water Project	13.0
——— North American Water and Power Alliance (NAWAPA)	110.0

Sources: Geographical Review, Jan. 1968 and Western States Water Council, 1969

Statute Miles
100   0   100   200   300

© WATER INFORMATION CENTER, INC.

PLATE 17 – PRINCIPAL RIVERS AND DRAINAGE BASINS

The map shows the names and locations of the principal rivers of the United States, and also identifies the major drainage basins in which these rivers are located. The amount of water from precipitation in a basin that eventually finds its way into the rivers of that basin is called runoff. These amounts and the land areas for each basin shown on the map are given in the table below. It should be noted that the indicated amounts of runoff do not take into account any diversions of water by man.

Region	Area (thousands of square miles)	Average runoff	
		Inches per year	Billions of gallons daily
New England	59	24	67
Delaware-Hudson	31	21	32
Chesapeake	57	19	51
South Atlantic	170	14	110
Eastern Gulf	109	19	99
Tennessee-Cumberland	59	21	59
Ohio	145	16	110
Eastern Great Lakes-St. Lawrence	47	18	40
Western Great Lakes	81	11	42
Hudson Bay	60	1.6	4.6
Upper Mississippi	182	7.2	62
Upper Missouri	458	1.0	24
Lower Missouri	62	7.8	23
Lower Mississippi	64	16	49
Upper Arkansas-Red	153	1.6	11
Lower Arkansas-Red-White	117	14	79
Western Gulf	341	3.2	52
Colorado	258	1.1	13
Great Basin	200	1.1	10
South Pacific	112	12	64
Pacific Northwest	257	13	159
Total:	3,022		1,200

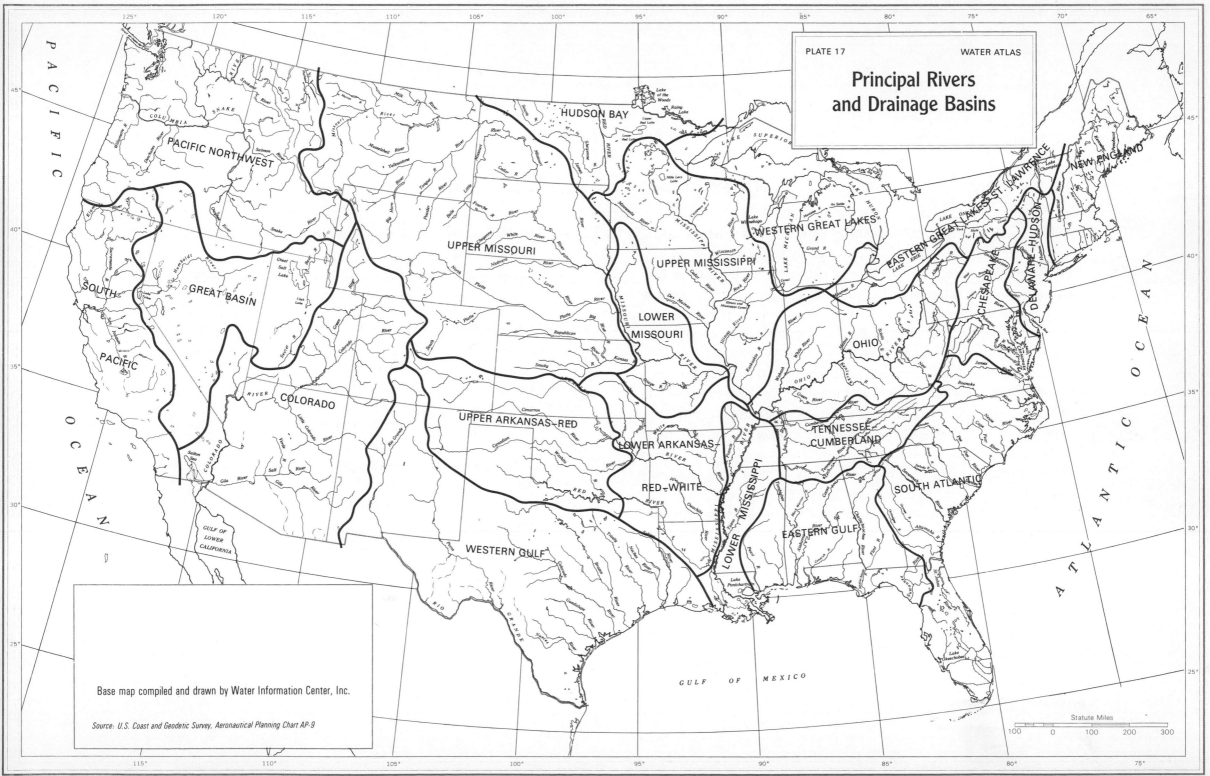

PLATE 17   WATER ATLAS

Principal Rivers and Drainage Basins

PACIFIC NORTHWEST

HUDSON BAY

NEW ENGLAND

WESTERN GREAT LAKES

EASTERN GREAT LAKES-ST. LAWRENCE

UPPER MISSOURI

UPPER MISSISSIPPI

GREAT BASIN

SOUTH PACIFIC

LOWER MISSOURI

OHIO

CHESAPEAKE

DELAWARE-HUDSON

COLORADO

UPPER ARKANSAS-RED

LOWER ARKANSAS-

TENNESSEE-CUMBERLAND

SOUTH ATLANTIC

RED-WHITE

LOWER MISSISSIPPI

EASTERN GULF

WESTERN GULF

GULF OF LOWER CALIFORNIA

GULF OF MEXICO

PACIFIC OCEAN

ATLANTIC OCEAN

Base map compiled and drawn by Water Information Center, Inc.

Source: U.S. Coast and Geodetic Survey, Aeronautical Planning Chart AP-9

Statute Miles

100   0   100   200   300

© WATER INFORMATION CENTER, INC.

PLATE 18 – MAJOR RESERVOIRS AND DAMS

To a large extent, the availability of water for industrial, urban, and agricultural development in the United States depends on how much storage capacity is available in natural or artificial reservoirs. In some parts of the country, as much as 75 percent of the total annual runoff takes place in a relatively short period of time, and if this water could not be saved in reservoirs, those regions would suffer severe water shortages much of the time.

Without artificial storage in reservoirs, less than half of the runoff in humid areas can be depended upon for regular use, and in arid and semi-arid areas, only about 25 percent of the total can be considered as a steady dependable supply. By storing the water in rivers at times of peak flows, damaging floods can be avoided, and releases can be made from the reservoirs to satisfy demands for municipal water supply, irrigation, power, and navigation.

Thus, the construction of dams and reservoirs makes possible the utilization of water that otherwise would be wasted into the sea, and it also allows streamflow to be regulated to suit the needs of man. Many of the large reservoirs in the United States store tremendous quantities of water.

The 10 largest, with their storage capacities, are listed below:

Name of Reservoir	State	Storage Capacity (billions of gallons)
Lake Mead	Arizona	9,700
Glen Canyon	Arizona	9,140
Oahe	South Dakota	7,690
Garrison	North Dakota	7,500
Fort Peck	Montana	6,320
Franklin D. Roosevelt	Washington	3,065
Rockland	Texas	2,220
Fort Randall	South Dakota	2,054
Lake Cumberland	Kentucky	1,985
Kentucky	Kentucky	1,956

PLATE 18

WATER ATLAS

Major Reservoirs and Dams

Sources: *T. W. Mermel, World Register of Dams, 1969 and U.S. Geological Survey, 1956*

Statute Miles

PLATE 19 – NAVIGABLE INLAND WATERWAYS

Historically, the rivers and lakes of the United States have served as vital avenues of transportation and commerce. The unimproved waterways of the country provided the earliest inhabitants with routes to areas otherwise inaccessible. The first settlers viewed these routes as a great blessing, and wasted no time in improving them to better suit the needs of a growing country. The first efforts were made around 1770, and many now-famous projects quickly followed, notably the Erie Canal in 1825 and the Louisville-Portland Canal in 1831.

There are at present approximately 23 thousand miles of improved waterways in the conterminous United States that are suitable for commercial navigation. These waterways and the depths of their channels are indicated on the map. There are also several thousand miles of waterways that are still used in their natural state; most notable among these are the Great Lakes. In 1965, the waterways carried 15.5 percent of the total inter-city traffic in the conterminous United States. Total domestic waterborne traffic was 830 million tons. In addition, foreign waterborne traffic within the nation amounted to 444 million tons.

Waterborne commerce is generally transported in three main types of carriers: deep-draft sea-going ships, Great Lakes ships of 20 to 27 feet draft, and barges and towboats of 5 to 12 feet draft. Most of the internal traffic is carried on the Mississippi River, the Ohio River, and the Gulf Intracoastal Waterway.

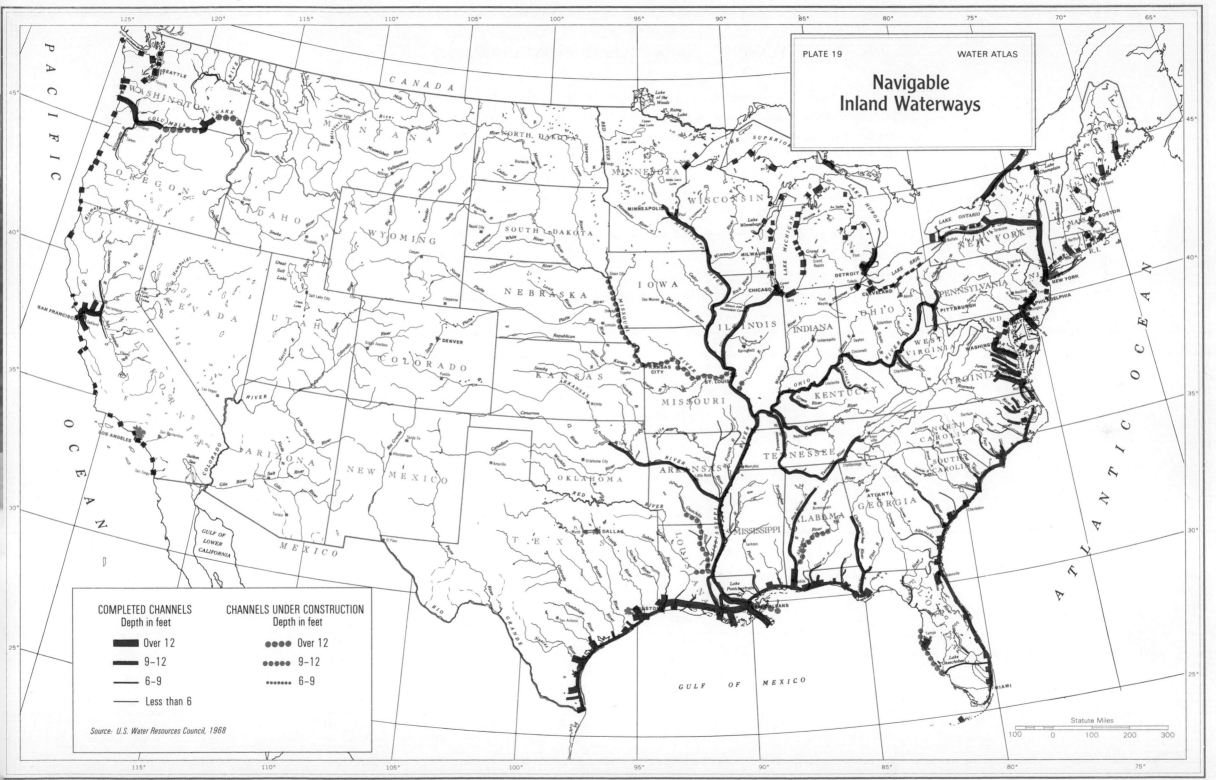

PLATE 19   WATER ATLAS

Navigable Inland Waterways

COMPLETED CHANNELS
Depth in feet

▬▬▬ Over 12

▬▬ 9-12

— 6-9

— Less than 6

CHANNELS UNDER CONSTRUCTION
Depth in feet

●●●● Over 12

●●●● 9-12

●●●●● 6-9

Source: U.S. Water Resources Council, 1968

Statute Miles
100 0 100 200 300

© WATER INFORMATION CENTER, INC.

PLATE 20 — AREA COVERED BY INLAND WATER

For statistical purposes, the inland water surface of the nation is defined as permanent bodies of water such as lakes, reservoirs, and ponds larger than 40 acres in area (Great Lakes excluded); streams, estuaries, and canals one-eighth of a statute mile or more in width; and deeply indented embayments, sounds, and coastal waters behind or sheltered by headlands or islands separated by less than one nautical mile of water. Inland water in the conterminous United States covers an area of 57,180 square miles, equivalent to two percent of the total land surface of the country.

The map shows the number of square miles covered by inland water in each state. The relatively large areas of inland water in North Carolina, Florida, Louisiana, and Texas largely reflect extensive coastal embayments.

The 10 largest fresh-water lakes (excluding the Great Lakes) are:

Lake	Location	Area in Square Miles
Lake of the Woods	Minnesota and Ontario	1,485
Okeechobee	Florida	700
Champlain	New York, Vermont, and Quebec	490
St. Clair	Michigan and Ontario	460
Upper and Lower Red	Minnesota	451
Rainy	Minnesota and Ontario	345
Winnebago	Wisconsin	215
Mille Lacs	Minnesota	207
Flathead	Montana	197
Tahoe	California and Nevada	193

The total areas of the Great Lakes and the portions of the lakes within the territories of Canada and the United States are shown below:

Lake	Areas in square miles		
	United States	Canada	Total
Superior	20,710	11,110	31,820
Michigan	22,400	0	22,400
Huron	9,110	13,900	23,010
Erie	4,990	4,950	9,940
Ontario	3,560	3,980	7,540
Total:	60,770	33,940	94,710

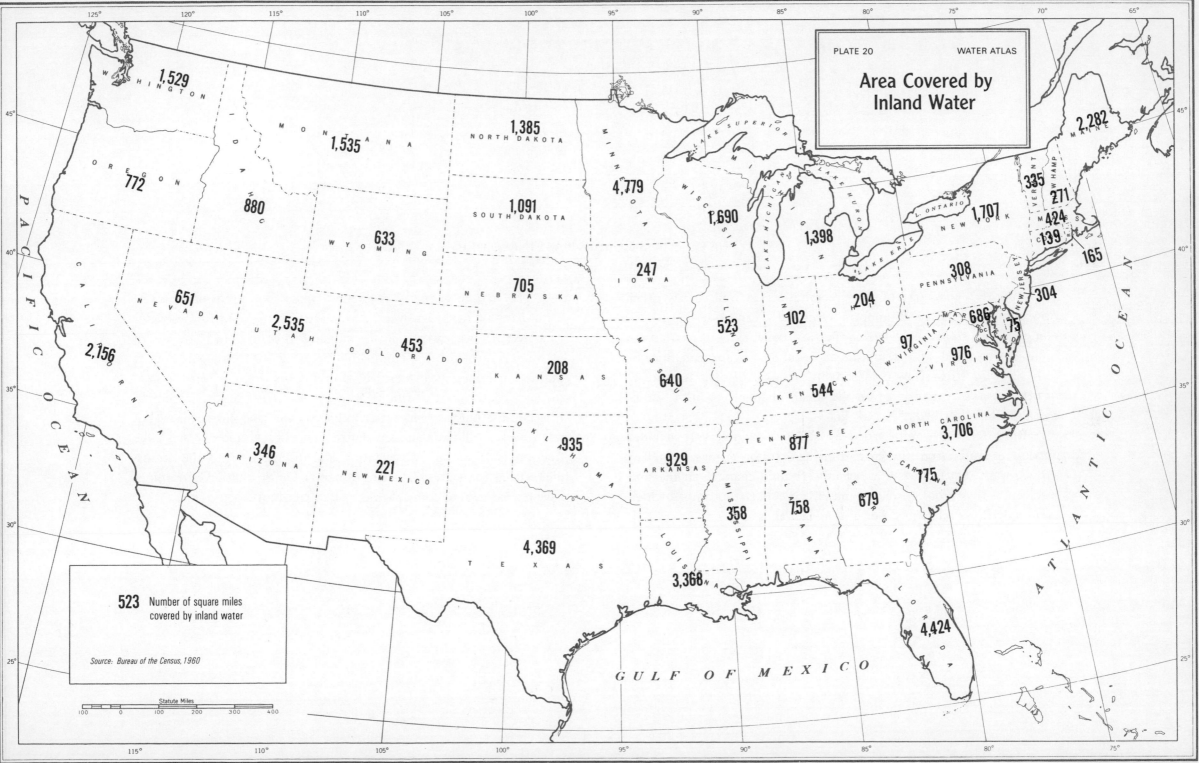

PLATE 20   WATER ATLAS

Area Covered by Inland Water

523 Number of square miles
     covered by inland water

Source: Bureau of the Census, 1960

Statute Miles

PACIFIC OCEAN

ATLANTIC OCEAN

GULF OF MEXICO

WASHINGTON 1,529
OREGON 772
IDAHO 880
MONTANA 1,535
NORTH DAKOTA 1,385
MINNESOTA 4,779
WYOMING 633
SOUTH DAKOTA 1,091
WISCONSIN 1,690
NEVADA 651
UTAH 2,535
COLORADO 453
NEBRASKA 705
IOWA 247
ILLINOIS 523
INDIANA 102
OHIO 204
PENNSYLVANIA 308
CALIFORNIA 2,156
ARIZONA 346
NEW MEXICO 221
KANSAS 208
MISSOURI 640
KENTUCKY 544
W. VIRGINIA 97
VIRGINIA 976
MARYLAND 686
DELAWARE 75
NEW JERSEY 304
NEW YORK 1,707
VERMONT 335
NEW HAMPSHIRE 271
MAINE 2,282
MASS. 424
CONN. 139
R.I. 165
MICHIGAN 1,398
OKLAHOMA 935
ARKANSAS 929
TENNESSEE 877
NORTH CAROLINA 3,706
S. CAROLINA 775
GEORGIA 679
ALABAMA 758
MISSISSIPPI 358
LOUISIANA 3,368
TEXAS 4,369
FLORIDA 4,424

Lake Superior
Lake Michigan
Lake Huron
Lake Erie
L. Ontario

Base Map by U.S.C.&G.S.

© WATER INFORMATION CENTER, INC.

PLATE 21 — SURFACE-WATER RUNOFF

Runoff is that part of the precipitation, as well as any other flow contributions, which appears in surface streams of either perennial or intermittent form. This is the flow collected from a drainage basin or watershed, and it appears at an outlet of the basin. Specifically, it is the streamflow unaffected by artificial diversions, storage, or other works of man in or on the stream channels, or in the drainage basin or watershed.

Runoff is the water carried by streams and rivers. It includes outflow of water from the ground in the form of springs, as well as surface wash that follows a heavy rain. Natural channels in the land surface, such as brooks, creeks, and rivers, collect the runoff, which eventually flows into the sea or into inland lakes or basins.

The volume of runoff is usually expressed in terms of inches of water in an average year over the drainage area that contributes water to a river. In other words, inches of runoff is equivalent to the depth of water with which the land would be covered if all the streamflow during an average year were to be evenly distributed over the land surface. The amount of runoff is always less than the total precipitation because much of the water falling on the land surface is evaporated back to the atmosphere almost immediately and another large fraction is taken up by vegetation and discharged into the atmosphere from the leaves and stems of plants. On the map, contour lines have been drawn to connect places of equal runoff.

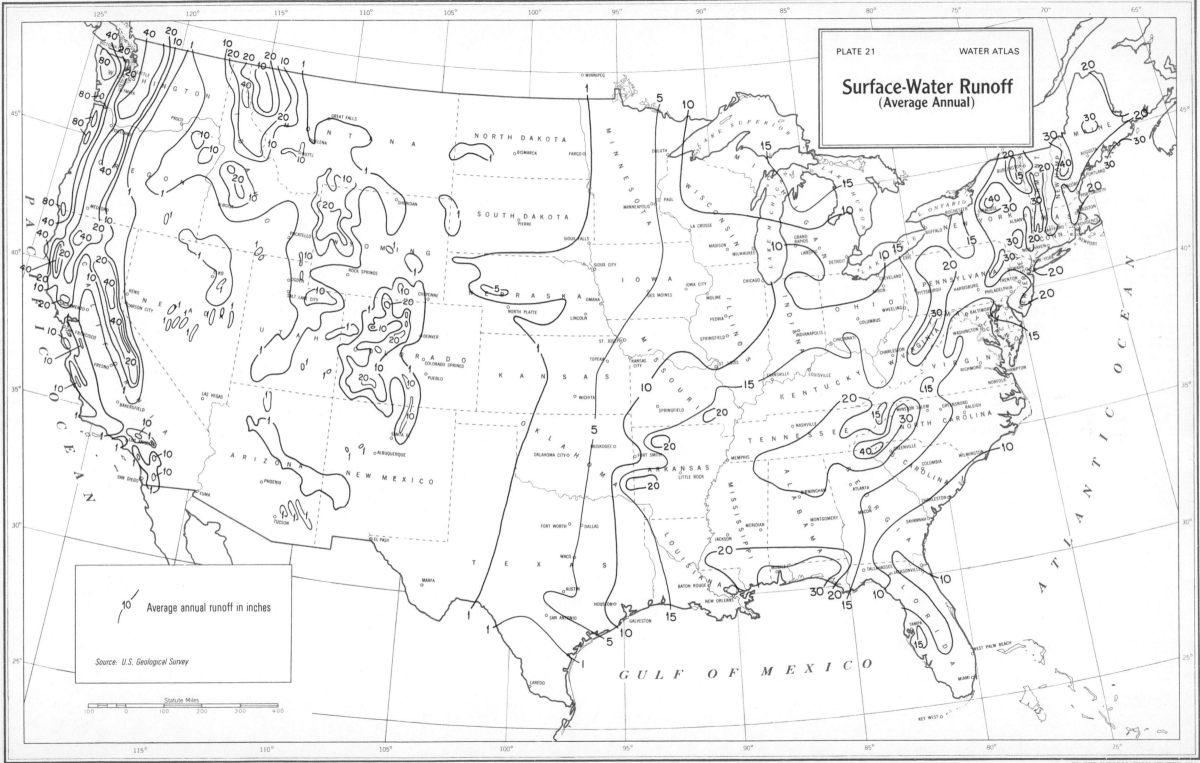

PLATE 21   WATER ATLAS

Surface-Water Runoff
(Average Annual)

Average annual runoff in inches

Source: U.S. Geological Survey

Statute Miles
100   0   100   200   300   400

GULF OF MEXICO

PLATE 22 – NORMAL DISTRIBUTION OF SURFACE-WATER RUNOFF

The graphs on the map show the percentage of annual runoff that normally occurs in each month of the year for 16 representative rivers of the United States. Each graph extends from October to September, which is the water year conventionally used by hydrologists. The 8-percent line shown on each graph represents the average monthly flow, 8 percent being approximately one-twelfth of an annual total of 100 percent. Most of the graphs show that streamflow in spring and summer is greater than the average, but that the high flows usually prevail for fewer months than the low flows. The most marked seasonal concentration is in the Central Rocky Mountain region, as illustrated by the graph for Roaring Fork in Colorado, where as much as 30 percent of the annual runoff takes place in June. The least seasonal variation is in the Southeastern States.

An interesting feature is that in some areas streams discharge almost the same quantity of water each month of the year. The Chattahoochie River in the southeastern part of the country, for example, seldom carries in a particular month more than twice as much water as it does in the lowest month of the year. By contrast, the Kings River in California discharges in the month of May more than 20 times as much water as it carries in September and October.

These variations reflect local differences in precipitation patterns, snowmelt, and seepage of ground water along the river channels. Almost all of the rivers show an increase in discharge in the spring and summer months, but it is interesting to note that the Kissimmee River in Florida displays a reversed pattern, in which the peak flows occur in September and October and the lowest flows occur in late spring. This is accounted for by the fact that Florida has very little rainfall between October and June.

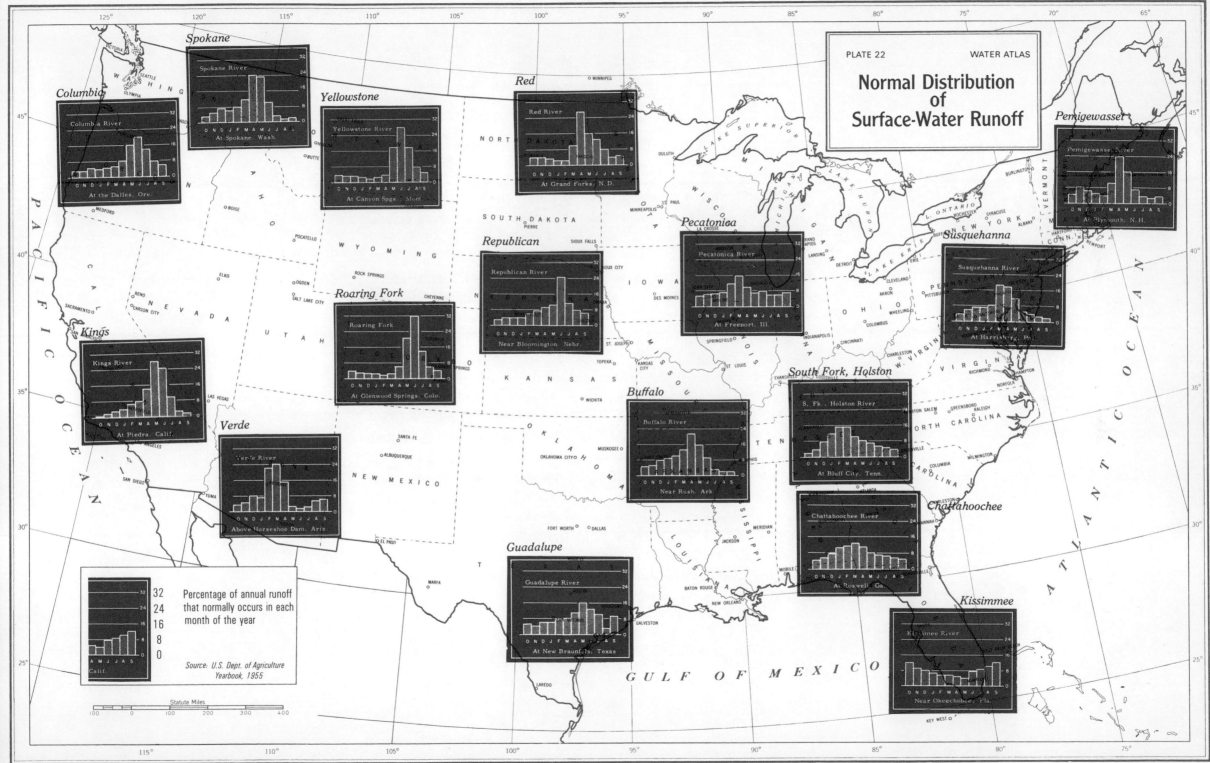

Plate 22   WATER ATLAS

Normal Distribution of Surface-Water Runoff

Percentage of annual runoff that normally occurs in each month of the year

Source: U.S. Dept. of Agriculture Yearbook, 1955

Base Map by U.S.C.&G.S.

© WATER INFORMATION CENTER, INC.

PLATE 23 – FLOWS OF LARGE RIVERS

The map shows, by means of colored bands, the flows of the major rivers of the conterminous United States. The width of the band at each point along a particular stream is a measure of the average flow of water at that point.

It can be seen from the map that the Mississippi River carries the largest quantity of water of any river in the country, and that its flow into the Gulf of Mexico is on the order of 620,000 cubic feet of water every second (a cubic foot of water is equal to 7.48 gallons). This fantastically large volume is accounted for by the tremendous land area drained by the river and its tributaries in the central part of the nation. The largest contributors to this flow are the Missouri River, which originates in the Rocky Mountains in Montana, and the Ohio River, which begins its flow in Pennsylvania. From the standpoint of total flow, the Columbia River and the St. Lawrence River are the second and third largest streams in the country.

It is interesting to note that many of the famous rivers in American literature, such as the Colorado River, the Hudson River, and the Delaware River, have almost insignificant flows when compared with the Mississippi, the Columbia, and the St. Lawrence. Many well-known streams, like the Rio Grande along the Texas-Mexico border, have too small a discharge to be shown on this map; the Rio Grande, for example, has an average flow of less than 10,000 cubic feet per second.

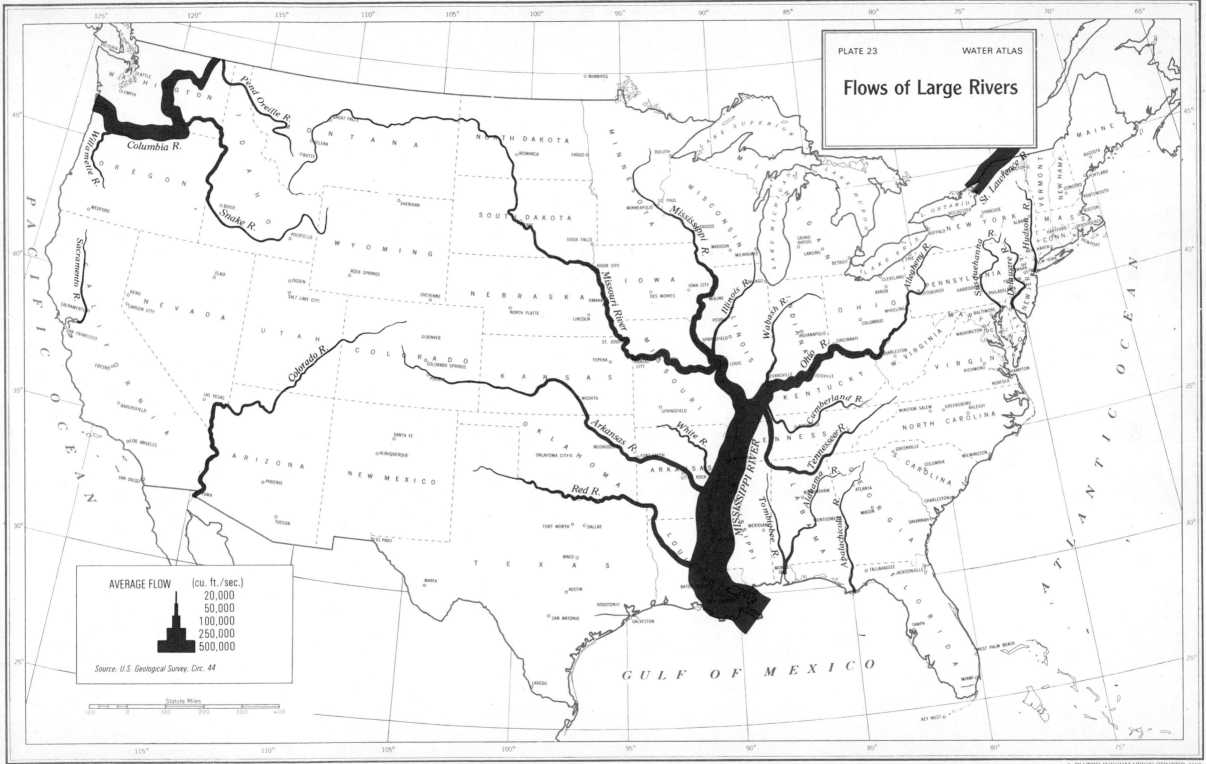

PLATE 23   WATER ATLAS

Flows of Large Rivers

AVERAGE FLOW (cu. ft./sec.)
20,000
50,000
100,000
250,000
500,000

Source: U.S. Geological Survey, Circ. 44

Statute Miles

Base Map by U.S.C.&G.S.

© WATER INFORMATION CENTER, INC.

PLATE 24 — SEASONS OF LOWEST STREAM FLOW

The map shows the seasons of the year when rivers and streams usually contain the least amounts of runoff. Generally, autumn and winter are the seasons of lowest flow in the conterminous United States. In the Eastern States and along the West Coast, the lowest streamflows are in the late summer and fall. In the Northeastern States, winter is also a season of low flow, but intermittent thaws maintain streamflow at rates generally above those of late summer and fall.

The winter low flows in the central part of the country are due to seasonally low rainfall. Winter is also the low-flow season in the western mountain area, where almost all precipitation is locked up in the form of snow until thawing begins in spring and summer. Low flows during June and November in Arizona streams coincide with dry months in that state.

Low flows determine to a large extent the minimum dependable supply of water in any particular region. Users who require a constant supply of water every day of the year receive no particular benefit from peak flows. In dry seasons, which usually last for several months, water supplies are commonly limited to the low flow of the streams, unless ground water is available or lakes and reservoirs are used to store surplus waters from the wet season.

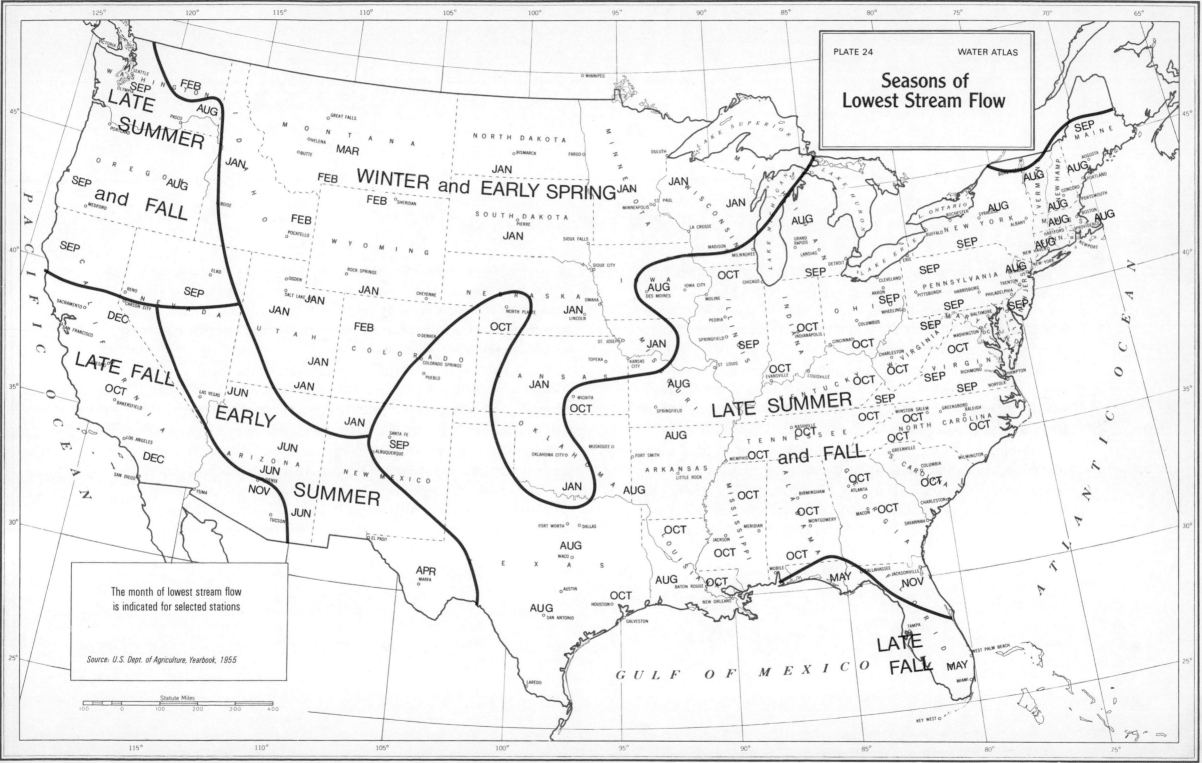

PLATE 24   WATER ATLAS

Seasons of
Lowest Stream Flow

The month of lowest stream flow
is indicated for selected stations

Source: U.S. Dept. of Agriculture, Yearbook, 1955

LATE SUMMER and FALL

WINTER and EARLY SPRING

LATE SUMMER and FALL

LATE FALL

EARLY SUMMER

LATE FALL

Base Map by U.S.C.&G.S.

© WATER INFORMATION CENTER, INC.

Statute Miles

PLATE 25 — SEASONS OF HIGHEST STREAM FLOW

This map shows the seasons during an average year when rivers and streams contain the greatest amounts of runoff. In all major runoff regions of the United States, there is a pronounced concentration of water in one season of the year. In arid and semi-arid parts of the country, as much as 75 percent of the year's runoff comes within a period of only a few weeks in the spring, owing to melting of snow on upland watersheds. Even in Florida, which has a rather evenly distributed runoff, 30 percent of the streamflow is concentrated within three months in an average year.

In humid regions, between 50 and 70 percent of total annual runoff occurs during intermittent stream rises resulting from rainstorms or melting snow. Many of the smaller streams have peak flows that are several hundred times greater than their average flows.

High flows can occur in any season of the year, depending upon the region. In southern areas, winter and early spring are the seasons of favorable conditions for runoff from rainfall. In northern regions and in high mountain areas, however, high flows are associated mainly with the melting of accumulated snow, which reaches a climax with the onset of the warm season.

Generally, peak runoff in the eastern part of the country shows a south-to-north progression, with high flows occurring in January, February, and March, in the Gulf States, and in April and May in the Great Lakes and New England States. In Florida, which is an exception, October is the month of high flow because that state has a rainy season extending from June to October. There is also a pronounced rainy season in the area bordering the Pacific Ocean, and this accounts for that region's high stream flows in February. Peak flows in parts of southern Arizona occur during sporadic summer storms.

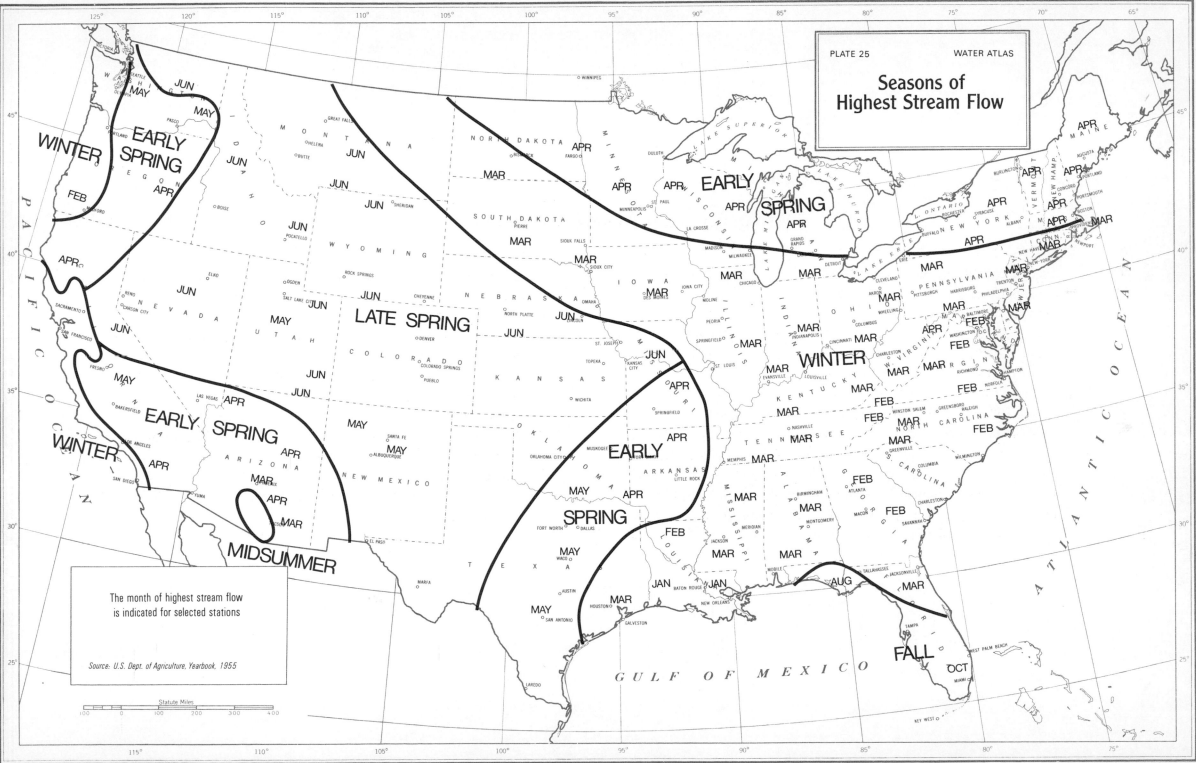

PLATE 26 – FLOOD LOSSES (1925-1968)

In general, the term "flood" refers to an overflow of a river or other body of water that causes or threatens to cause loss of life or damage to goods and services in immediate and adjacent areas. Floods on the mainstem and major tributaries are classified as downstream floods, and those experienced on creek and headwater areas as upstream floods.

Estimates of total flood damage in major river systems for the period 1925-1968 are presented on the map. As may be seen, the basins in which the heaviest flood losses have taken place are those of the Missouri and Ohio Rivers and the Pacific and North Atlantic slopes.

Although a complete inventory of nationwide flood damage has never been undertaken, damage surveys for major floods have been made on a national scale for more than 60 years. Before 1940, most major floods causing heavy property damage also resulted in heavy loss of life (more than 20 thousand lives lost between 1831 and 1940). Since then, the loss of life has been much less, probably as a result of better flood and hurricane warning systems. Sixty percent of the floods causing 100 or more deaths were hurricane-associated.

With the enactment of the Flood Control Act of 1936, the Federal Government accepted a high degree of responsibility for controlling floods. Control programs have prevented about $14.6 billion in flood losses in downstream areas and $191 million in upstream areas. However, land requirements of the expanding urban economy have been reflected in more intense development and use of flood plains, and this has contributed to the continual increase in flood losses in spite of flood-control programs.

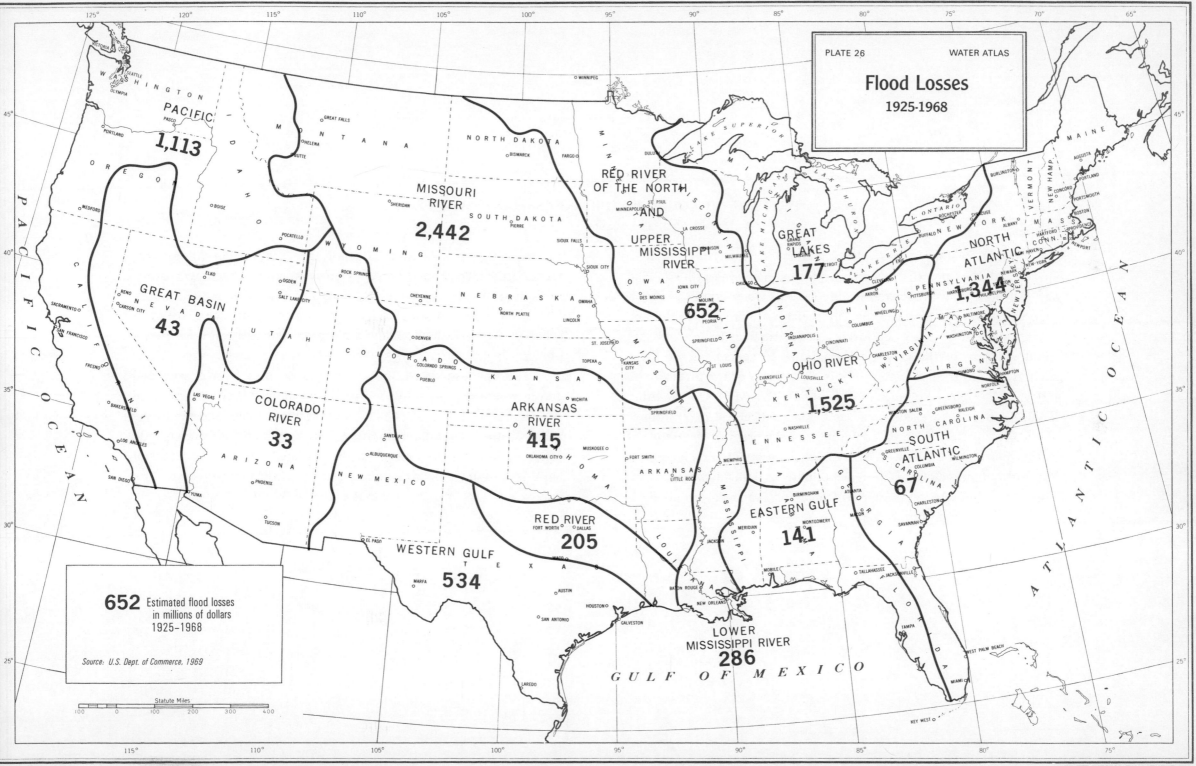

PLATE 26   WATER ATLAS

Flood Losses
1925-1968

652 Estimated flood losses
in millions of dollars
1925-1968

Source: U.S. Dept. of Commerce, 1969

Statute Miles

PACIFIC
1,113

MISSOURI RIVER
2,442

GREAT BASIN
43

COLORADO RIVER
33

ARKANSAS RIVER
415

RED RIVER OF THE NORTH AND UPPER MISSISSIPPI RIVER
652

GREAT LAKES
177

NORTH ATLANTIC
1,344

OHIO RIVER
1,525

SOUTH ATLANTIC
67

EASTERN GULF
141

RED RIVER
205

WESTERN GULF
534

LOWER MISSISSIPPI RIVER
286

Base Map by U.S.C.&G.S.   © WATER INFORMATION CENTER, INC.

PLATE 27 – GROUND-WATER AREAS (MAJOR AQUIFERS)

Ground water is the water contained in the saturated pore spaces and fractures of hard rocks and sediments beneath the land surface. Beds that yield water readily to wells are referred to as aquifers. Ground water is replenished by seepage of rainfall into the soil, and its abundance in a given locality is determined in large measure by the nature of the geologic formations. In general, dense rocks such as granite contain water only in thin cracks or fractures and do not yield very large supplies to individual water wells. On the other hand, aquifers such as beds of loose sand and gravel may produce abundant supplies of water, sometimes on the order of thousands of gallons per minute, to a well. Many of the consolidated rock aquifers can yield hundreds of gallons per minute to individual wells, and some of them, such as porous volcanic rocks and cavernous lime-stones, may yield thousands of gallons per minute. The colored patterns on the map show the areal extent and nature of geologic formations that supply comparatively large quantities of ground water. The areas shown in white are mostly underlain by dense rocks or other formations which seldom yield more than 50 gallons per minute to a single well.

The unconsolidated aquifers are made up of loose sand and gravel; where these deposits are partly cemented, they are described as semi-consolidated. Rocks such as limestone, shale, and sandstone make up the consolidated aquifers. The map is not necessarily indicative of how much water might be obtained on a specific tract of land. Its usefulness is in defining the parts of the country where productive aquifers of wide areal extent can be found.

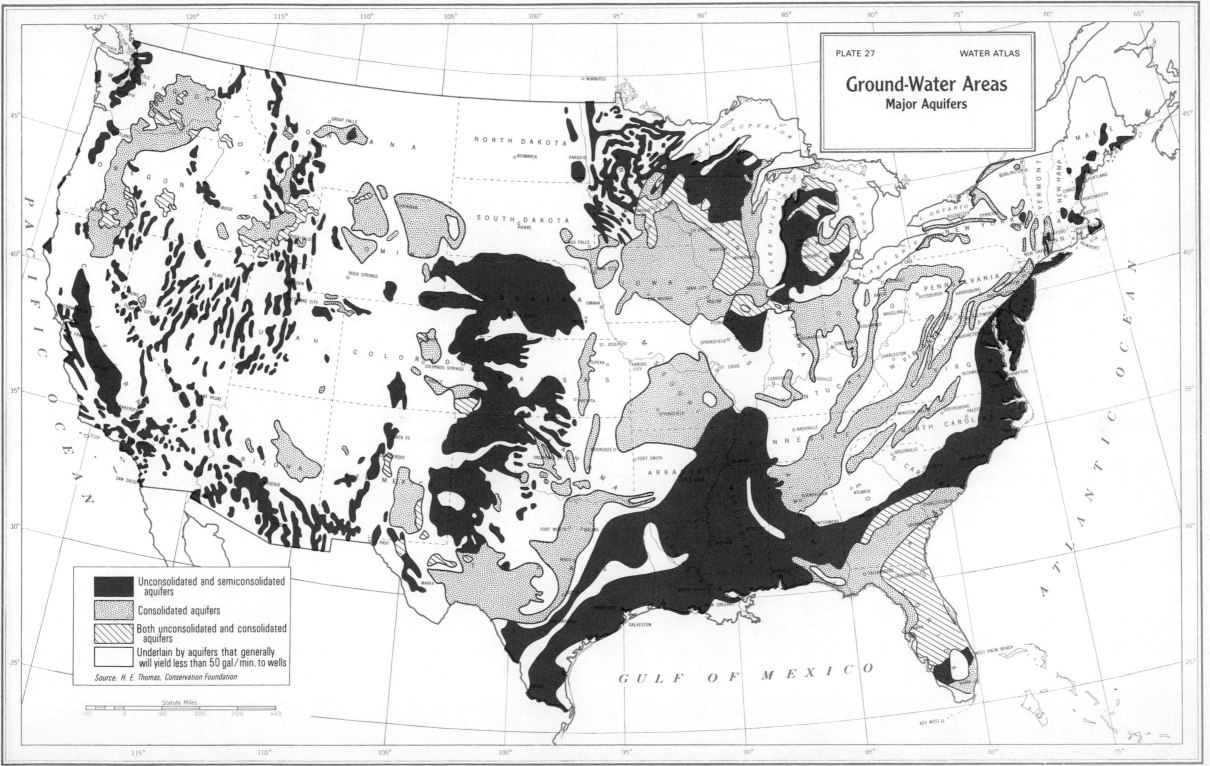

PLATE 27   WATER ATLAS

Ground-Water Areas
Major Aquifers

Legend:

- Unconsolidated and semiconsolidated aquifers
- Consolidated aquifers
- Both unconsolidated and consolidated aquifers
- Underlain by aquifers that generally will yield less than 50 gal/min. to wells

Source: H. E. Thomas, Conservation Foundation

Statute Miles
100 0 100 200 300 400

Base Map by U.S.C.&G.S.

© WATER INFORMATION CENTER, INC.

PLATE 28 – GROUND-WATER AREAS (NARROW AQUIFERS RELATED TO RIVER VALLEYS)

The map shows those areas that are known to be underlain by water-bearing sand and gravel deposits associated with existing or ancient stream channels. The deposits in these narrow channels consist of fragments of rock carried by running water and deposited along the channels in the form of terraces, flood plains, and sand bars. Over the centuries, a typical stream accomplishes a great deal of erosional and depositional work, which accounts for the fact that many stream channels are underlain by sand, gravel, and clay.

Only those channels are shown which have been reasonably well defined and are believed to be capable of supplying at least 50 gallons per minute to an average well. Undoubtedly, other such channels exist, and will be located through future geologic investigations and the drilling of test wells. Most of the narrow aquifers are associated with existing river systems. Where the stream deposits were laid down by ancient rivers that are no longer in existence, they are often more difficult to locate because there may be little evidence of their presence at the land surface. Many of the ancient valley-fill deposits are in the glaciated northern part of the country, where the topography underwent considerable changes during the Great Ice Age.

Because sand and gravel beds are among the most productive aquifers, yields of individual wells in valley-fill deposits are commonly large. Moreover, the lowering of ground-water levels caused by pumping from wells near a stream usually induces a flow of water from the stream into the water-bearing deposits, which helps to sustain the yield of the aquifer and to increase the supply available for withdrawal.

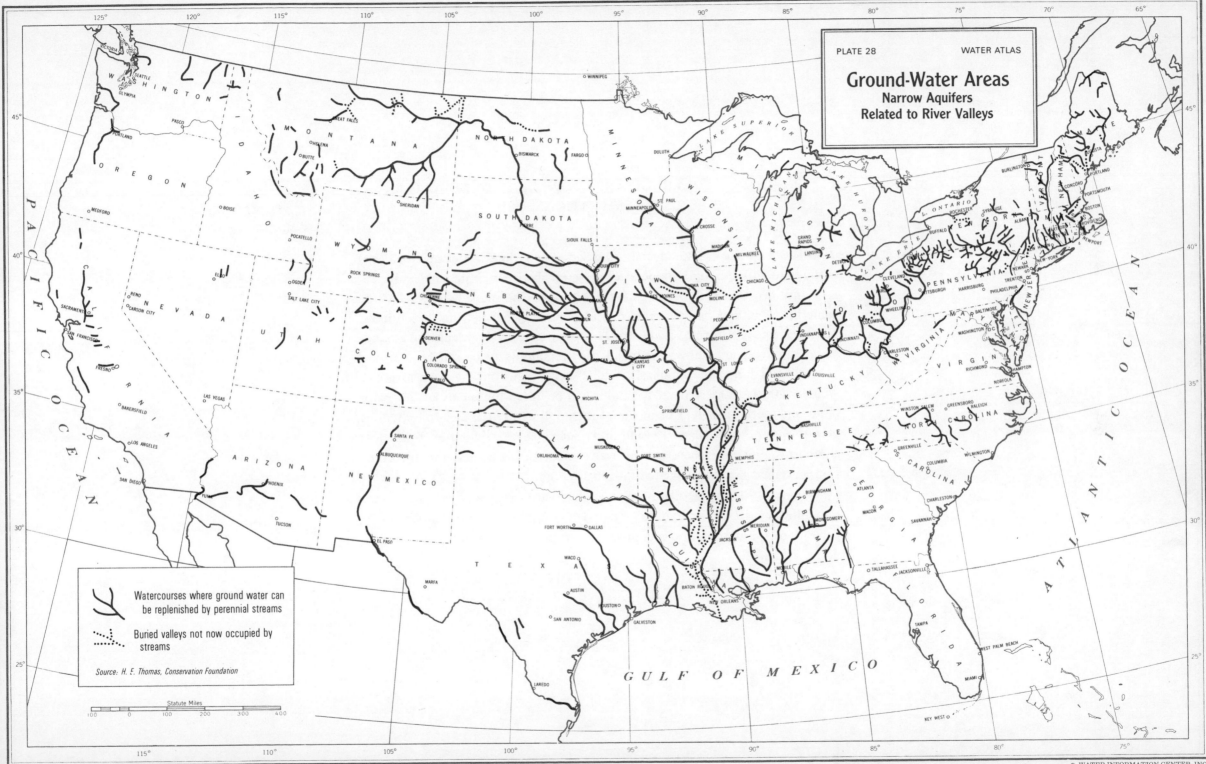

PLATE 28   WATER ATLAS

Ground-Water Areas
Narrow Aquifers
Related to River Valleys

Watercourses where ground water can be replenished by perennial streams

Buried valleys not now occupied by streams

Source: H. E. Thomas, Conservation Foundation

Statute Miles

Base Map by U.S.C.&G.S.

© WATER INFORMATION CENTER, INC.

PLATE 29 – COVERAGE AND SCOPE OF GROUND-WATER INVESTIGATIONS

The map shows the coverage and scope of ground-water investigations carried out through joint cooperative programs between State and local agencies and the U.S. Geological Survey. Although the map does not include some investigations being carried on independently by such states as Illinois, Missouri, and California, it illustrates the pattern of knowledge of ground-water resources and shows the major gaps remaining to be filled.

By and large, the emphasis in this survey work has been on localities where water is in great demand, and it will be noted that many of the major cities and metropolitan areas of the country fall within the areas of extensive ground-water knowledge. In addition, such places as central Texas and southern California, where ground water is used in large amounts for irrigation, have also been investigated thoroughly.

Under a long-range plan, the U.S. Geological Survey is working toward obtaining, by 1973, generalized or detailed ground-water information for 75 percent of the nation, and reconnaissance-type information for the remainder.

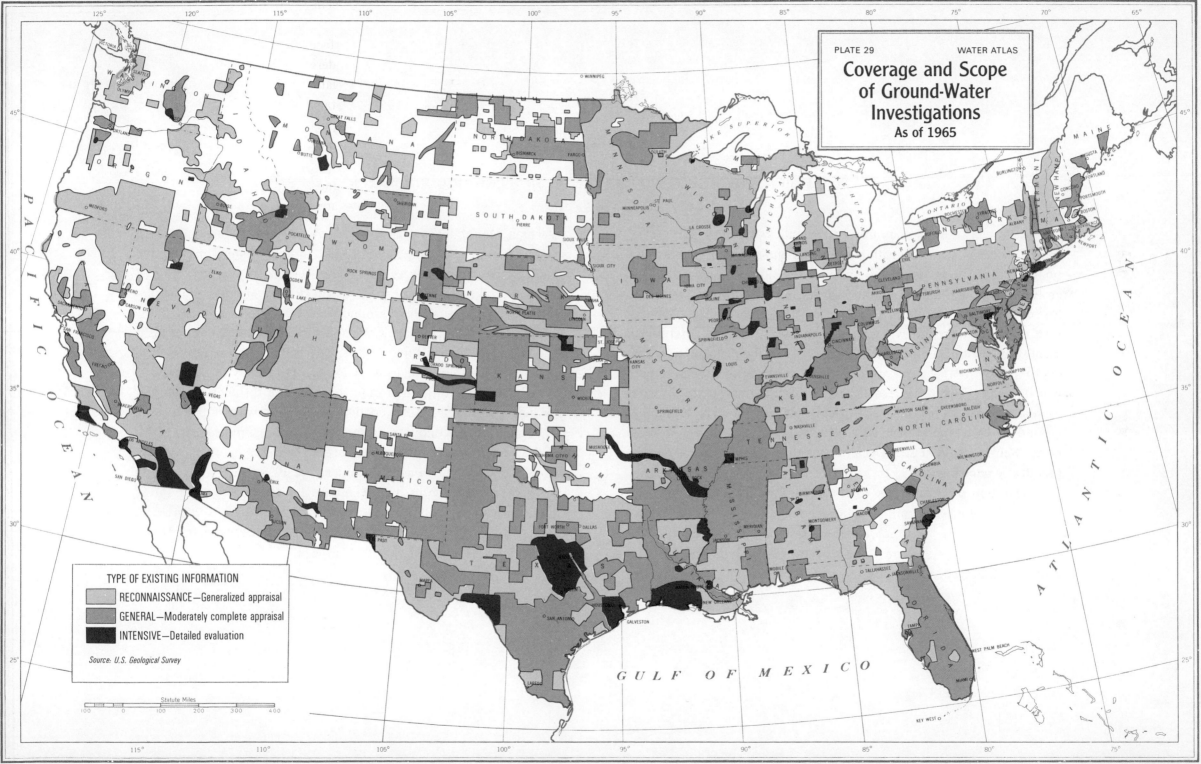

PLATE 29   WATER ATLAS

Coverage and Scope of Ground-Water Investigations
As of 1965

TYPE OF EXISTING INFORMATION

RECONNAISSANCE—Generalized appraisal

GENERAL—Moderately complete appraisal

INTENSIVE—Detailed evaluation

Source: U.S. Geological Survey

Statute Miles
100   0   100   200   300   400

Base Map by U.S.C.&G.S.

© WATER INFORMATION CENTER, INC.

PLATE 30 – AVERAGE TEMPERATURE OF SHALLOW GROUND WATER

Although the temperature of ground water may vary from freezing (in caves and beneath snow fields and glaciers) to above the boiling point (in super-heated geysers), the normal temperature of ground water at shallow depths in the United States ranges from a low of about 37 degrees F. to a high of 77 degrees F. The temperature of shallow ground water in a particular locality is determined mainly by the mean annual air temperature of the region. At greater depths, the internal heat of the earth controls the temperature, which on the average, increases approximately one degree F. with each additional 50 to 100 feet of depth below land surface. Normal ground-water temperatures at a depth of 30 to 60 feet seldom vary more than a degree or so all year long, and at greater depths, remain practically unchanged.

The map shows that the lowest ground-water temperatures are in northern Minnesota and the highest temperatures are in the extreme southern tip of Florida. In the eastern part of the country, the temperature shows a more or less regular increase from north to south. A deflection of the contour lines is apparent all along the Appalachian Mountains, owing to the relatively low average annual air temperature at these higher altitudes. In the western part of the country, temperatures vary irregularly because of the very rugged topography. In the highest parts of the Rocky Mountains in Colorado and Wyoming, shallow ground waters have temperatures as low as 42 degrees F., in contrast with temperatures some 10 degrees higher in adjacent lowlands and valleys. The belt of comparatively high temperatures in California is in the low Central Valley of that state.

The stability of ground-water temperature throughout the year is a highly desirable characteristic wherever the water is to be used for cooling or air-conditioning purposes. Some appreciation of this can be gained by comparing the accompanying map with Plate 10, which indicates the range in temperature of surface-water bodies during the warm months of July and August. The comparison shows that temperatures in lakes and rivers are from 10 to 20 degrees F. higher than those in shallow aquifers during the warm season, when demands for cooling water are at their peak.

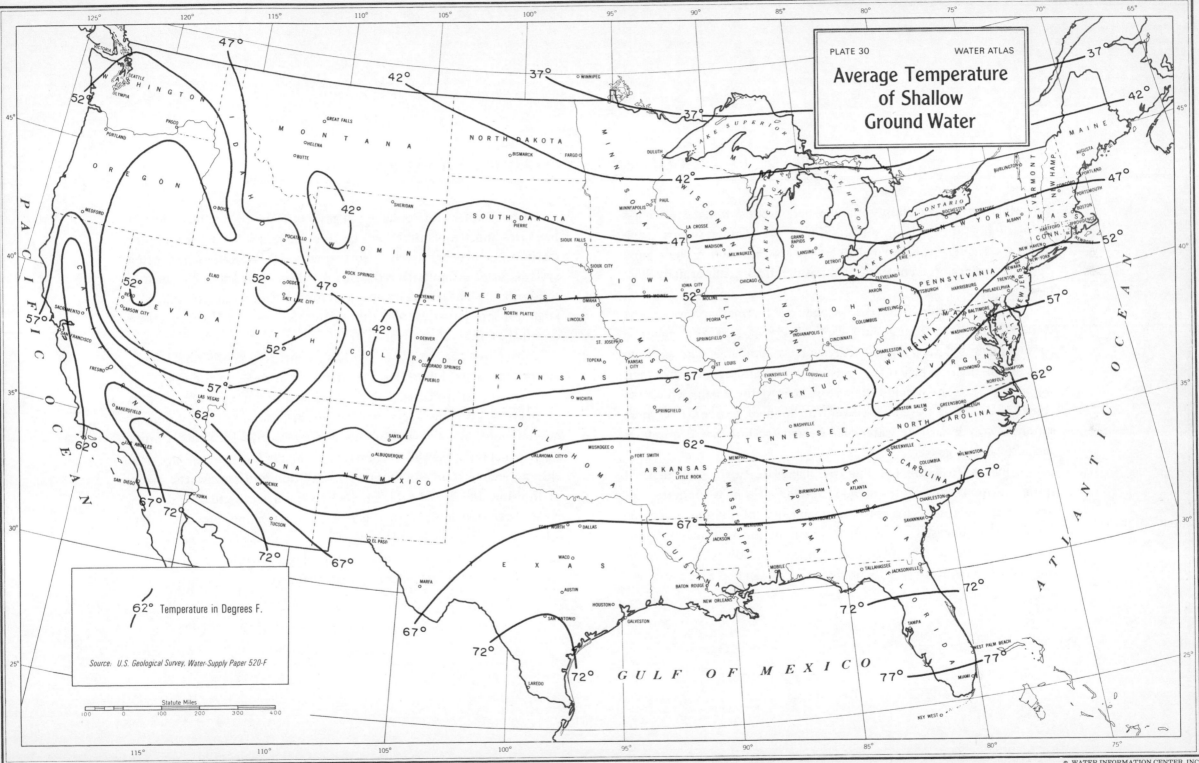

PLATE 30   WATER ATLAS

Average Temperature of Shallow Ground Water

62° Temperature in Degrees F.

Source: U.S. Geological Survey, Water-Supply Paper 520-F

Statute Miles

100   0   100   200   300   400

Base Map by U.S.C.&G.S.

© WATER INFORMATION CENTER, INC.

PLATE 31 — THERMAL SPRINGS AND GEOTHERMAL ENERGY

Most springs are simply places where ground water is discharging naturally at the land surface. Thus, the temperature of such springs is usually the same as that of the ground water in the region. Thermal springs, by contrast, yield water having abnormally high temperatures.

Nearly two-thirds of the recognized thermal springs in the United States issue from granitic varieties of rock that are thought to be underlain by deep-seated heat sources. Available data indicate that the thermal springs of the western mountain region derive their water chiefly from precipitation seeping into the earth, which becomes heated as it travels downward to the heat source. If the heat supply is very great, the water may become so hot that it erupts at the surface as a geyser.

It has been estimated that the aggregate flow of all thermal springs in the United States is about 500,000 gallons per minute, and some of the largest springs produce many tens of millions of gallons per day. The largest thermal spring in the nation is probably Warm Spring in Montana, which has a discharge of 80,000 gallons per minute, but a temperature of only 68 degrees F.

Geothermal heat contained in gases or fluids having high enough pressures and temperatures can be of economic value in energy production. In a general way, geothermal fields are either hot-spring systems or deep insulated reservoirs that have little leakage of heated fluids to the surface. Yellowstone National Park is an example of a large hot-spring system, while the Salton Sea area in California is an example of an insulated system.

Over five percent of the world's resources of geothermal energy are in the United States, most of it stored in rocks in the upper six miles of the earth's crust. The U. S. Geological Survey estimates that as much as 1.5 million acres of land appear promising for geothermal development, mostly within the western portions of the United States, including Hawaii and possibly Alaska. Such areas may provide an energy source of from 15 to 30 thousand megawatts. Many of the sites are on Federal land. Six very good geothermal fields have been discovered in California, Nevada, and Wyoming. The only operating power station is at The Geysers in California. Its generating capacity, as of May 1973, is 302,000 kilowatts with a projected increase to 412,000 kilowatts in the near future.

PLATE 31   WATER ATLAS

Thermal Springs and Geothermal Energy

Thermal springs

Geothermal field

Sources: U.S. Geological Survey Prof. Paper 492 and
J. B. Koenig, Calif. Div. of Mines and Geology

Statute Miles
100 0 100 200 300 400

PLATE 32 – GROUND-WATER USE (AS PERCENT OF TOTAL WATER USE – 1970)

This map shows the percentage of all water withdrawn (excluding water used for water power) that is taken from natural underground water sources in each state. Ground-water use is steadily increasing in importance, and in 1970, the total fresh ground-water withdrawal in the nation (including Alaska and Hawaii) was 68 billion gallons per day or 21 percent of all fresh water withdrawn. An additional one billion gallons per day of saline ground water was also withdrawn. The total ground-water withdrawal was obtained from tens of millions of water wells. Some 500,000 new water wells are drilled each year in all parts of the nation.

Generally speaking, ground water is more heavily developed in states west of the Mississippi River than it is in the eastern part of the country. In Arizona, New Mexico, Arkansas, Oklahoma, Kansas, Nebraska and South Dakota, 50 percent or more of all water withdrawn is from water wells.

In the drier regions, where surface waters are not abundant, a great reliance is placed on underground water reserves. In many parts of the West, where irrigation is extensively practiced, it is generally more economic to obtain water supplies from wells than it is to construct facilities for importing surface water over large distances. The high percentage of ground-water use in the Southwestern and Central States reflects in large measure the heavy demand for irrigation water. Vermont shows an unusually high percentage from ground-water sources owing to the largely rural nature of its population.

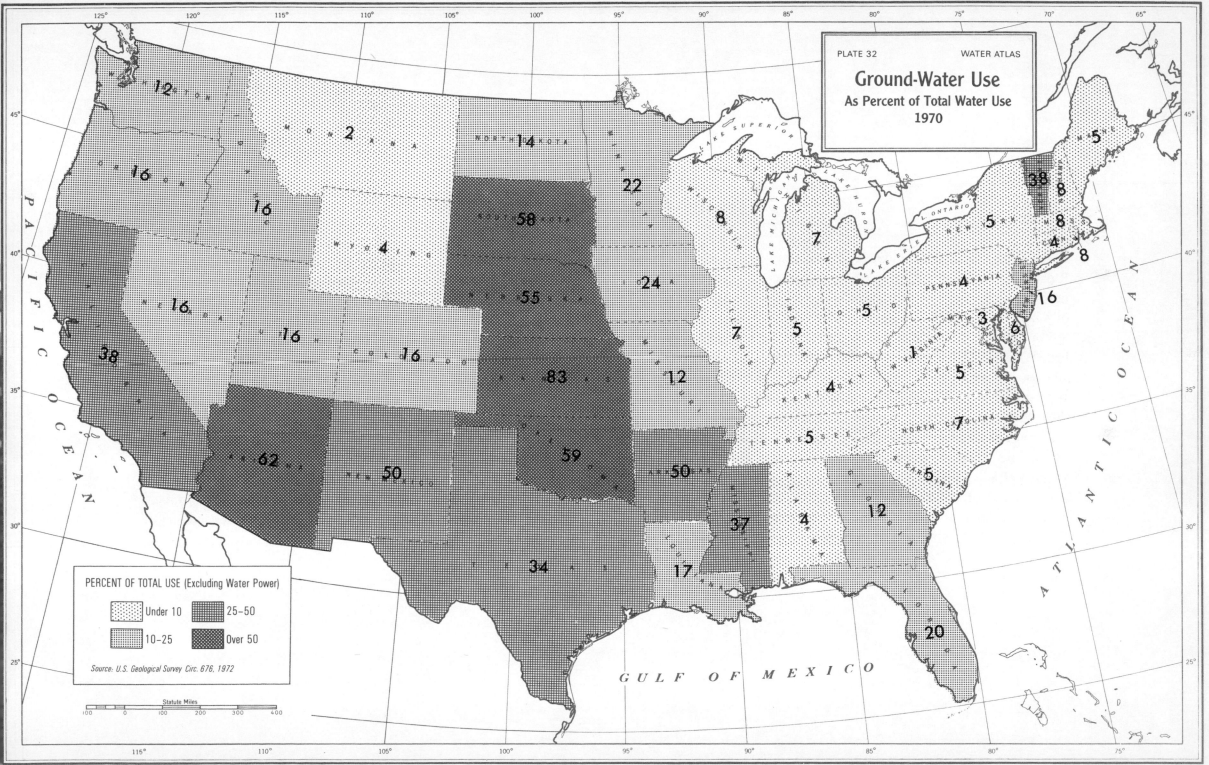

PLATE 32   WATER ATLAS

Ground-Water Use
As Percent of Total Water Use
1970

PERCENT OF TOTAL USE (Excluding Water Power)

Under 10

10-25

25-50

Over 50

Source: U.S. Geological Survey Circ. 676, 1972

Statute Miles

100   0   100   200   300   400

Base Map by U.S.C.&G.S.   © WATER INFORMATION CENTER, INC.

PACIFIC OCEAN

ATLANTIC OCEAN

GULF OF MEXICO

LAKE SUPERIOR   LAKE MICHIGAN   LAKE HURON   L. ONTARIO   LAKE ERIE

PLATE 33 – SURFACE-WATER LAWS

In all parts of the country, water laws are largely based on the Riparian Doctrine, the Appropriation Doctrine, or a combination of both. A riparian right to withdraw water is based on the ownership of land next to a surface-water body. The right is independent of the use or non-use of the water. An appropriation right is based upon the beneficial use of the water. In other words, the first to appropriate and use the water has a priority over others who come along and appropriate at a later time. An appropriation right is independent of the location of the land with respect to the water.

The map shows that all states roughly east of the 95th meridian follow the Riparian Doctrine exclusively, with the exception of Mississippi and Florida. This eastern half of the country coincides with the area of water surplus shown on Plate 15. In this humid region, the Riparian Doctrine requires a land owner to allow the stream to flow by or through his land in its natural state. Thus, in its strict sense, the right does not allow for the consumptive use of the water except for small domestic needs. When irrigation becomes necessary in a riparian state, the courts modify the doctrine to allow reasonable use in relation to neighboring users. No riparian user can take all the water of a stream and allow none to flow down to his neighbor. This contrasts sharply with the appropriator's right in other parts of the country to consume all that he needs.

The Mountain States follow the Appropriation Doctrine exclusively; other states recognize both doctrines. In those states that recognize both, the relative importance of each doctrine varies considerably.

In addition to riparian and appropriation rights, there is a third kind of right based on need. Some examples of this type are Indian water rights, Federal Reserve rights, and, in some cases, municipal rights.

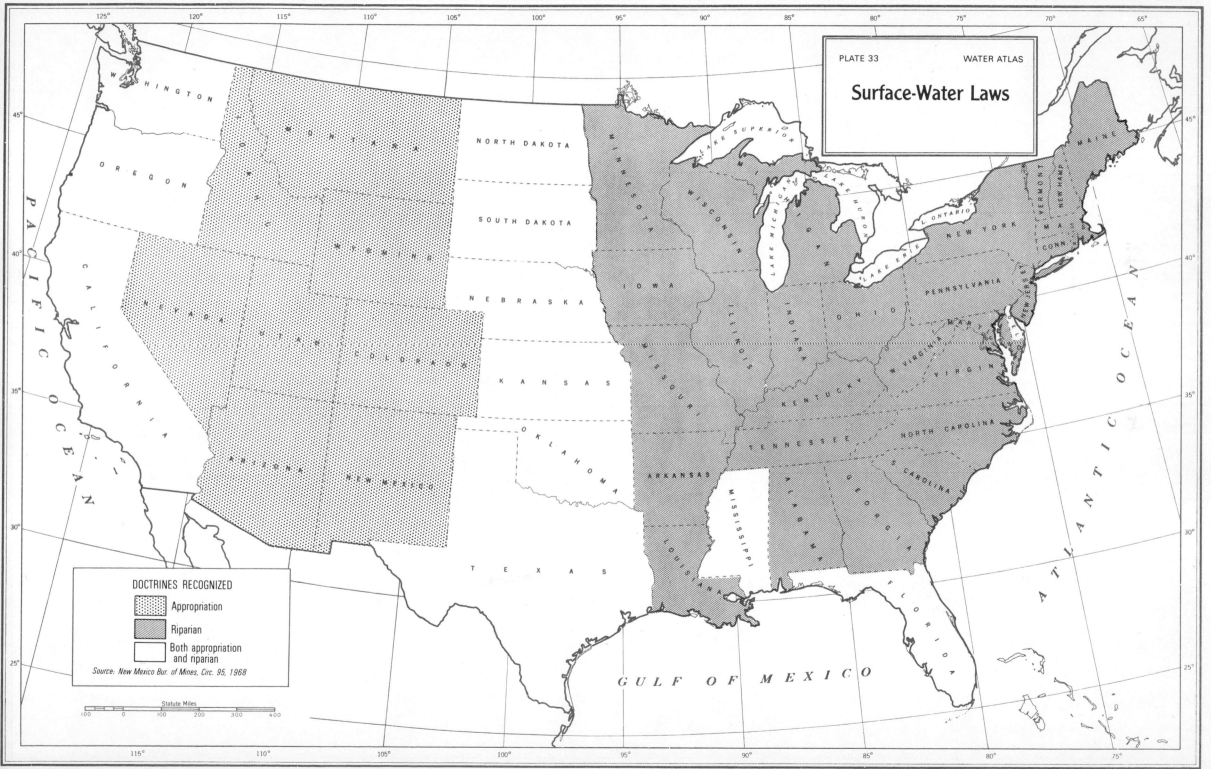

PLATE 33   WATER ATLAS

Surface-Water Laws

DOCTRINES RECOGNIZED

- Appropriation
- Riparian
- Both appropriation and riparian

Source: New Mexico Bur. of Mines, Circ. 95, 1968

Statute Miles
100   0   100   200   300   400

PLATE 34 — GROUND-WATER LAWS

In all states, water laws relating to ground waters generally are based on either the Riparian Doctrine or the Appropriation Doctrine (an explanation of these doctrines is given in the text accompanying Plate 33). The Eastern States generally use the English common-law version of the Riparian Doctrine, which gives absolute ownership of ground water to the land owner. Fifteen states modify this version and apply the American rule of "reasonable use", which restricts the landowner's rights in relation to others. California goes one step further in the modification of the Riparian Doctrine with its doctrine of "correlative rights". Here, the landowner's use must not only be reasonable, but must be correlated with the uses of others during times of shortage. When the supply is limited, use is restricted to the lands directly overlying the common supply.

While the Appropriation Doctrine seems to function easily for surface-water supplies in the arid states, it runs into some difficulty when it is applied to ground water. The main reason for this is that ground water is a hidden resource, whose occurrence and movement are poorly understood by most people.

Many states, in recent years, have begun to expand their control and regulation of ground-water use, and this has resulted in the creation of many special rules and regulations. Some of these apply to methods of well construction, monitoring of changes in ground-water levels and ground-water quality, periodic submission of data on ground-water use, and preventive measures to minimize contamination and pollution.

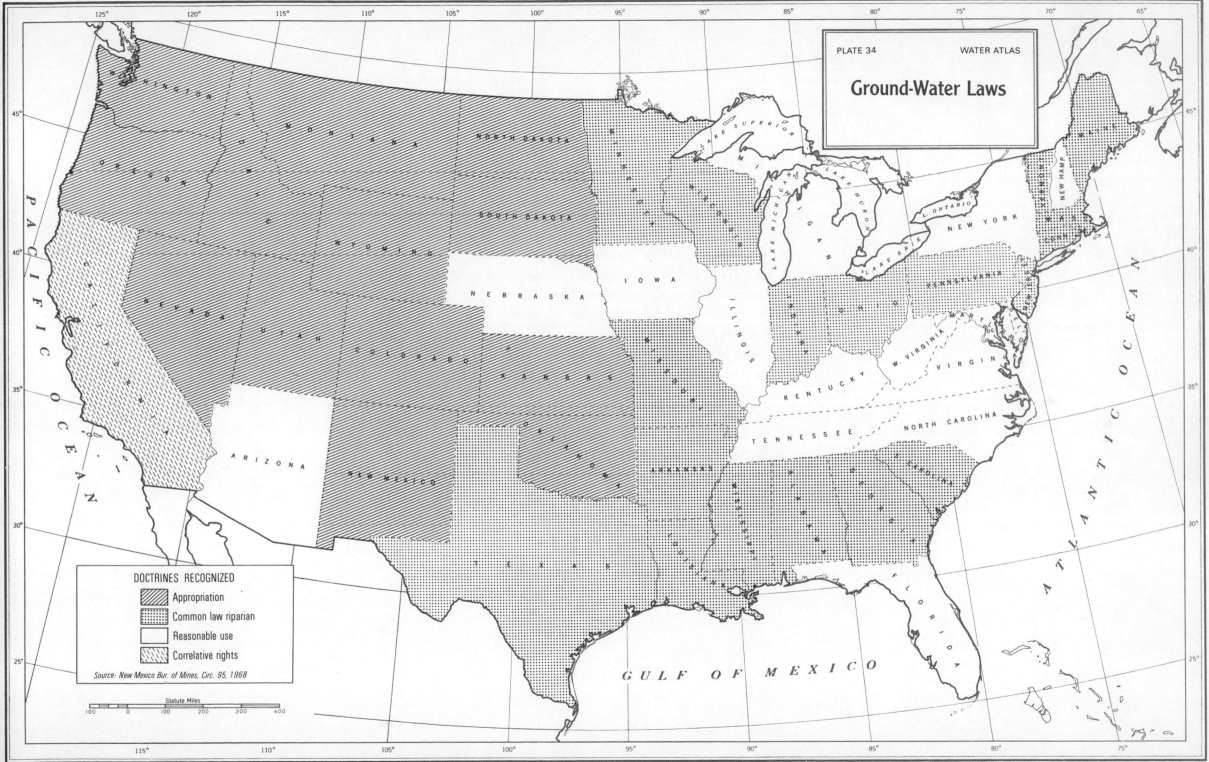

PLATE 34   WATER ATLAS

Ground-Water Laws

DOCTRINES RECOGNIZED

- Appropriation
- Common law riparian
- Reasonable use
- Correlative rights

Source: New Mexico Bur. of Mines, Circ. 95, 1968

Statute Miles
100   0   100   200   300   400

PLATE 35 — WEATHER MODIFICATION LAWS

This map shows the states that so far have enacted specific legislation dealing with weather modification. Such statutes regulate persons engaged in "rain-making" and provide for the administration of these activities.

Many scientists feel that the licensing and regulation of weather modification should be carried on at the federal level instead of at the state level. Weather modification does not simply mean "rain-making", but also includes fog dissipation, hail suppression, and the control of severe storms. Because the effects of such operations cannot be limited to specific land areas, it seems that federal legislation would be required to cope with problems of indemnification and litigation arising from weather modification. However, such federal legislation is unlikely in the near future, and if a law is ever written, it probably will gradually emerge as a result of decisions rendered in test cases based on established water law.

The social and legal implications of weather modification appear insurmountable at times, especially when one considers examples like these: if it were possible to change the direction of a hurricane away from a city, to where would the hurricane be diverted? Who would make the decision to spare the city and direct the disaster to the rural areas? How would the farmers be compensated for losses in life, crops, and livestock?

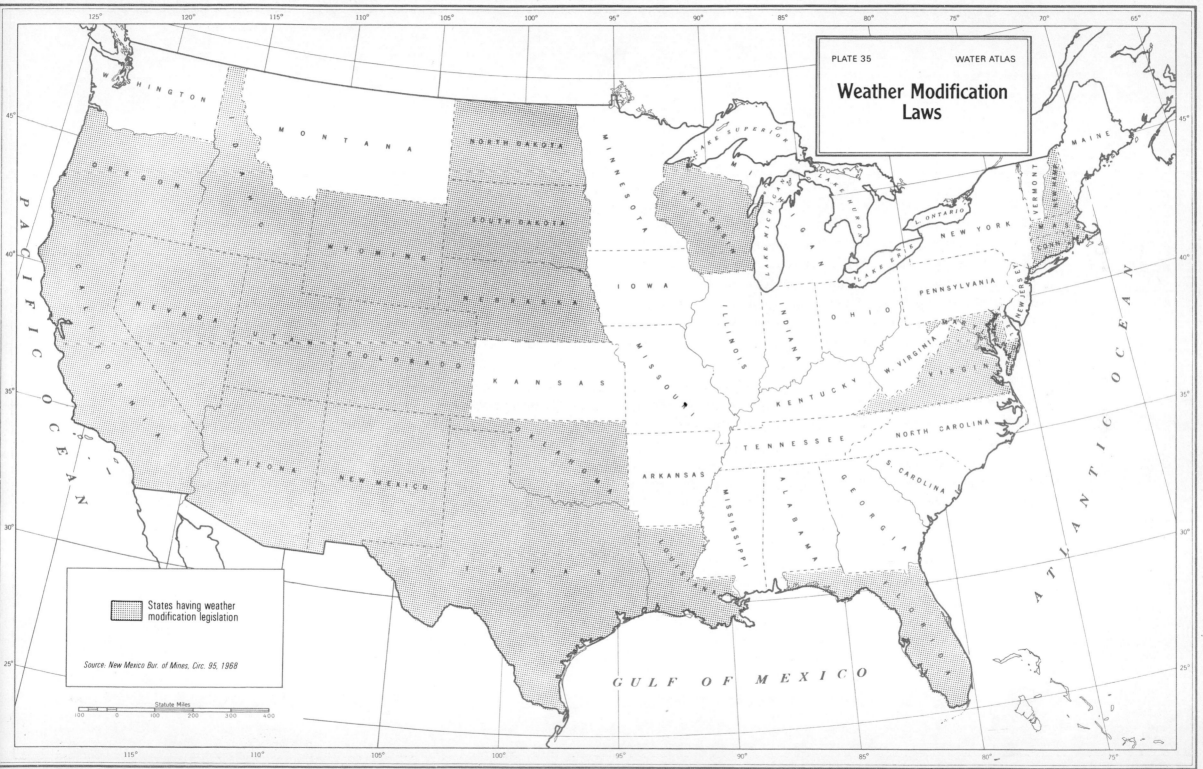

PLATE 35   WATER ATLAS

Weather Modification Laws

States having weather
modification legislation

Source: New Mexico Bur. of Mines, Circ. 95, 1968

Statute Miles

PLATE 36 — DEEP WELL DISPOSAL LAWS

In recent years, the practice of injecting industrial or municipal liquid wastes through wells into deep geologic formations, as a relatively inexpensive way of overcoming the disposal problem, has been growing in the United States. For the most part, wells of this kind discharge the wastes into beds that naturally contain salty water unfit for human consumption and that are hydraulically separated from other beds that could serve as sources of water supply.

The subtle nature of vertical and horizontal migration of fluids in the subsurface environment has created some very tough problems for the country's lawmakers. Although a waste-disposal well can be responsible for, or contribute to, pollution and contamination, it may be very difficult to obtain enough sound data to prove the case. With the burden of proof on the plaintiff, only companies or people with adequate financial resources are in a position to conduct the necessary investigations.

Jurisdiction over the installation and operation of injection well systems is basically the responsibility of individual states; there is no specific Federal legislation regarding deep well disposal. However, where radioactive wastes are to be dealt with in this manner, a license must be obtained from the Atomic Energy Commission.

No state is known to have legislation that automatically denies the installation of wastewater injection systems. However, eight states subscribe to a policy of either rejecting applications (Arizona, Idaho, New Jersey, and Wisconsin) or discouraging them (Alaska, South Carolina, South Dakota, and New York). New York, for example, recently declared that its policy will be one of regarding liquid-waste injection as a "last resort".

Present policy in the remaining states for which information is available is to permit the practice of subsurface disposal. However, only five of these states — Michigan, Ohio, West Virginia, Missouri, and Texas — are reported to have specific legislation pertaining to the regulation of industrial wastewater injection. Several states, among which are Colorado, Mississippi, and Georgia, are in the process of preparing policy statements and regulations governing disposal wells.

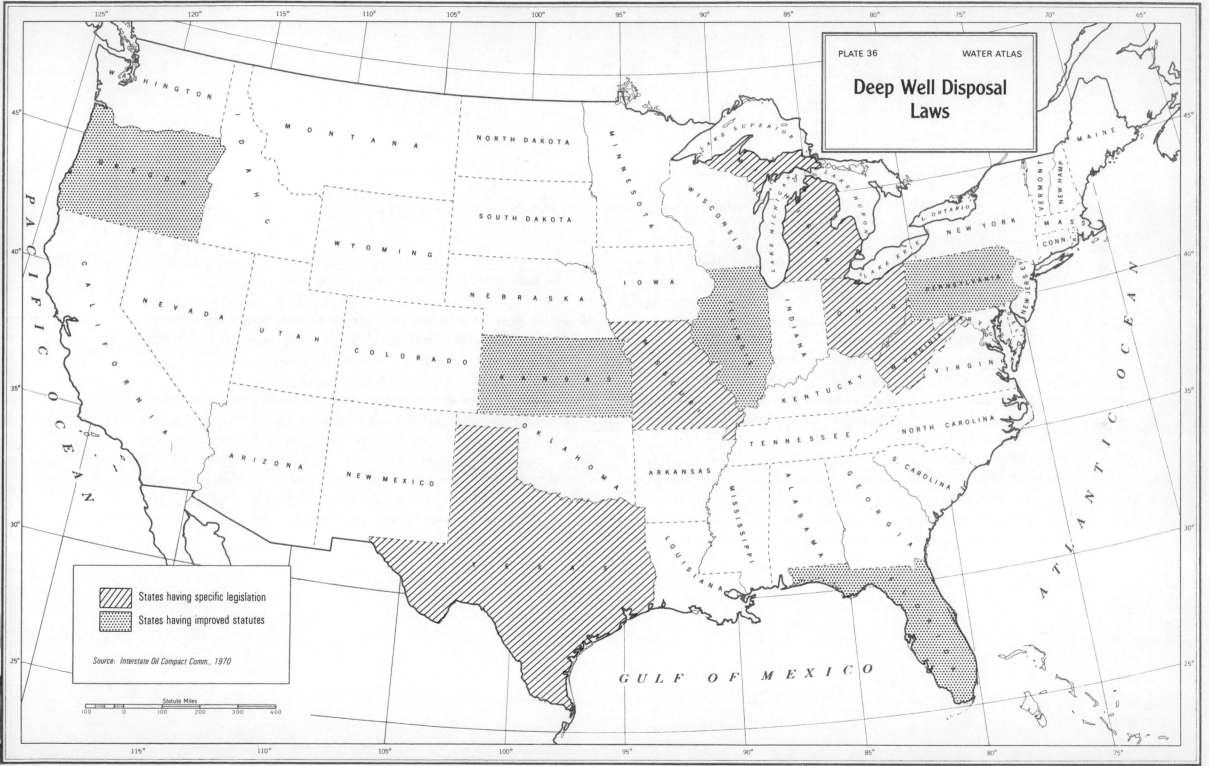

PLATE 36   WATER ATLAS

Deep Well Disposal Laws

States having specific legislation

States having improved statutes

Source: Interstate Oil Compact Comm., 1970

Statute Miles

Base Map by U.S.C.&G.S.

© WATER INFORMATION CENTER, INC.

PLATE 37 – DISSOLVED SOLIDS CONTENT OF SURFACE WATER

Although rain and snow contain only traces of dissolved mineral matter, waters that flow in rivers, streams, and through ground-water systems always contain a significant percentage of dissolved solids. These constituents in water originate from the weathering of soils and rocks. Generally, sedimentary rocks are more soluble than igneous or metamorphic rocks and contribute significant concentrations of sodium, calcium, magnesium, chloride, and sulfate ions to the water. This is especially true where the waters are associated with evaporites and with other sediments retaining saline water from former marine environments.

The map shows the concentrations of dissolved solids in fresh-water streams across the nation. The concentrations are given in parts per million (ppm) and refer to the number of units of mineral matter contained in one million units of water. A million units of normal ocean water, for example, contains about 35,000 units of mineral matter. In some places, the mineral content of inland surface waters is several times that of ocean water.

There are four commonly used classifications for water, based on the concentration of total dissolved solids. Fresh water has between 0 and 1000 ppm, brackish water ranges from 1000 to 10,000 ppm, salty water is defined as between 10,000 and 100,000 ppm, and brine contains more than 100,000 ppm.

Concentrations of dissolved solids in fresh-water streams tend to be low in areas of abundant rainfall such as in the East and the Northwest, and high in the Southwest where the rocks are not as completely leached. The average concentration for all the country's surface water discharged to the oceans is about 130 ppm, or 225 million tons of mineral matter per year. It is the equivalent of 82 tons per year removed from each square mile of land area.

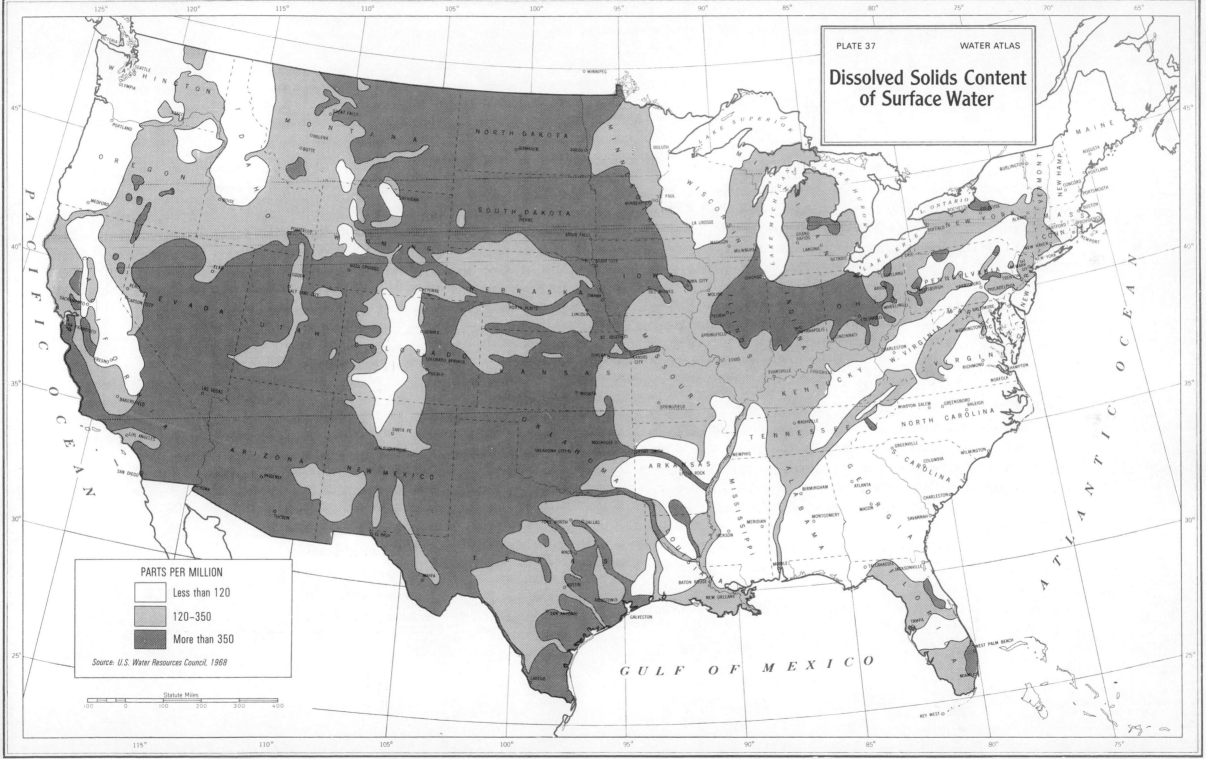

PLATE 37   WATER ATLAS

Dissolved Solids Content of Surface Water

PARTS PER MILLION

Less than 120

120–350

More than 350

Source: U.S. Water Resources Council, 1968

Statute Miles

PLATE 38 – SALINE SURFACE WATER

The map shows those areas in the United States where streams and lakes contain saline water. The term "saline" refers to water containing more than 1000 ppm (parts per million) of dissolved solids. All waters defined as brackish, salty, or brine fall into this category (see text for Plate 37 for a more detailed explanation of these terms).

Saline water is generally considered to be unsuitable for human consumption or for irrigation. There are, however, a few locations in the Southwest where water containing more than 4,000 ppm of dissolved solids is used continuously for irrigation. In some areas of the Southwest and the Great Plains, supplies containing as much as 2,500 ppm are used for drinking by people who have become accustomed to such water.

The high concentrations of dissolved solids in saline water are usually related to the types of underlying rock formations. In some regions, beds of salt deposited in the ancient basins of dried-up seas are the source of the mineral matter. In other areas, limestone, gypsum, and similar soluble rocks are responsible for heavy concentrations of minerals.

In closed topographic basins having no surface-water outlets, evaporation of water causes an increase in the concentration of dissolved solids. Many lakes in such areas contain water that has been concentrated by evaporation or that has redissolved accumulated salts left by receding water.

Saline waters occur in tidal streams along the coast where the mixing of sea water and surface water may extend several miles inland. Near the mouth of a stream, the concentration of dissolved solids may approach that of sea water. Successive reuse for irrigation may increase the dissolved solids content of the water draining from irrigated land; the increase may amount to several thousand ppm. Oilfield, municipal, and industrial wastes also may contribute to the salinity of surface water in some localities.

The 10 largest saline lakes in the country are listed below:

Lake	Location	Present Area (square miles)
Great Salt	Utah	1,000
Pontchartrain	Louisiana	625
Salton Sea	California	350
Pyramid	Nevada	180
Walker	Nevada	107
Goose	California and Oregon	100
Sabine	Louisiana and Texas	95
Calcasieu	Louisiana and Texas	90
Maurepas	Louisiana and Texas	90
Salvador	Louisiana and Texas	70

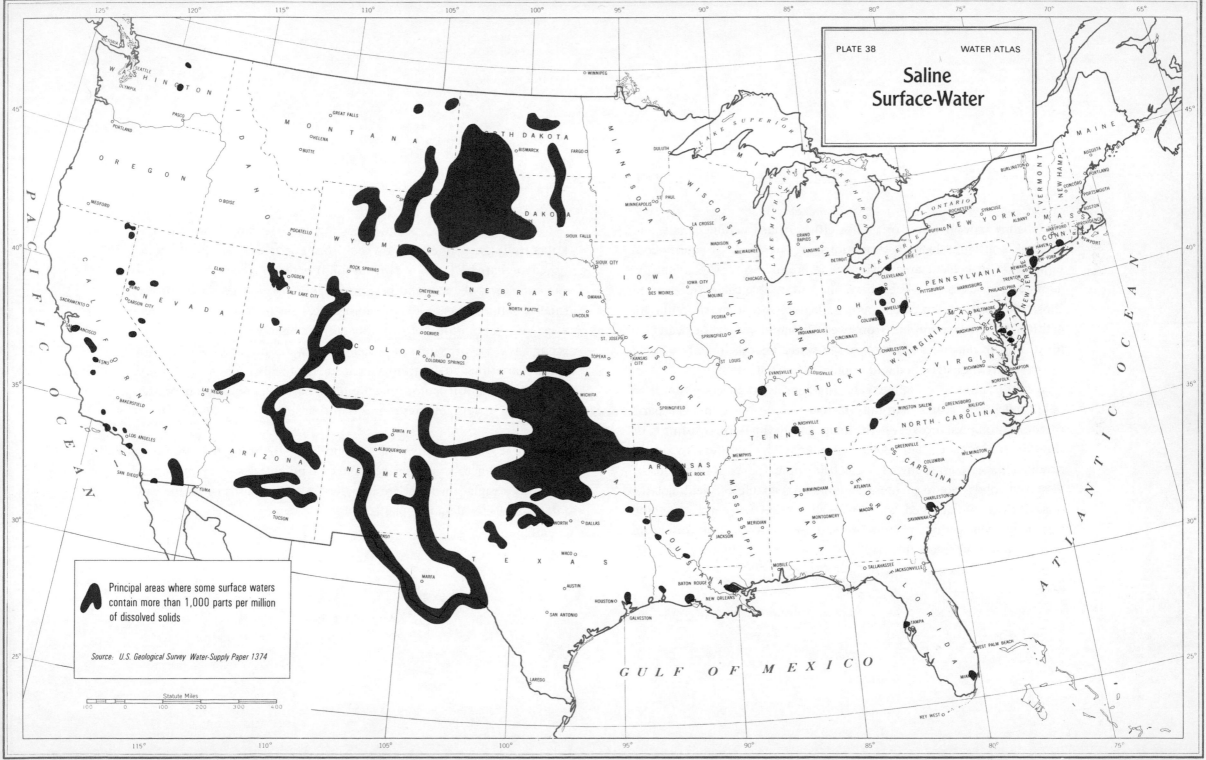

PLATE 38   WATER ATLAS

Saline Surface-Water

Principal areas where some surface waters contain more than 1,000 parts per million of dissolved solids

Source: U.S. Geological Survey Water-Supply Paper 1374

Statute Miles

Base Map by U.S.C.&G.S.

© WATER INFORMATION CENTER, INC.

PLATE 39 — DEPTH TO SALINE GROUND WATER

Saline ground water originates either from leaching of salts and minerals contained in rock formations, or as a result of aquifer contamination in coastal areas. The saline ground waters in inland regions are residues left over from ancient geological periods when those areas were submerged under saline seas. In some shoreline localities, excessive pumping from wells has induced saline water to move inland causing problems of salt-water encroachment in some of the highly industrialized and populated coastal cities.

Large amounts of saline water (perhaps as much as 40 thousand cubic miles) are stored naturally in rocks at various depths in parts of the nation. As shown on the map, approximately two-thirds of the conterminous United States is underlain by aquifers known to produce water containing at least 1000 ppm (parts per million) of dissolved solids. Some of these aquifers are capable of yielding large quantities of mineralized water to wells. Areas with wells yielding less than seven gallons per minute and areas with little information have been left blank on the map.

The large saline ground-water region extending from the Dakotas to Texas is underlain by rock formations that are partly composed of natural beds of salt. Ground water entering these formations dissolves the salt and becomes highly mineralized. Some of the smaller saline areas in the Western States are in regions where high rates of evaporation help to concentrate dissolved minerals in the ground waters. In general, the salinity of water increases with depth. Local variations in hydrology and geology, however, may modify this pattern, and it is not uncommon in coastal regions to encounter alternating layers of fresh and salty ground water in the aquifers.

Saline ground water, once considered to be of no value and even a nuisance, now represents a vast potential source of water, either as a replacement of fresh water for certain uses or as the raw intake water for desalting plants.

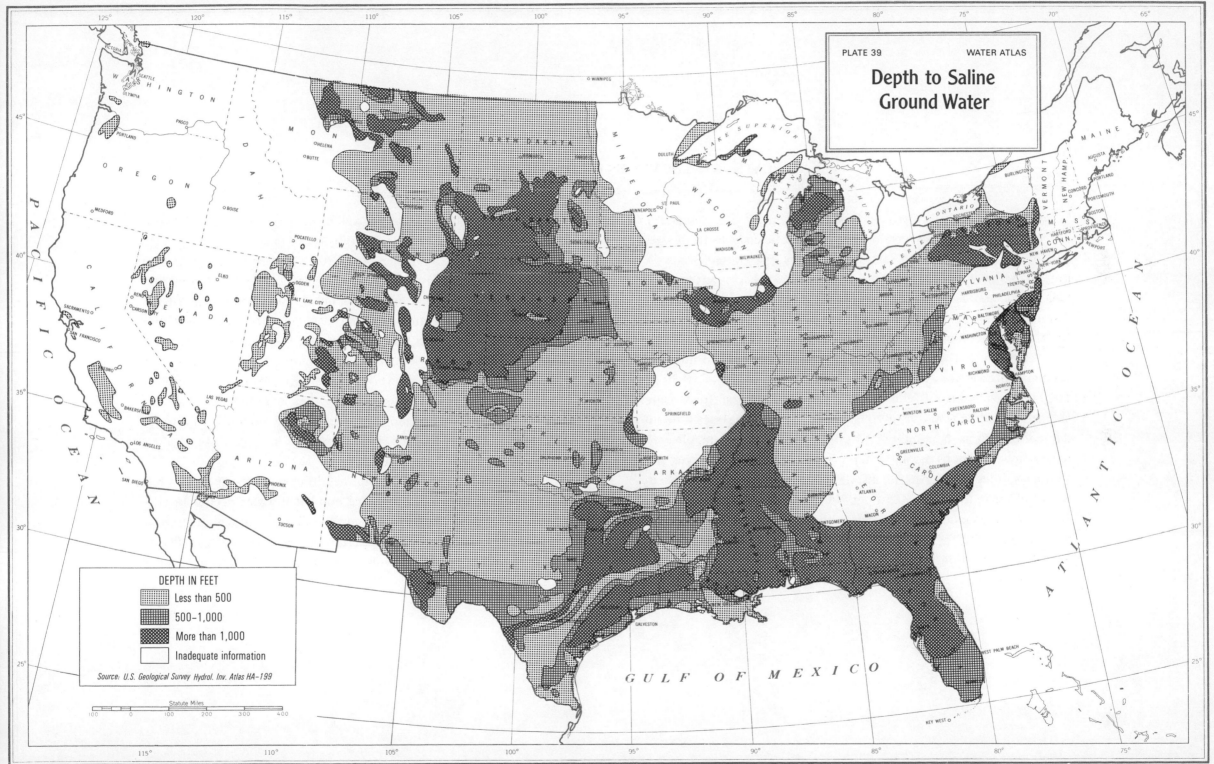

PLATE 39   WATER ATLAS

Depth to Saline Ground Water

DEPTH IN FEET

- Less than 500
- 500–1,000
- More than 1,000
- Inadequate information

Source: U.S. Geological Survey Hydrol. Inv. Atlas HA-199

Statute Miles

PLATE 40 – LOCATIONS OF DESALTING PLANTS

In recent years, a new emphasis has been given to research in salt-water conversion because of a growing deficiency in fresh-water supplies in many arid and semi-arid parts of the United States. At present, saline-water conversion is an expensive process, but in places like islands and deserts, it may be the only way of providing drinking water. In addition, many industries requiring extremely pure water for processing and manufacturing utilize demineralizing plants.

Research and development has been directed toward new conversion processes that can produce fresh water at a cost of $0.30 per 1000 gallons, which is the average price for natural fresh water charged by public water-supply systems in the United States. Present-day conversion costs are about $1.00 per 1000 gallons (undelivered) for one mgd (millions of gallons daily) capacity plants. However, projections of desalting costs in distillation plants of 10-mgd capacity would lower it to about $0.50 per 1000 gallons by 1975. One weakness in some economic evaluations is that the quoted figures almost never include the cost of delivering the water. In most cases, delivery is the major portion of the total cost of water. A good municipal well, for instance, can produce large quantities of water for only a few cents per 1000 gallons at the well head. The storage and delivery costs push the rate up into the $0.20 to $0.30 range.

On January 1, 1969, there were 307 desalting plants of 25,000 gallons per day capacity or greater in operation or under construction in the country (including Alaska and Hawaii), comprising a total capacity of about 43 million gallons per day. Practically all of the plants use the distillation process; a few use the membrane and crystallization processes. The two largest plants, each producing 2.6 mgd., are at San Diego, California and at Key West, Florida; both process water for municipal supplies. Other large installations with a capacity of one mgd or more are located at San Diego, California; Siesta Key, Florida; Roswell, New Mexico; Clairton, Pennsylvania; and in Freeport and Texas City, both in Texas.

About 25 percent of the total desalting capacity in the United States is for the purpose of meeting municipal water needs. An estimated 2 percent of the total is used for military and demonstration purposes, and the remaining 73 percent is for industrial use. Plants located along the coast desalt sea water, but inland plants use brackish or saline water as a source.

PLATE 40   WATER ATLAS

Locations of Desalting Plants

FRESH WATER CAPACITY
(thousands of gallons per day)

- · Less than 100
- • 100–500
- ● 500–1,000
- ⬤ Over 1,000
- ○ Office of Saline Water
  Pilot Plant Facility

Source: U.S. Office of Saline Water, 1969

Statute Miles

Base Map by U.S.C.&G.S.

© WATER INFORMATION CENTER, INC.

PLATE 41 – HARDNESS OF SURFACE WATER

The term "hardness" is applied to the soap-neutralizing power of a water. It is the characteristic of water that shows itself in the increased quantity of soap required to produce a lather, and by the insoluble mineral scale deposited in boilers and kettles when such water is heated or evaporated. For the most part, hardness is attributable to calcium and magnesium in the water. Water having a hardness of less than 60 ppm (parts per million) is considered soft. A hardness of 60 to 120 ppm does not seriously interfere with the use of water for most purposes, although the consumption of soap is increased somewhat. Water having a hardness of more than 120 ppm is rated as hard, and is commonly softened when used for domestic and some industrial purposes. The map shows five separate patterns for the hardness of surface waters in the United States.

Hardness is due mainly to the composition of the soils and rocks over which the water moves. In general, rocks of the limestone variety, which are readily soluble, are the basic source of much of the hard water in the nation. In addition, regions where saline waters are naturally present (see Plates 37, 38, and 39) also have higher percentages of hard water.

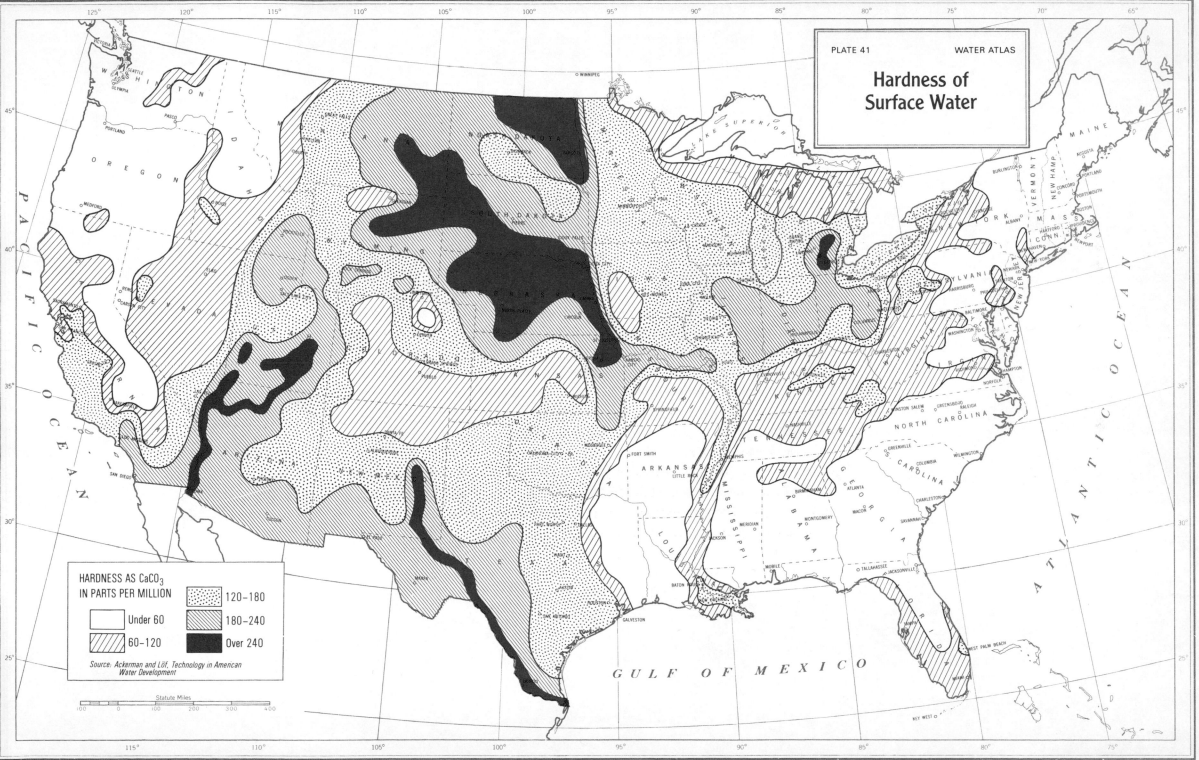

PLATE 41   WATER ATLAS

Hardness of Surface Water

HARDNESS AS CaCO₃
IN PARTS PER MILLION

	120–180
Under 60	180–240
60–120	Over 240

Source: Ackerman and Löf, Technology in American Water Development

Statute Miles

Base Map by U.S.C.&G.S.   © WATER INFORMATION CENTER, INC.

PLATE 42 – HARDNESS OF GROUND WATER

The map shows the general pattern of hardness of ground waters in the United States (the term "hardness" is explained in the text accompanying Plate 41). The large hard-water area in the north-central part of the country is underlain mainly by limestone. The Florida peninsula is also composed mostly of limestone, which accounts for the relatively high hardness of ground water there. Only a few sections of the country, notably the New England States, some areas along the Atlantic and Gulf Coastal Plains, and large parts of the States of Oregon and Washington, fall into the soft ground-water category.

The patterns shown on the map do not necessarily mean that all ground waters in a specific area have exactly the same hardness. Some of the ground waters in localities indicated as hard-water areas may be soft, for example, and vice versa. The map patterns simply mean that most of the ground water in any given region displays the indicated hardness range.

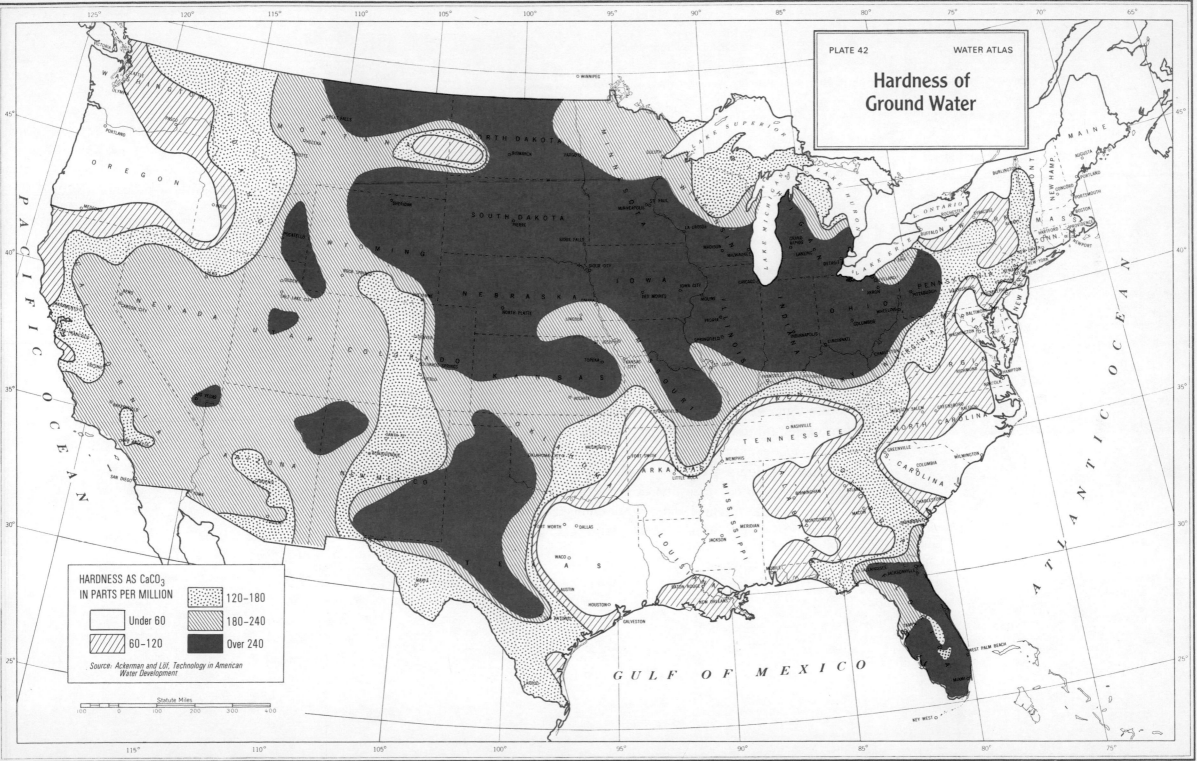

PLATE 42   WATER ATLAS

Hardness of Ground Water

HARDNESS AS CaCO₃
IN PARTS PER MILLION

- Under 60
- 60–120
- 120–180
- 180–240
- Over 240

Source: Ackerman and Löf, Technology in American Water Development

Statute Miles

Base Map by U.S.C.&G.S.

© WATER INFORMATION CENTER, INC.

PLATE 43 – HARDNESS OF UNTREATED PUBLIC WATER SUPPLIES

The map depicts, by individual states, the average hardness of raw, untreated municipal water supplies (the term "hardness" is explained in the text accompanying Plate 41). No distinction is made as to whether the water comes from surface-water or ground-water sources.

The information is based on data from 1,596 municipal water systems serving about 102 million people, or roughly 80 percent of the urban population and about 57 percent of the total population. As shown by the map, soft water containing less than 60 ppm (parts per million) of hardness is obtained for municipal use only in some states along the Atlantic and Gulf Coasts, and in Oregon and Washington. It should be kept in mind that the map shows only average water hardness, and does not depict the natural wide range in hardness that normally shows up when all of the water resources of any particular state are examined.

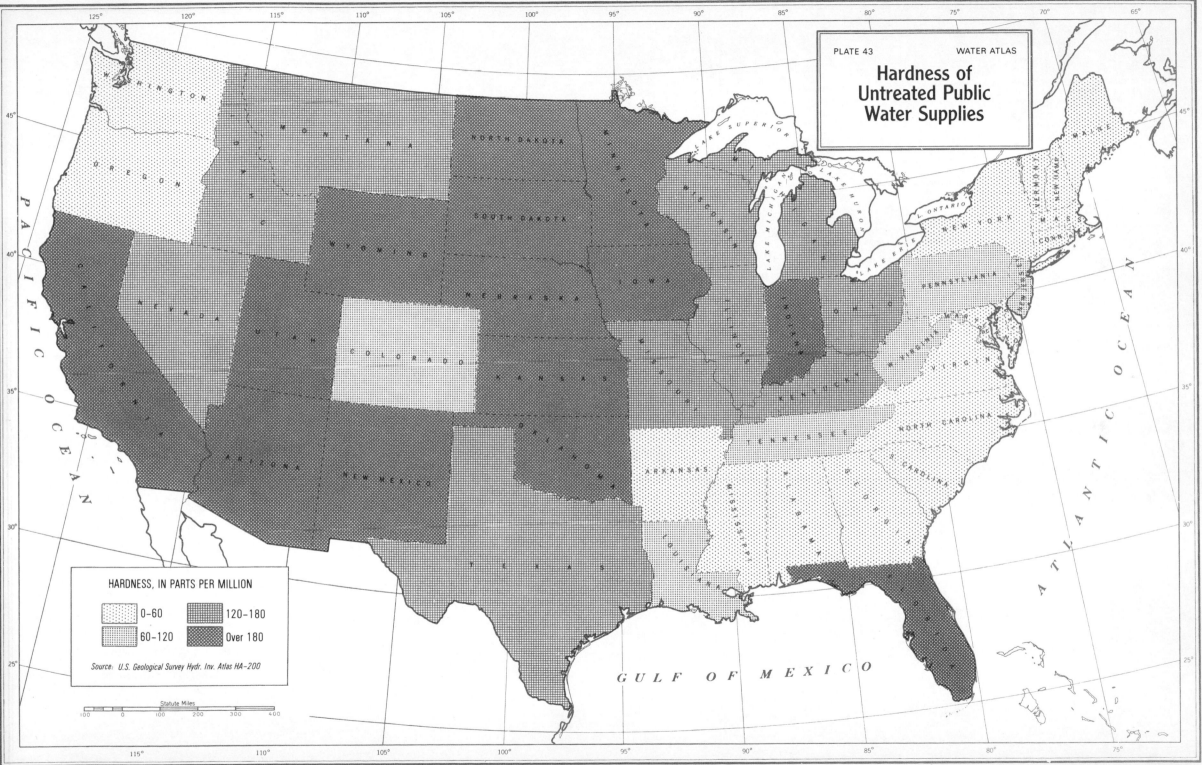

PLATE 43   WATER ATLAS

Hardness of Untreated Public Water Supplies

HARDNESS, IN PARTS PER MILLION

- 0-60
- 60-120
- 120-180
- Over 180

Source: U.S. Geological Survey Hydr. Inv. Atlas HA-200

Statute Miles
100   0   100   200   300   400

PLATE 44 – HARDNESS OF FINISHED PUBLIC WATER SUPPLIES

Many municipalities in the nation, particularly in localities where natural or raw waters are very hard, treat their water supplies to reduce the degree of hardness. Thus, the finished water, which is the water actually delivered to homes after treatment, may be softer than the raw, untreated water. The principal softening agents are lime and lime-soda ash, which convert the dissolved calcium and magnesium into precipitates that settle out of the water as a sludge.

For the 1,596 cities with a total population of about 102 million people, on which the map is based, the overall average hardness of finished water is 111 ppm (parts per million). Data collected in 1960-61 for the 100 largest cities show that 29 of them, serving more than 21 million people, obtain soft raw water in the range of 0-60 ppm and do not soften these supplies. Sixteen other cities, serving more than 15 million people, have moderately hard raw water in the range of 60-120 ppm, and also do not soften their supplies. Twenty-two cities with about 16 million people use hard water in the range of 120-180 ppm; about half of these do not soften their water. Twenty-seven cities, having about 8 million people, tap very hard water containing more than 180 ppm; only 15 of these artificially soften their supplies.

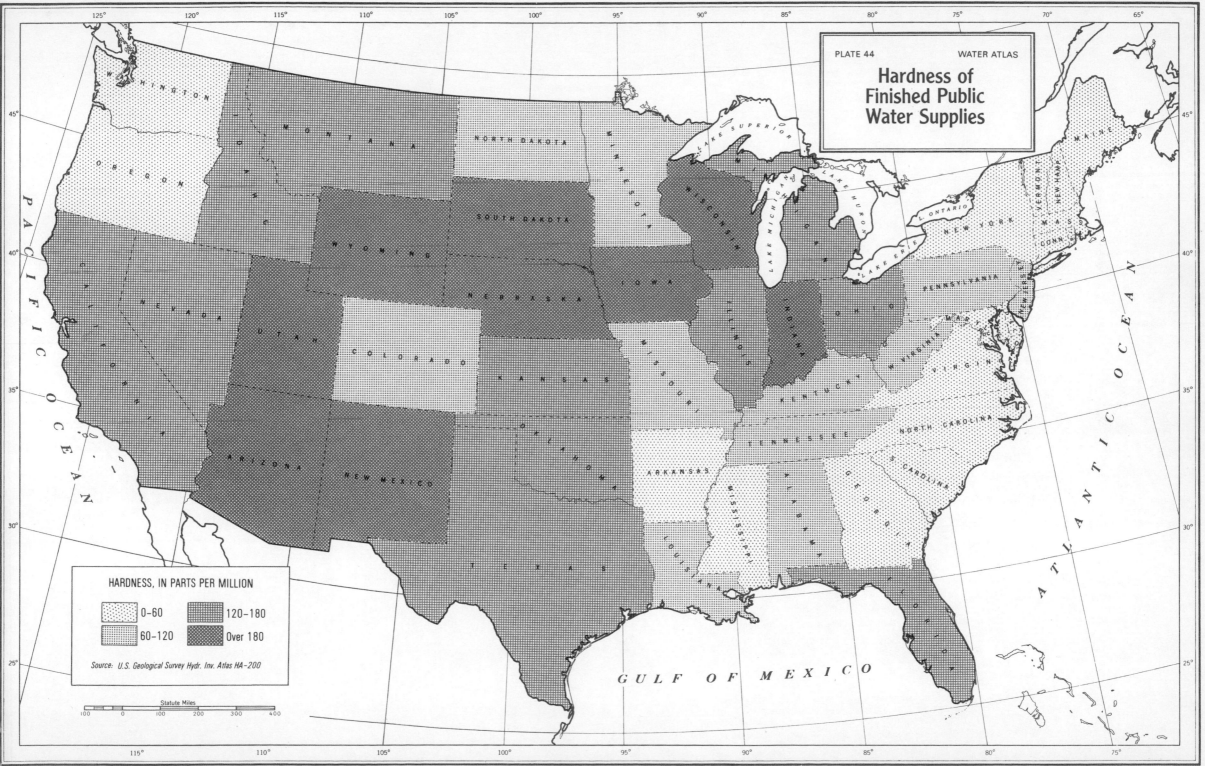

PLATE 44

WATER ATLAS

Hardness of Finished Public Water Supplies

HARDNESS, IN PARTS PER MILLION

0-60	120-180
60-120	Over 180

Source: U.S. Geological Survey Hydr. Inv. Atlas HA-200

Statute Miles
100 0 100 200 300 400

Base Map by U.S.C.&G.S.

© WATER INFORMATION CENTER, INC.

PLATE 45 – SODIUM IN UNTREATED PUBLIC WATER SUPPLIES

The map shows the average sodium content in untreated public water supplies by state, weighted by population served. Data for Wisconsin and Wyoming are insufficient to give reliable averages.

The sodium content of water is of concern to persons on sodium-restricted diets. In certain areas, where sodium concentrations in public water supplies are high enough to seriously affect such diets, precautions should be taken.

Sodium is a very active metal that does not occur freely in nature, although sodium compounds comprise 2.83 percent of the earth's crust. Sodium is generally found in much smaller concentrations than calcium and magnesium. Since nearly all sodium salts are extremely soluble in water, sodium leached from soil or originating from industrial waste tends to remain in solution. Certain ion-exchange reactions between sodium in soils and calcium and magnesium in ground water result in high sodium concentrations and low hardness. Other reactions may decrease sodium concentrations.

Common municipal water-treatment methods usually raise the sodium content of water. Sodium carbonate, a compound used to raise the pH and a softening agent when used with lime, increases the amount of sodium in solution. Ion-exchange methods of treatment for hardness also raise sodium concentrations in treated water. Sodium, along with other dissolved minerals, may be removed from water by either demineralization or distillation, but neither of these processes is commonly used in municipal water treatment.

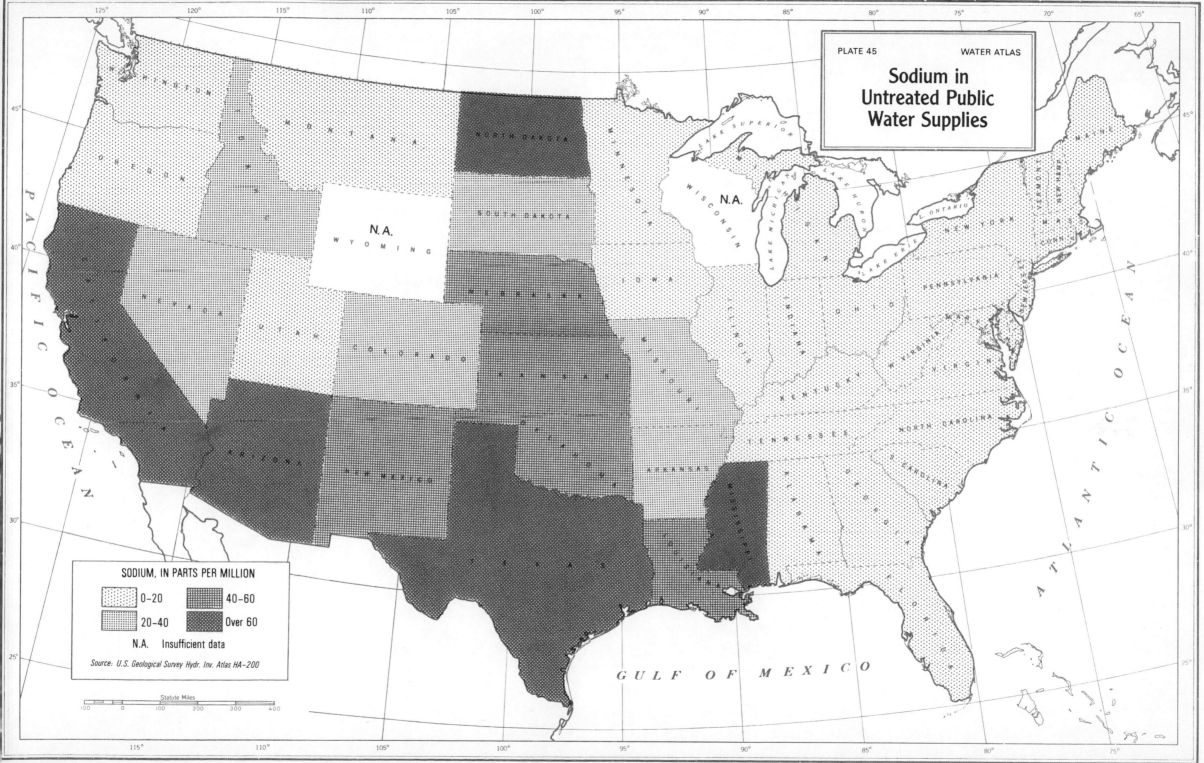

PLATE 45   WATER ATLAS

Sodium in
Untreated Public
Water Supplies

SODIUM, IN PARTS PER MILLION

0-20   40-60

20-40   Over 60

N.A.   Insufficient data

Source: U.S. Geological Survey Hydr. Inv. Atlas HA-200

Statute Miles
100   0   100   200   300   400

Base Map by U.S.C.&G.S.   © WATER INFORMATION CENTER, INC.

PLATE 46 – SODIUM IN FINISHED PUBLIC WATER SUPPLIES

The map shows the average sodium content in finished public water supplies by state, weighted by population served. Averages for Wisconsin and Wyoming are omitted due to insufficient data.

The nature and significance of sodium are discussed in the text for Plate 45. It is noteworthy that the finished public water supplies of Florida, Iowa, Kansas, Kentucky, Ohio and South Dakota contain more sodium than their respective untreated water supplies.

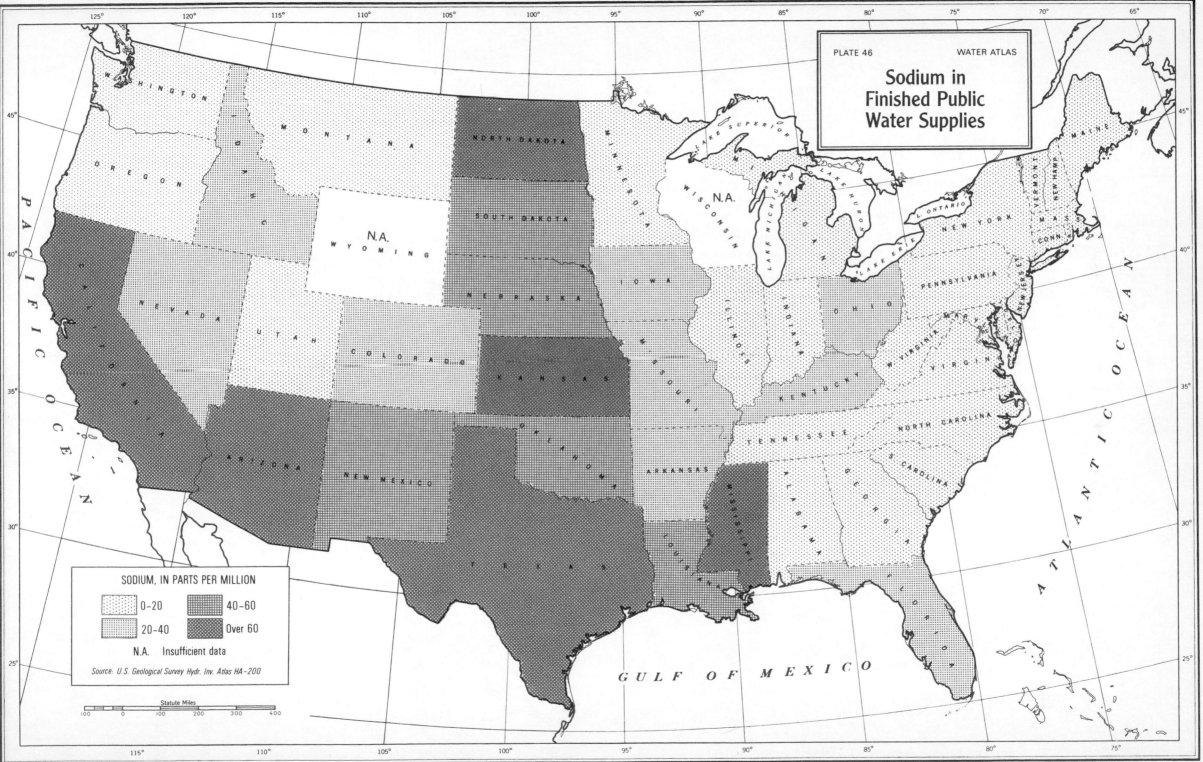

PLATE 46   WATER ATLAS

Sodium in Finished Public Water Supplies

SODIUM, IN PARTS PER MILLION

- 0–20
- 20–40
- 40–60
- Over 60

N.A.   Insufficient data

Source: U.S. Geological Survey Hydr. Inv. Atlas HA-200

Statute Miles
100   0   100   200   300   400

Base Map by U.S.C.&G.S.

© WATER INFORMATION CENTER, INC.

PLATE 47 – NATURAL FLUORIDE IN WATER SUPPLIES

Each dot on this map represents a community having at least one water source that contains 0.7 ppm (parts per million) or more of natural fluoride. The U.S. Public Health Service and medical authorities believe that 0.7 ppm is the minimum concentration of fluoride needed to provide optimum protection against tooth decay. This recommended optimal concentration varies from 0.7 to 1.2 ppm, depending on the annual average maximum daily air temperature in the community (higher air temperatures require a lower concentration of fluoride). In 1970, a total of 2,624 communities in the United States had one or more sources of drinking water containing this minimum concentration.

Approximately 8.4 million people reside in the communities shown on the map; forty percent of these people live in Texas. Most of the water supplies contain concentrations of fluoride of less than 1.5 ppm. Fluoride levels greater than 5.0 ppm have been reported for only 13 communities.

Fifty-two percent of the communities shown are in Illinois, Indiana, Iowa, Ohio, South Dakota, and Texas. In addition to those shown on the map, many other towns and cities in the nation add fluoride to drinking water as a tooth-decay preventive (see Plate 48).

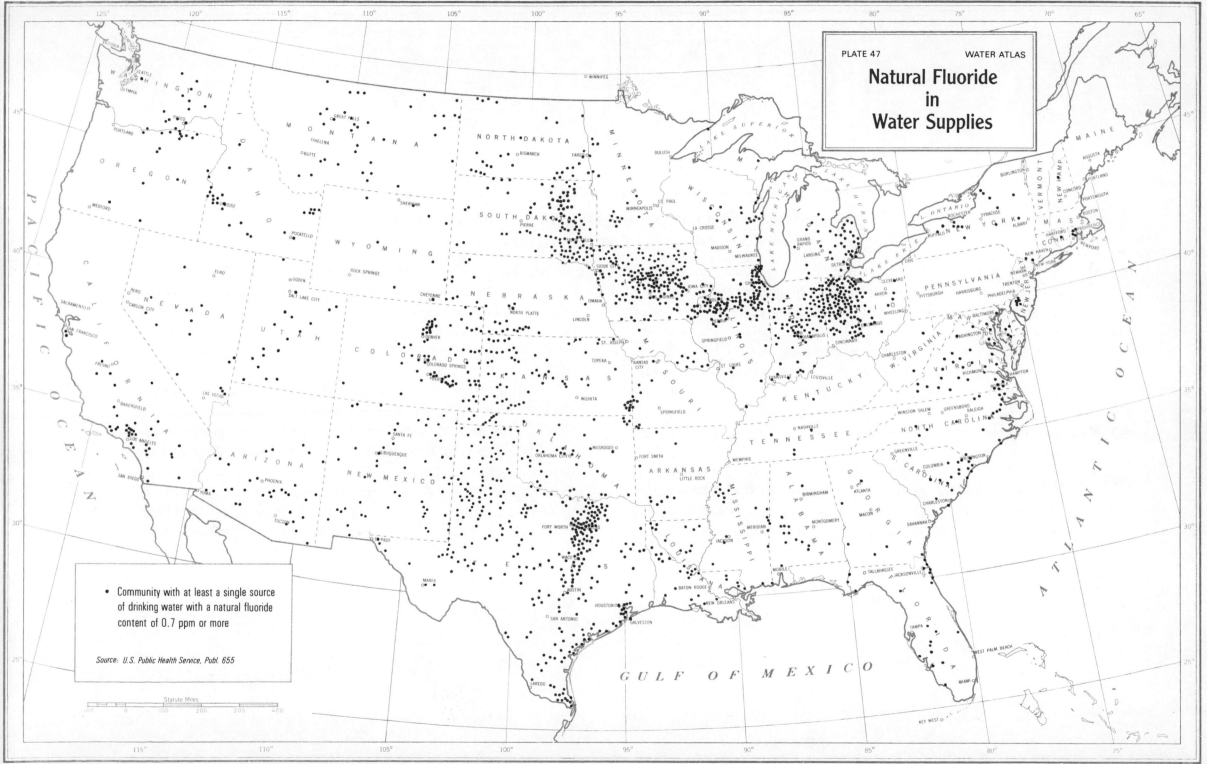

PLATE 47   WATER ATLAS

Natural Fluoride
in
Water Supplies

• Community with at least a single source
of drinking water with a natural fluoride
content of 0.7 ppm or more

Source: U.S. Public Health Service, Publ. 655

Statute Miles

Base Map by U.S.C.&G.S.   © WATER INFORMATION CENTER, INC.

PLATE 48 – POPULATION SERVED WITH FLUORIDATED WATER

The map shows the total population of each state and the percentage of that population served with fluoridated water. In some instances, as discussed in the text for Plate 47, the fluorides are of natural origin. In others, they are deliberately added to the water to maintain an optimal fluoride concentration. Artificial fluoridation may be accomplished by adding fluoride chemicals to fluoride-deficient water; by blending two or more sources of water naturally containing fluoride to the optimal concentration; or by defluoridation, that is, removing fluorides that are present in concentrations in excess of the recommended level.

Early in 1945, Grand Rapids, Michigan, and Newburgh, New York, were the first communities to adjust the fluoride content of their water-supply systems as a measure to prevent tooth decay. As of 1970, over 80 million people in 4,834 communities received water with a fluoride concentration adjusted to the optimal level. An additional 8.4 million people in 2,624 communities enjoyed the protection of an adequate natural fluoride content in their water supplies. In 1970, approximately 56 percent of the nation's public water supplies had access to water with a dentally significant concentration of fluoride.

It is interesting to note that every state in the country has fluoridated communities. In Maryland, Wisconsin, Virginia, Illinois, and Connecticut, over 90 percent of the population on public water supplies has access to fluoridated water. Furthermore, Connecticut, Minnesota, Illinois, Delaware, Michigan, South Dakota, and Ohio have statewide fluoridation laws. The total number of people receiving fluoridated water in Connecticut has more than tripled since 1965, when it became the first state to enact fluoridation legislation.

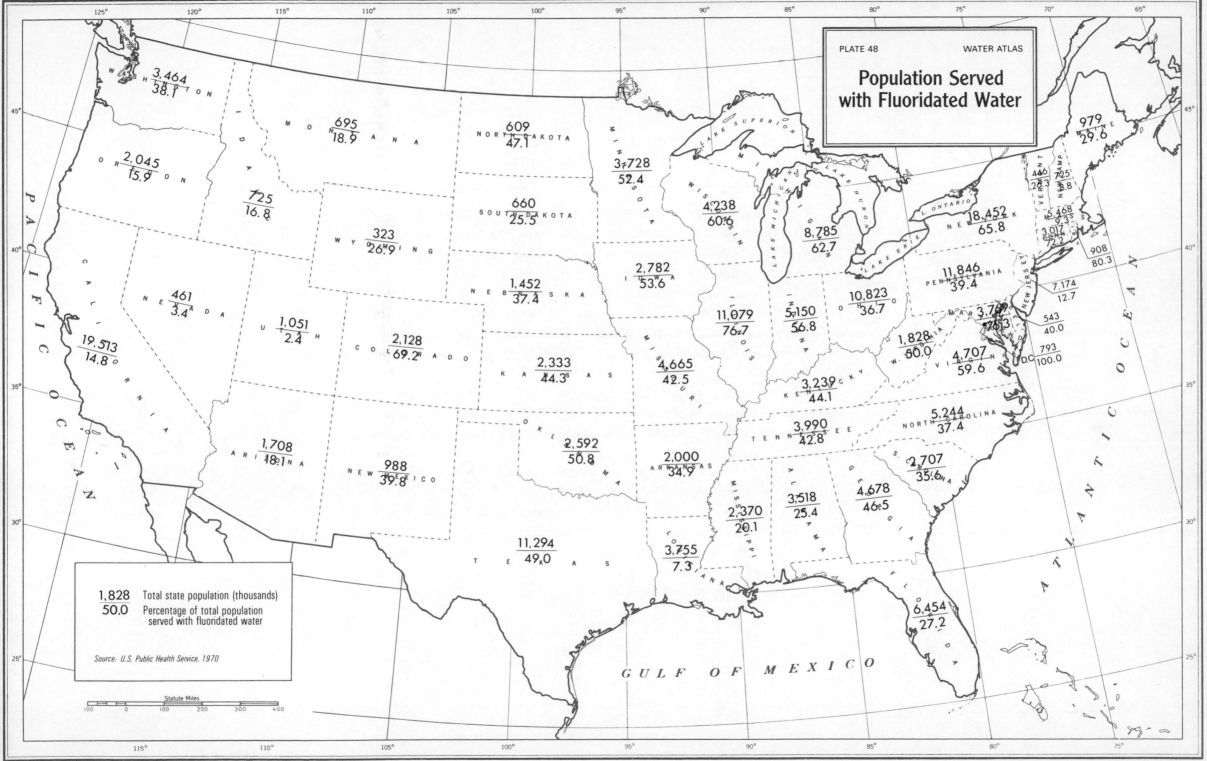

PLATE 48   WATER ATLAS

Population Served with Fluoridated Water

$\dfrac{3,464}{38.1}$ WASHINGTON

$\dfrac{2,045}{15.9}$ OREGON

$\dfrac{695}{18.9}$ MONTANA

$\dfrac{609}{47.1}$ NORTH DAKOTA

$\dfrac{3,728}{52.4}$ MINNESOTA

$\dfrac{4,238}{60.6}$ WISCONSIN

$\dfrac{8,785}{62.7}$ MICHIGAN

$\dfrac{979}{29.6}$ MAINE

$\dfrac{446}{28.3}$ VERMONT

$\dfrac{725}{8.8}$ NEW HAMPSHIRE

$\dfrac{5,468}{9.3}$ MASS

$\dfrac{3,017}{2.2}$ CONN

$\dfrac{908}{80.3}$ R.I.

$\dfrac{725}{16.8}$ IDAHO

$\dfrac{323}{26.9}$ WYOMING

$\dfrac{660}{25.5}$ SOUTH DAKOTA

$\dfrac{1,452}{37.4}$ NEBRASKA

$\dfrac{2,782}{53.6}$ IOWA

$\dfrac{18,452}{65.8}$ NEW YORK

$\dfrac{11,846}{39.4}$ PENNSYLVANIA

$\dfrac{7,174}{12.7}$ NEW JERSEY

$\dfrac{461}{3.4}$ NEVADA

$\dfrac{1,051}{2.4}$ UTAH

$\dfrac{2,128}{69.2}$ COLORADO

$\dfrac{2,333}{44.3}$ KANSAS

$\dfrac{4,665}{42.5}$ MISSOURI

$\dfrac{11,079}{76.7}$ ILLINOIS

$\dfrac{5,150}{56.8}$ INDIANA

$\dfrac{10,823}{36.7}$ OHIO

$\dfrac{1,828}{50.0}$ W. VA.

$\dfrac{3,749}{76.3}$ MD.

$\dfrac{543}{40.0}$ DEL.

$\dfrac{793}{100.0}$ D.C.

$\dfrac{19,513}{14.8}$ CALIFORNIA

$\dfrac{4,707}{59.6}$ VIRGINIA

$\dfrac{3,239}{44.1}$ KENTUCKY

$\dfrac{3,990}{42.8}$ TENNESSEE

$\dfrac{5,244}{37.4}$ NORTH CAROLINA

$\dfrac{1,708}{18.1}$ ARIZONA

$\dfrac{988}{39.8}$ NEW MEXICO

$\dfrac{2,592}{50.8}$ OKLAHOMA

$\dfrac{2,000}{34.9}$ ARKANSAS

$\dfrac{2,370}{20.1}$ MISSISSIPPI

$\dfrac{3,518}{25.4}$ ALABAMA

$\dfrac{4,678}{46.5}$ GEORGIA

$\dfrac{2,707}{35.6}$ SOUTH CAROLINA

$\dfrac{11,294}{49.0}$ TEXAS

$\dfrac{3,755}{7.3}$ LOUISIANA

$\dfrac{6,454}{27.2}$ FLORIDA

PACIFIC OCEAN

ATLANTIC OCEAN

GULF OF MEXICO

LAKE SUPERIOR · LAKE MICHIGAN · LAKE HURON · LAKE ERIE · L. ONTARIO

$\dfrac{1,828}{50.0}$ Total state population (thousands)
Percentage of total population served with fluoridated water

Source: U.S. Public Health Service, 1970

Statute Miles
100   0   100   200   300   400

PLATE 49 – DISSOLVED SOLIDS IN UNTREATED PUBLIC WATER SUPPLIES

The map shows the concentrations of dissolved solids, in ppm (parts per million), in untreated public water supplies in the United States. The U.S. Public Health Service recommends that water containing more than 500 ppm of dissolved solids should not be used for drinking purposes if other less mineralized supplies are available. However, it is recognized by the U.S. Public Health Service that a considerable number of supplies with dissolved solids in excess of the recommended limit are being used without any obvious ill effects. (For a discussion of the origin of dissolved solids, refer to the text accompanying Plate 37).

The dissolved-solids content of ground water is fairly stable, unlike that of surface water, which is constantly changing. Also, the concentration in a stream is generally less at the headwaters than at the mouth. For example, Minneapolis draws raw water from the Mississippi River that contains only half as much dissolved solids as the raw water drawn off by New Orleans at the mouth of the river.

Streams generally carry their lowest concentrations of dissolved solids during times of highest flow or flood. Many cities impound water in reservoirs at this time for use later on when consumption exceeds stream-flow, and consequently, the impounded water usually has a lower dissolved-solids content than the annual average for the stream.

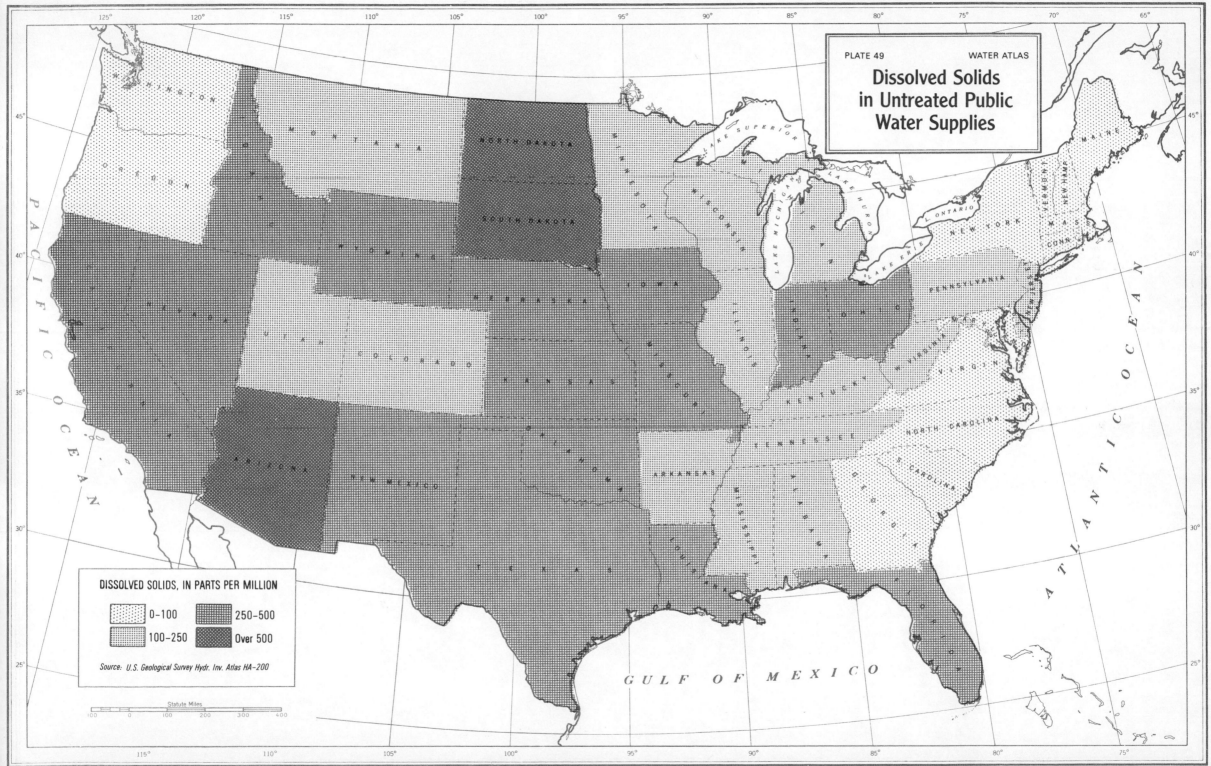

PLATE 49   WATER ATLAS

Dissolved Solids in Untreated Public Water Supplies

DISSOLVED SOLIDS, IN PARTS PER MILLION

0–100		250–500
100–250		Over 500

Source: U.S. Geological Survey Hydr. Inv. Atlas HA-200

Statute Miles
100   0   100   200   300   400

Base Map by U.S.C.&G.S.

© WATER INFORMATION CENTER, INC.

PLATE 50 — DISSOLVED SOLIDS IN FINISHED
PUBLIC WATER SUPPLIES

The map shows the concentrations of dissolved solids, in ppm (parts per million), in treated or finished public water supplies in the United States. Most municipalities treat their raw-water supplies before distribution to the consumer. Chlorination, filtration, pH adjustment, aeration, and softening are common methods of treatment. Softening processes using lime and processes for the removal of iron and manganese generally lower the dissolved-solids content; most other methods of treatment tend to increase it slightly. Additional information on the dissolved-solids content of water is given in the texts accompanying Plates 37 and 49.

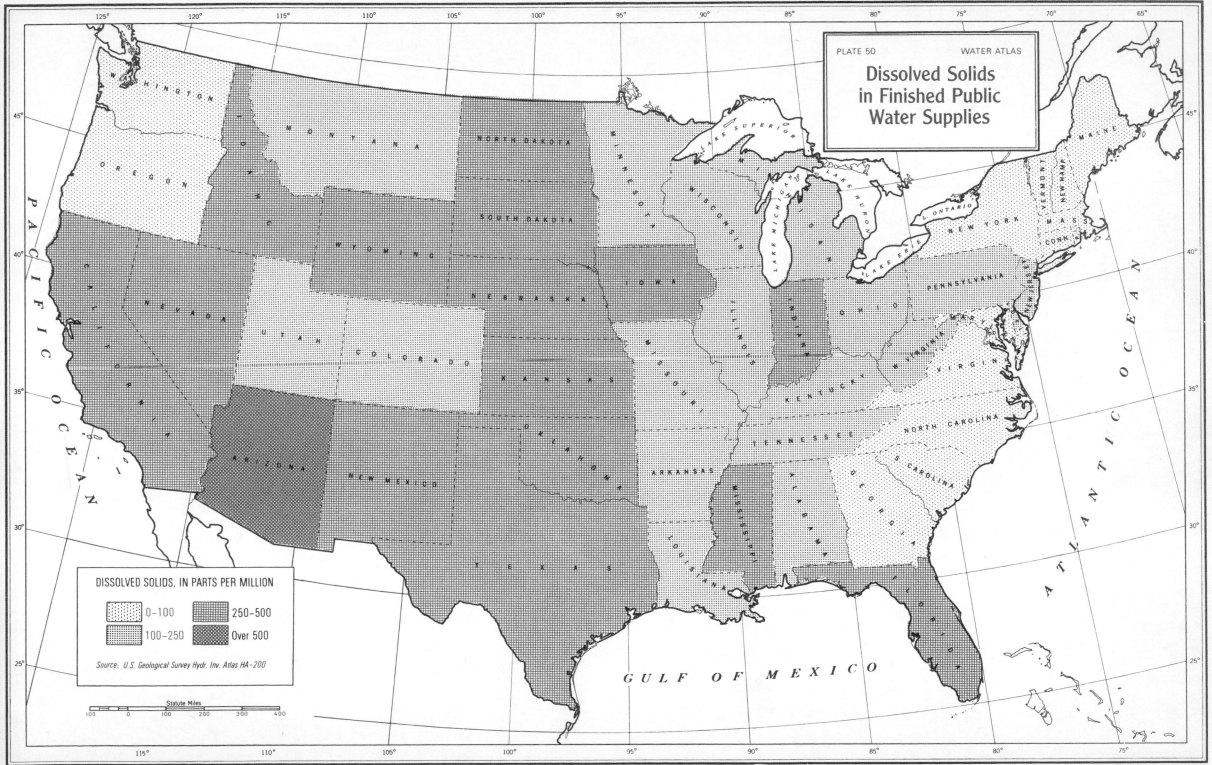

PLATE 50   WATER ATLAS

Dissolved Solids
in Finished Public
Water Supplies

DISSOLVED SOLIDS, IN PARTS PER MILLION

0-100

100-250

250-500

Over 500

Source: U.S. Geological Survey Hydr. Inv. Atlas HA-200

Statute Miles

100   100   200   300   400

PACIFIC OCEAN

ATLANTIC OCEAN

GULF OF MEXICO

LAKE SUPERIOR

LAKE MICHIGAN

LAKE HURON

L. ONTARIO

LAKE ERIE

WASHINGTON

OREGON

CALIFORNIA

NEVADA

IDAHO

MONTANA

WYOMING

UTAH

COLORADO

ARIZONA

NEW MEXICO

NORTH DAKOTA

SOUTH DAKOTA

NEBRASKA

KANSAS

OKLAHOMA

TEXAS

MINNESOTA

IOWA

MISSOURI

ARKANSAS

LOUISIANA

WISCONSIN

ILLINOIS

MICHIGAN

INDIANA

OHIO

KENTUCKY

TENNESSEE

MISSISSIPPI

ALABAMA

GEORGIA

FLORIDA

S. CAROLINA

NORTH CAROLINA

VIRGINIA

W. VIRGINIA

PENNSYLVANIA

NEW YORK

MARYLAND

MAINE

VERMONT

NEW HAMP.

MASS.

CONN.

PLATE 51 – PRINCIPAL AREAS OF WATER POLLUTION

Many streams, lakes, and estuaries in the nation receive large quantities of industrial, domestic, or animal wastes that have undergone little or no treatment by man. The degree of pollution caused by these discharges varies widely, depending on a broad range of hydrological, biological, and chemical considerations. Some rivers, for example, especially downstream of cities discharging large amounts of sewage, are plagued by excessive nutrients that cause growth of objectionable algae. Another kind of problem arises where pesticide residues end up in waterways and poison fish and livestock. Acid mine drainage, excess heat from power plants, and oil spills are other serious water pollutants.

The Environmental Protection Agency (EPA) estimates that almost one-third of U.S. stream-miles are characteristically polluted, in the sense that they violate federal water quality criteria. Less than ten percent of U.S. watersheds were characterized by EPA regional offices as unpolluted or even moderately polluted. However, these estimates, and the estimates upon which the map is drawn, are quite subjective and are not based on actual monitoring data. The attached map, while being the best generalized map available, should be used with the realization that the basic data are subjective and that actual records in the possession of local or state agencies can modify the picture substantially.

The map does not attempt to pinpoint the innumerable local problems and it is also restricted to showing only surface-water pollution. Ground-water pollution is generally localized, owing to the very slow rates at which liquids move through geologic formations. Nevertheless, underground contamination can be quite serious because the wastes remain in the subsurface for very long periods of time and cannot be removed easily.

The rivers referred to as the "ten dirtiest waterways" in the United States are listed below:

Ohio River	Passaic River, New Jersey
Houston Ship Canal, Texas	Arthur Kill, New Jersey
Cuyahoga River, Ohio	Merrimack River, New Hampshire
River Rouge, Michigan	Androscoggin River, Maine
Buffalo River, New York	Escambia River, Florida

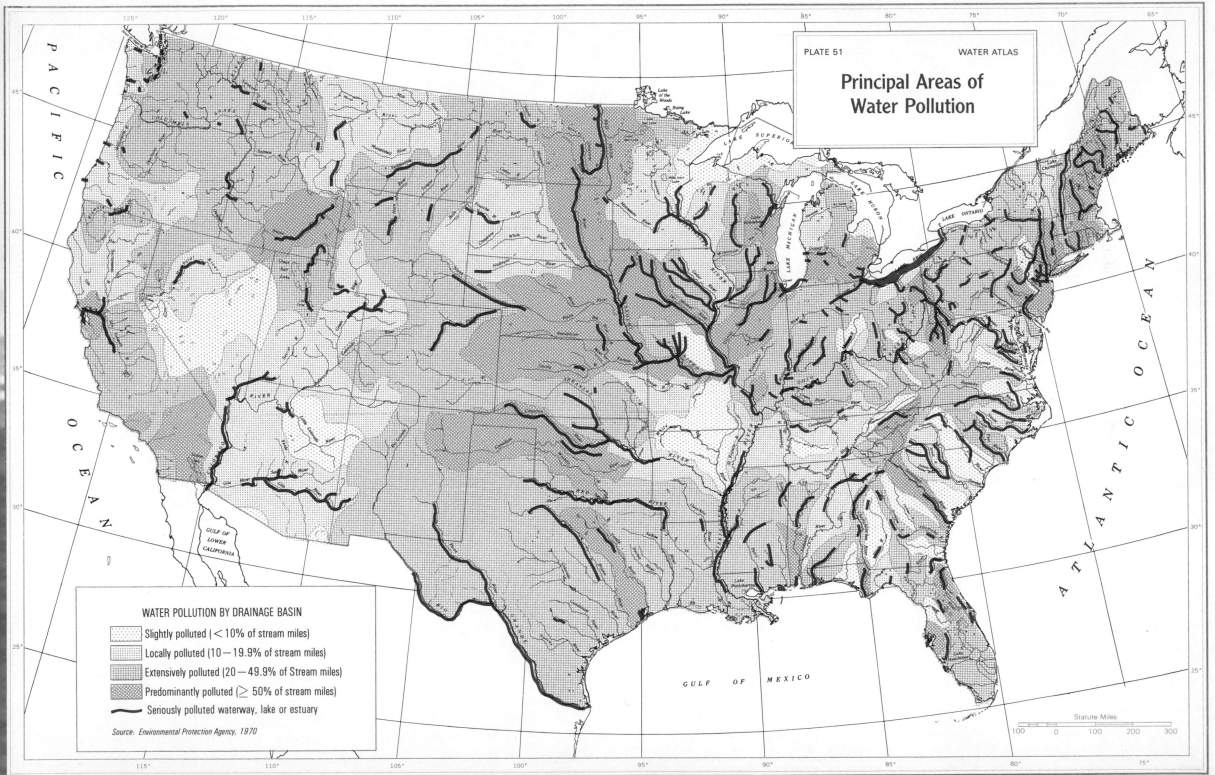

PACIFIC OCEAN

ATLANTIC OCEAN

GULF OF LOWER CALIFORNIA

GULF OF MEXICO

PLATE 51   WATER ATLAS

Principal Areas of Water Pollution

WATER POLLUTION BY DRAINAGE BASIN

Slightly polluted (< 10% of stream miles)

Locally polluted (10 — 19.9% of stream miles)

Extensively polluted (20 — 49.9% of Stream miles)

Predominantly polluted (≥ 50% of stream miles)

Seriously polluted waterway, lake or estuary

Source: Environmental Protection Agency, 1970

Statute Miles

100   0   100   200   300

© WATER INFORMATION CENTER, INC.

PLATE 52 — AMOUNTS OF MUNICIPAL SEWAGE

Two-thirds of the population of the United States, or about 125 million people, are served by municipal sewers. Sewage from about 10 percent of these people is discharged raw, and that from more than another 25 percent is discharged after only primary treatment. Thus, thousands of communities still dump their raw or inadequately treated sewage into convenient surface waters.

Combined sewers, which are very common throughout the urban areas of the country, especially in the older cities, carry a combination of storm runoff and sanitary sewage, usually to a treatment plant designed to handle only the dry-weather flow plus some storm flow. Many such systems commonly overflow into surface waters during storms or periods of prolonged rainfall. During storm peaks, as much as 95 percent of the sanitary sewage may overflow into the receiving stream. It is estimated that perhaps 5 percent of the total pollutional discharges into the nation's waters comes from these overflows.

The numbers shown on the map represent estimated sewage loads for 1962 and 1980. The numbers are expressed as population equivalents, each unit of which represents the amount of waste having a specific BOD (biochemical oxygen demand) produced by one person each day. This amount is approximately one-sixth of a pound. The BOD is a widely used standard method of evaluating the demands on the ability of a body of water to keep itself clean and balanced. It is described as "the oxygen required during the stabilization of decomposable organic matter by aerobic bacterial action." As an example, the 1962 figure for population equivalents for the North Atlantic region means that the amount of municipal waste that has a biochemical oxygen demand is equivalent to a human population of 45.8 million. In actuality, the population is smaller than this, and the difference represents other organic materials carried by the municipal sewer systems.

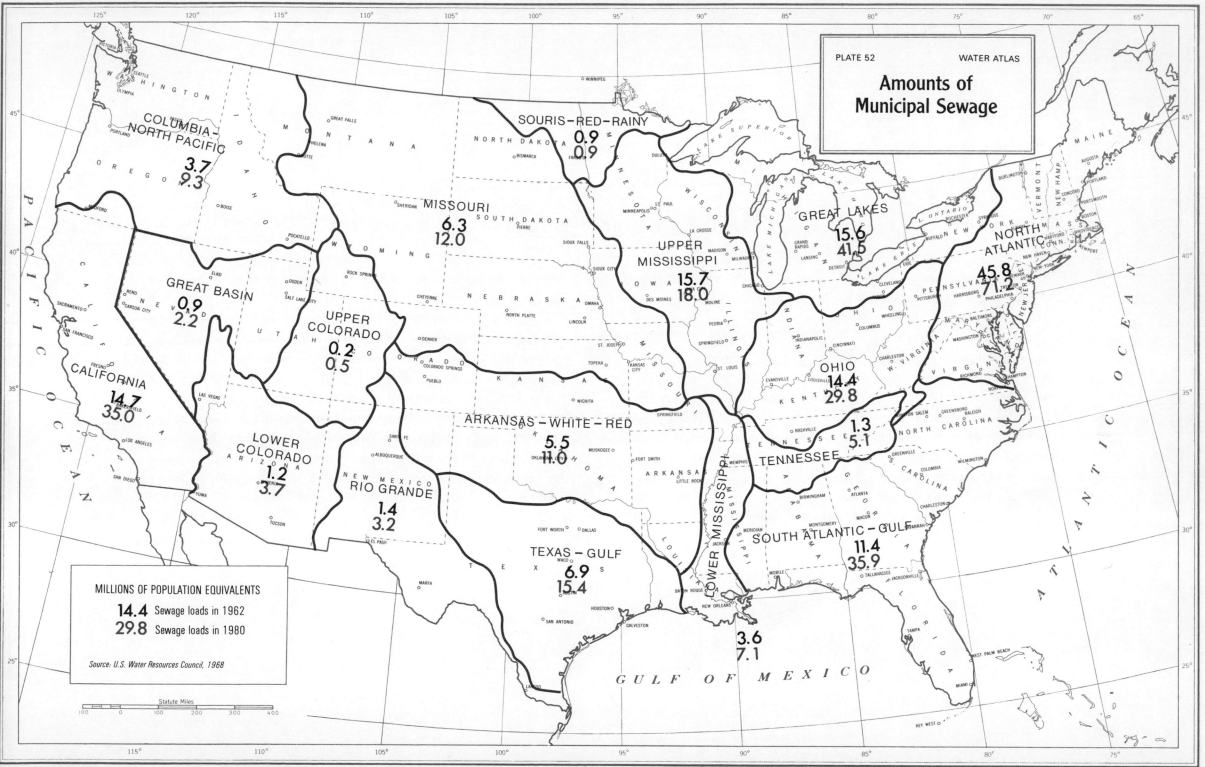

PLATE 52   WATER ATLAS

Amounts of Municipal Sewage

COLUMBIA-
NORTH PACIFIC
3.7
9.3

SOURIS–RED–RAINY
0.9
0.9

MISSOURI
6.3
12.0

GREAT LAKES
15.6
41.5

NORTH
ATLANTIC
45.8
71.2

GREAT BASIN
0.9
2.2

UPPER
COLORADO
0.2
0.5

UPPER
MISSISSIPPI
15.7
18.0

CALIFORNIA
14.7
35.0

OHIO
14.4
29.8

LOWER
COLORADO
1.2
3.7

NEW MEXICO
RIO GRANDE
1.4
3.2

ARKANSAS–WHITE–RED
5.5
11.6

TENNESSEE
1.3
5.1

TEXAS–GULF
6.9
15.4

LOWER
MISSISSIPPI
3.6
7.1

SOUTH ATLANTIC–GULF
11.4
35.9

MILLIONS OF POPULATION EQUIVALENTS

14.4   Sewage loads in 1962
29.8   Sewage loads in 1980

Source: U.S. Water Resources Council, 1968

Statute Miles
100   0   100   200   300   400

PACIFIC OCEAN

ATLANTIC OCEAN

GULF OF MEXICO

PLATE 53 — POTENTIAL WATER POLLUTION FROM FARM ANIMAL WASTES

Both the increasing number of animals being raised in the nation and some of the modern methods used in the livestock industry contribute to the growing pollution of waters caused by animal wastes. Beef cattle, poultry, and swine-feeding operations, along with dairy farms, are the major sources of actual or potential water pollution of this kind.

In the past two decades, production of animal products has been increasing rapidly. The technology of this rising production requires that animals be confined in a minimum space and fed a concentrated ration, both of which tend to increase the pollution potential of the wastes.

When animal wastes find their way into water, they add large amounts of excessive nutrients that can unbalance natural ecological systems, causing excessive aquatic plant growth and fish kills. They also load water-filtration systems with solids, complicating water treatment; cause undesirable tastes and odors in waters; add chemicals that are detrimental to both man and animals; increase consumption of dissolved oxygen, producing stress on aquatic populations and occasionally resulting in septic conditions; and add micro-organisms that are pathogenic to animals and to man.

Between 500 and 600 million animals are being raised today on feedlots in the United States. The wastes produced by these animals are equivalent to the wastes of two billion people. This figure should not be interpreted as an estimate of the water pollution caused by feedlots however, since most of the animal wastes never reach open water.

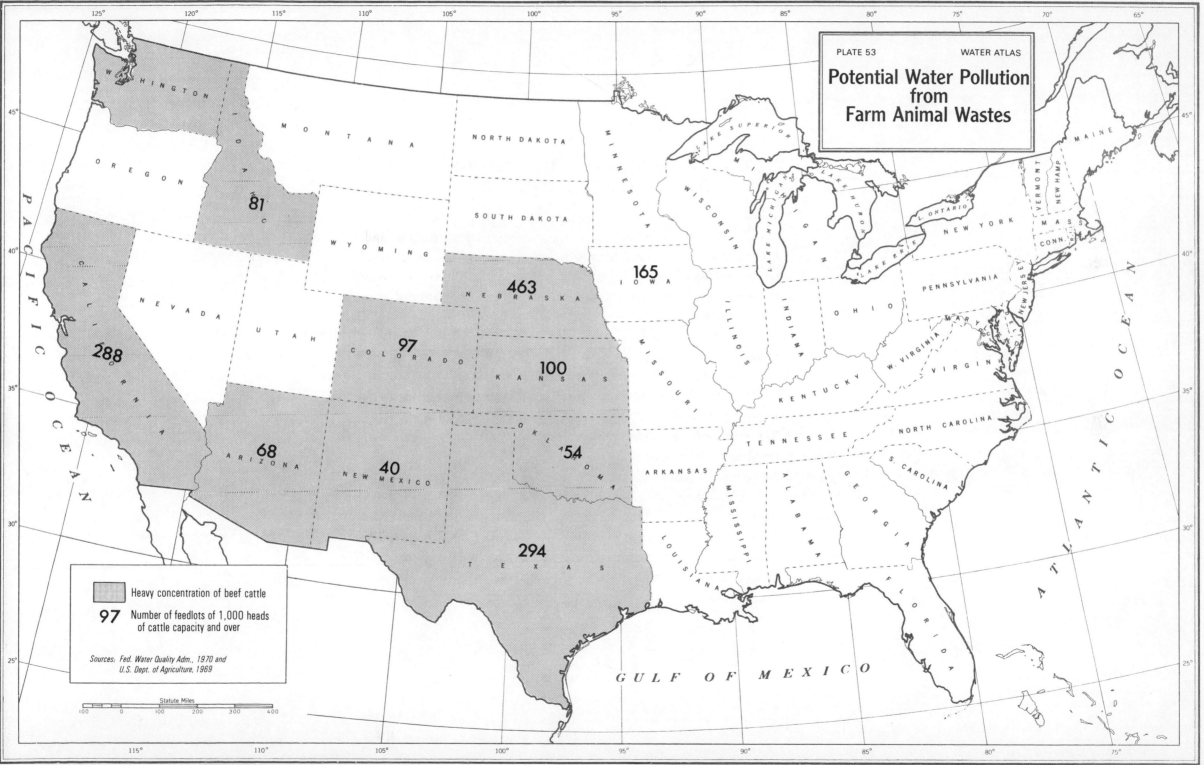

PLATE 53   WATER ATLAS

Potential Water Pollution from Farm Animal Wastes

Heavy concentration of beef cattle

97 Number of feedlots of 1,000 heads of cattle capacity and over

Sources: Fed. Water Quality Adm., 1970 and
U.S. Dept. of Agriculture, 1969

Statute Miles

PLATE 54 – POTENTIAL WATER POLLUTION
FROM COMMERCIAL FERTILIZERS

Commercial chemical fertilizers used for improving crops contain phosphates, nitrates, and other plant nutrients, and consequently, agricultural runoff into the nation's lakes, streams, and waterways is believed to be an important contributing factor to water pollution and eutrophication. Eutrophication is the progressive increase in biological productivity in a body of water as a result of the input of nutrients. It often results in stimulated growth of algae and other aquatic vegetation. Eutrophication is a natural phenomenon and occurs at slow rates in the "natural aging" of lakes. Accelerated eutrophication, on the other hand, is caused by man through his pollution of waters with sewage, industrial wastes, and agricultural runoff.

The use of chemical fertilizers in the United States has increased rapidly over the last decade. The total amount of fertilizers consumed in the nation during the 1969-70 period was 39 million tons. Of this, phosphate materials, which are a major contributor to algal growth, accounted for some 3 million tons or 9 percent. In terms of total tonnage, Illinois was the leading state with 3.3 million tons, followed by California with 3.1 million tons. As shown on the map, the heaviest concentrations of fertilized land are in the Midwest, Texas, and the Sacramento and San Joaquin Valleys of California.

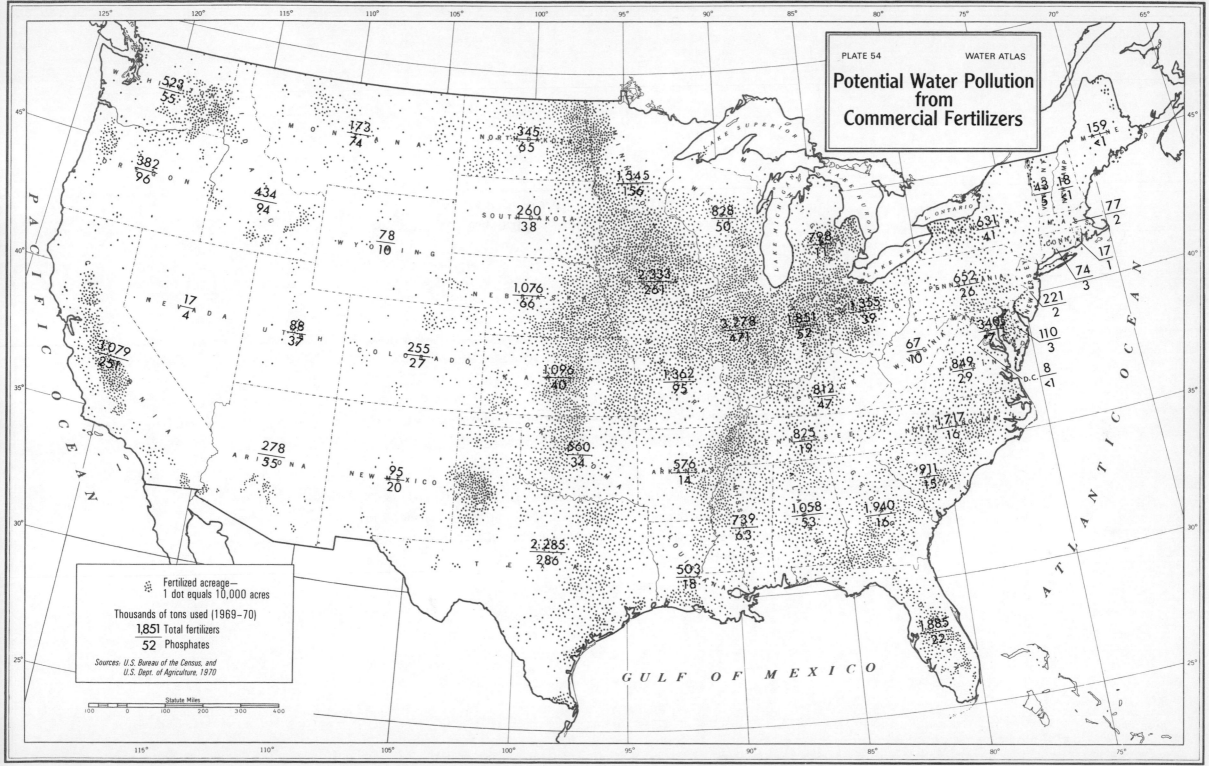

PLATE 54   WATER ATLAS

Potential Water Pollution from Commercial Fertilizers

Fertilized acreage—
1 dot equals 10,000 acres

Thousands of tons used (1969-70)
$\frac{1,851}{52}$ Total fertilizers
        Phosphates

Sources: U.S. Bureau of the Census, and
U.S. Dept. of Agriculture, 1970

Statute Miles

Base Map by U.S.C.&G.S.

© WATER INFORMATION CENTER, INC.

PLATE 55 — NUTRIENT-ASSOCIATED PROBLEMS IN MUNICIPAL WATER SUPPLIES

Nutrients contained in wastewaters are a stimulant to the growth of algae in surface-water bodies receiving such wastes. Problems stemming from this cause have been growing rapidly in all parts of the country, and specialists in the field are anticipating the time when requirements for wastewater treatment will have to be revised to include removal of nutrients. The two major offenders are nitrogen and phosphorus, both of which are abundant in water drained from land surfaces, in rainwater itself, in waste discharges from cities and industries, and in agricultural runoff. One of the principal effects of the overproduction of algae is a deterioration in the taste and odor of drinking water.

More than half of the surface-water bodies in the country are believed to be affected to some degree by nutrient-rich wastewater. To cope with the problem, chemicals must be used to retard the growth of algae. The map shows the areas where problems of this kind are of serious concern to public water-supply systems.

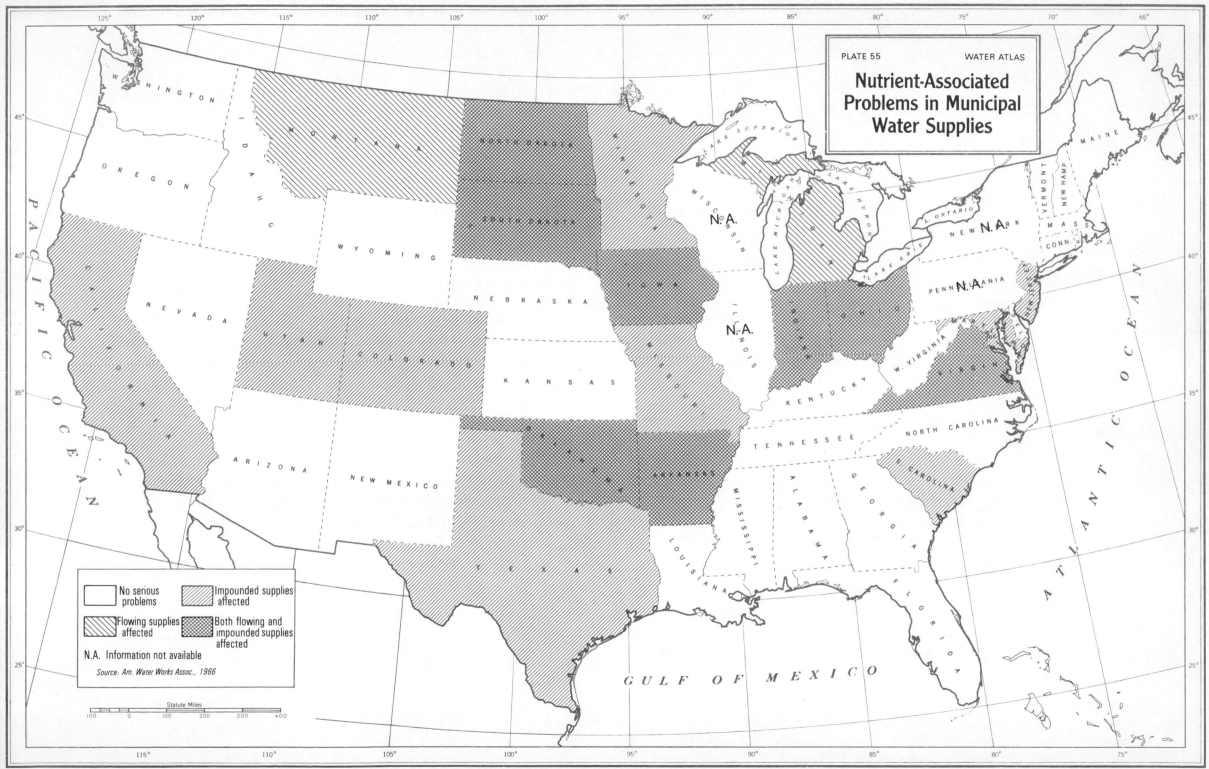

PLATE 55   WATER ATLAS

Nutrient-Associated Problems in Municipal Water Supplies

No serious problems

Flowing supplies affected

Impounded supplies affected

Both flowing and impounded supplies affected

N.A. Information not available

Source: Am. Water Works Assoc., 1966

Statute Miles

Base Map by U.S.C.&G.S.

© WATER INFORMATION CENTER, INC.

PLATE 56 – CONCENTRATION OF SEDIMENT IN STREAMS

Sediment, from man's viewpoint, can be thought of as a major pollutant of surface water, and a listing of the adverse effects caused by its presence is quite impressive. Excess sediment in water reduces its recreational value, fish propagation is adversely affected, the cost for treating the water for public supply is increased, nutrients adsorbed on sediment particles contribute to undesirable algae conditions in lakes, the penetration of sunlight into sediment-laden waters is reduced, stream temperatures are affected, stream channels are clogged, reservoirs are filled in, and hydroelectric-power turbines are damaged.

The dollar amount of damages caused by sediment is hard to evaluate. For example, harm done to the quality of recreational areas and the environment in general does not lend itself to easy calculation. Roughly, however, it is believed that damages resulting from sediment are in excess of $500 million per year.

Approximately four billion tons of soil are picked up each year by the nation's streams, and 25 percent of this total tonnage is discharged into the oceans. The rest is simply moved around from place to place within drainage basins.

Any soil not covered with vegetation or otherwise protected will erode. Some of the principal sources of sediment are farmlands, road construction, roadside erosion, and areas of urban development.

The map shows that the greatest sediment loads are found where the land is heavily farmed or in the drier parts of the country where the protecting ground cover is sparse. Steep stream gradients in some of these areas also aggravate the problem. In the relatively level and thickly vegetated State of Florida, soil and slope conditions do not favor heavy sediment loads, even though the rainfall is among the highest in the country (see Plates 2 and 3).

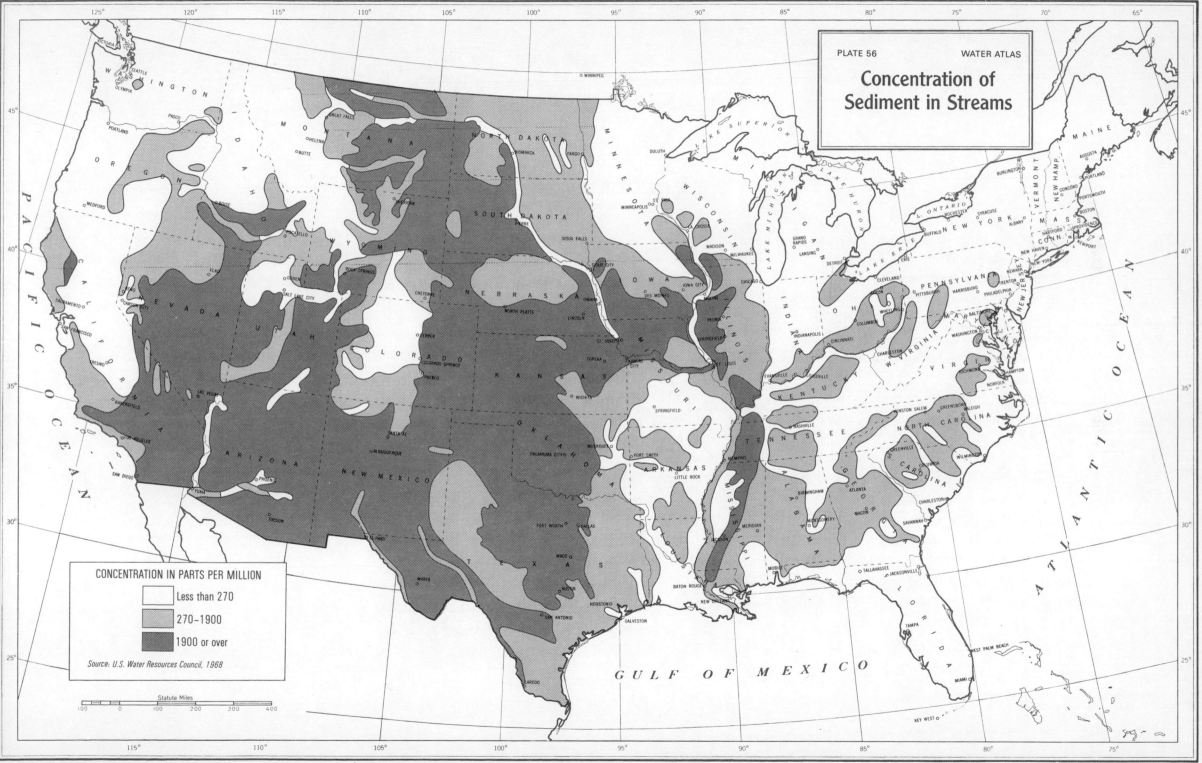

PLATE 56   WATER ATLAS

Concentration of Sediment in Streams

CONCENTRATION IN PARTS PER MILLION

Less than 270

270–1900

1900 or over

Source: U.S. Water Resources Council, 1968

Statute Miles

Base Map by U.S.C.&G.S.

© WATER INFORMATION CENTER, INC.

PLATE 57 – ACID MINE DRAINAGE

Acid mine drainage is a serious pollutant to the nation's streams, especially in Appalachia and the Ohio River Basin. Acid formation occurs when water and air react with the sulfur-bearing minerals in mines or mine refuse piles to form sulfuric acid and iron compounds. An estimated four million tons of acid flows into 11 thousand miles of streams and other waters each year, and nearly half of the 50 states are affected to some extent by this type of water pollution.

Although acid mine drainage is sometimes associated with other minerals, such as lead, zinc, manganese, and even gold, critical areas are where coal production has been heaviest. States hardest hit by acid coal mine drainage are Pennsylvania, Maryland, West Virginia, Ohio, Indiana, Illinois, Kentucky, and Tennessee.

The individual states are increasing their regulation of active mining operations to curb acid pollution, but well over half of this pollution comes from abandoned mines, estimated to number about 20 thousand in Appalachia alone. For example, in the relatively small Kanawha-New River system in West Virginia, approximately 67 million gallons of acid mine water enter the river system every day. A single large coal mine may spew out as much as 10 million gallons of contaminated water a day. The thousands of abandoned mine openings thus pose a stark pollution threat to streams, lakes and reservoirs.

Sometimes, whole waterways become sterile—void of all life except acid-loving algae. Fish and their food organisms disappear and recreational and aesthetic values suffer. Piers, bridges, culverts, industrial equipment, pipes, and boat hulls are corroded rapidly by acid waters, and these waters first must undergo expensive treatment to be made usable by cities and industries.

Control of acid mine drainage would help to reclaim large quantities of water that are now unsuitable for some uses. Reclamation of the acid-polluted streams for recreation and fishing would provide great benefits to many now economically depressed areas.

PLATE 57   WATER ATLAS

Acid Mine Drainage

Principal coal deposits

Streams affected by acid mine drainage

Source: U.S. Geological Survey, Hydrol. Inv. Atlas HA–198, 1965

Statute Miles

© WATER INFORMATION CENTER, INC.

PLATE 58 – THERMAL POLLUTION

Many industrial plants in the nation use large amounts of water for cooling purposes. At the end of the cooling cycle, the heated water is commonly discharged into rivers, lakes, or estuaries, where it may create problems. The hot water not only may harm the fish in the stream, but can make the water less valuable to farmers, factories, or cities downstream. This unfavorable situation is generally referred to as thermal pollution.

The electric power industry uses more water for cooling than any other industry and its projected growth illustrates the problem that lies ahead in thermal pollution. By 1980, when 65 percent of electric power production will come from nuclear plants, nearly 250 billion gallons of water per day will be needed by those plants for cooling purposes. Fresh-water sources will be used for 200 billion gallons of the cooling water, which is equivalent to one-fifth of all the fresh surface water available in the country.

At present, electric generating plants account for 70 percent of the hot water discharged into rivers and lakes in the nation. This water is often 10 to 20 degrees F. warmer than the receiving stream. A temperature change of only three or four degrees can, under certain conditions, have serious effects on fish and other aquatic life.

Also, fish are affected by the level, duration, and rapidity with which the temperature change takes place.

Thermal pollution can modify the entire ecological balance of a stream. For example, the addition of warm water may cause fish eggs to hatch so early in the spring that the natural food organisms needed by the young fish are not available. Also, fish generally depend on temperature changes as a signal for migration and spawning. Trout eggs will not hatch or incubate in water that is too warm, and salmon may not spawn. Fish double their consumption of oxygen for each 10-degree rise in water temperature; but as the water warms up, it can hold less oxygen. Thus, as the amount of oxygen that can dissolve in water dwindles with the rising temperature, the demand for oxygen increases.

The value of water for drinking and for recreational and industrial uses usually decreases at higher temperatures. Thermally polluted water is less capable of assimilating other wastes. Irrigation waters that are too hot may affect seedlings, plant growth rate, and crop yield. As temperature rises, nuisance plants and rough fish flourish, while useful life dies. The quality of the water deteriorates even further as foul odors and algal slime appear.

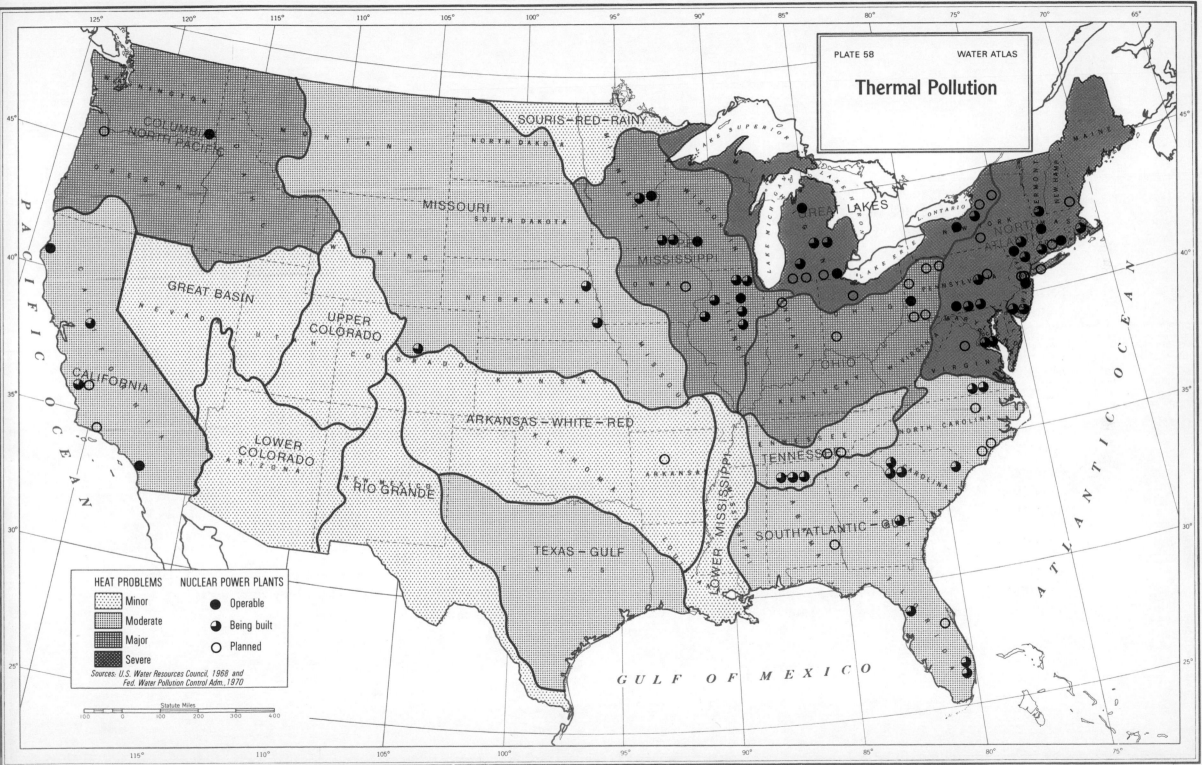

PLATE 58   WATER ATLAS

Thermal Pollution

HEAT PROBLEMS   NUCLEAR POWER PLANTS

Minor   ● Operable
Moderate   ◖ Being built
Major   ○ Planned
Severe

Sources: U.S. Water Resources Council, 1968 and
Fed. Water Pollution Control Adm., 1970

Statute Miles
100   0   100   200   300   400

Base Map by U.S.C.&G.S.

© WATER INFORMATION CENTER, INC.

PLATE 59 – POTENTIAL WATER POLLUTION FROM DDT

The common pesticidal chemicals fall into three general categories: inorganic, synthetic organic, and natural organic. Most inorganic pesticides are toxic to plants and humans as well as insects. The use of inorganic pesticides has declined and the trend today is toward the use of powerful synthetic organic pesticides which can be adapted to more specific uses. The natural organics are somewhat limited in supply and popularity.

DDT, a synthetic organic pesticide of the chlorinated hydrocarbon family, has been used so extensively that it is stored to some degree in almost every living human body in the United States. DDT has been very popular because it can control a large number of pests at moderate cost.

The map shows how many millions of pounds of DDT were used on farms in the United States in 1966. In that year, the total estimated use was 40 million pounds. Farmers were the major users, accounting for more than 26 million pounds, or two-thirds of the total. Most of the DDT used on farms, about 95 percent, was applied to crops, of which cotton, tobacco, and fruits received the heaviest applications (2.7 to 4.8 pounds per acre). Farmers in Alabama, Florida, Georgia, and South Carolina were the largest users of DDT.

DDT is not normally decomposed by sunlight and is very stable in soil, where it decomposes at a rate of only five percent per year.

The compound is picked up by the surface runoff and carried to streams, rivers, lakes, and the oceans; it can also contaminate ground water. Starting in the water, DDT enters the various food chains, accumulating in greater amounts as it works its way up the chain. Sometimes, the chain ends with an eagle or falcon that has fed on contaminated fish. A great danger here is that man is at the end of many of these food chains.

The spraying of pesticides is aimed at the total local destruction of a pest species. Although there have been undeniable benefits for man from the use of pesticides, there have been almost none for wildlife. Pesticide spraying has been responsible for a considerable amount of wildlife death. Probably far more important, however, is the question of whether pesticide use is leading to a cumulative long-term poisoning of the total environment. The spreading of DDT has certainly been great, extending far beyond areas where it has been applied. DDT has been found in the milk of Arctic reindeer and in the eggs of Antarctic penguins. The results of recent Federal government surveys of chlorinated hydrocarbons in surface water and fish are shown on Plates 60 and 61.

The general use of DDT is no longer legal in the United States. The ban, effective Dec. 31, 1972, ended nearly three decades of application of the pesticide.

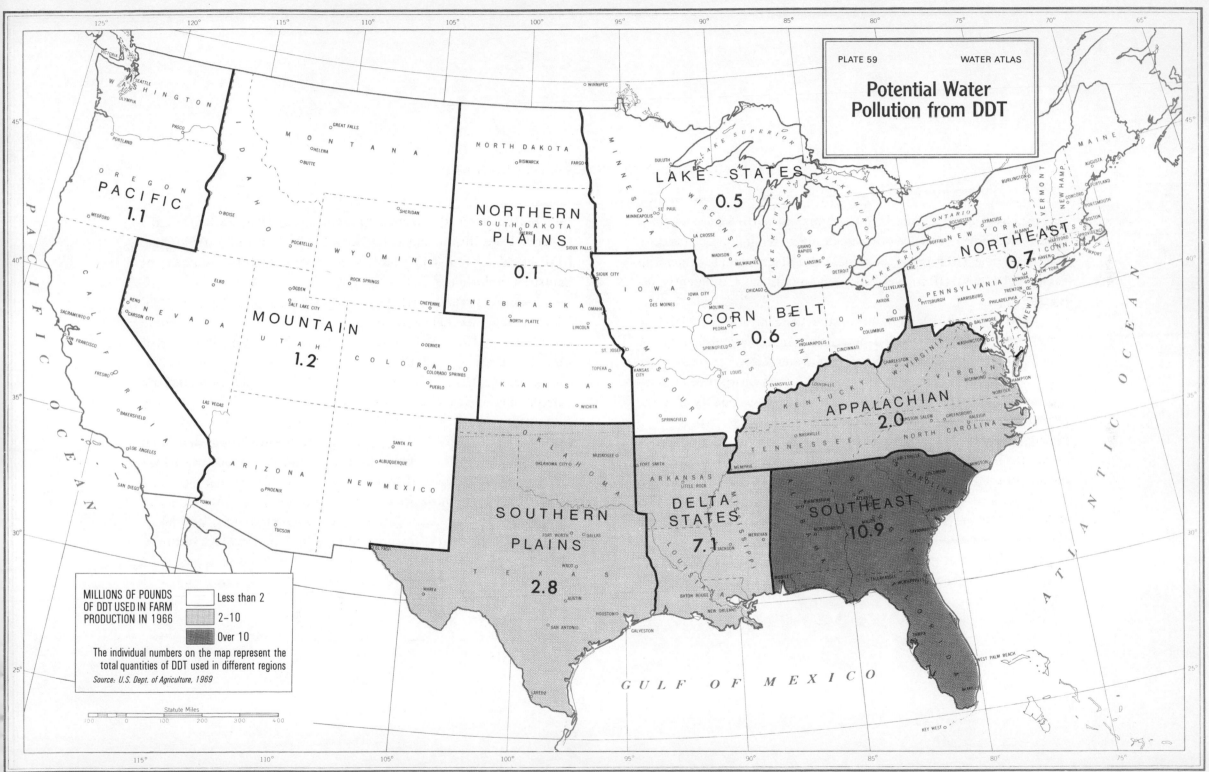

PLATE 59 WATER ATLAS

Potential Water Pollution from DDT

MILLIONS OF POUNDS
OF DDT USED IN FARM
PRODUCTION IN 1966

- Less than 2
- 2–10
- Over 10

The individual numbers on the map represent the
total quantities of DDT used in different regions

Source: U.S. Dept. of Agriculture, 1969

Statute Miles

PLATE 60 – DDT IN SURFACE WATERS AND FISH

Analyses made by the U.S. Government in 1968 have shown a rather widespread presence of pesticides in water and in fish (see also Plate 61). The DDT group of pesticides (which includes chemicals named DDE and DDD) were the compounds most frequently detected.

In the period 1964-68, maximum concentrations of DDT in surface waters did not exceed permissible limits established by the U.S. Public Health Service for drinking water. However, they often exceeded the environmental limit of 0.05 ppm (parts per million) recommended by the Federal Committee on Water Quality Criteria. In 1968, for instance, water samples from the Beauclair River in Florida, the Monongahela River in Pennsylvania, the Missouri River in South Dakota, and the Mississippi River in Mississippi, all exceeded this limit.

Results of the 1967-68 pesticide analyses for DDT residues in water and fish are shown on the map. DDT was found in 584 of the 590 composite fish samples, with values ranging to 45 ppm (wet weight, whole fish). Relatively high residues of DDT, above 1.0 ppm, were found consistently in fish during all sampling periods in the Hudson River, the Sacramento River, the Delaware River, Lake Ontario, Lake Huron, and Lake Michigan. Most of the fish with high DDT levels are found in waters subject to agricultural drainage or industrial pollution.

Federal interim guidelines call for a maximum of 5.0 ppm total DDT residues (including derivatives) in fish shipped in interstate commerce. In 1968, DDT levels in fish exceeded this limit at 8 of the 50 monitoring stations.

Concentrations of some of the insecticide residues in fish are considerably higher than those established by the Food and Drug Administration (FDA) for milk, meat, fruits, vegetables, and other food and feed crops. Much of the residue accumulation may be in portions of the fish not normally consumed by humans, but which are consumed by, and might be hazardous to fish-eating birds and other animals. The high pesticide concentrations encountered in fish compared with the relatively low concentrations in rivers and lakes, illustrate the cumulative nature and danger of pesticides in our food chain.

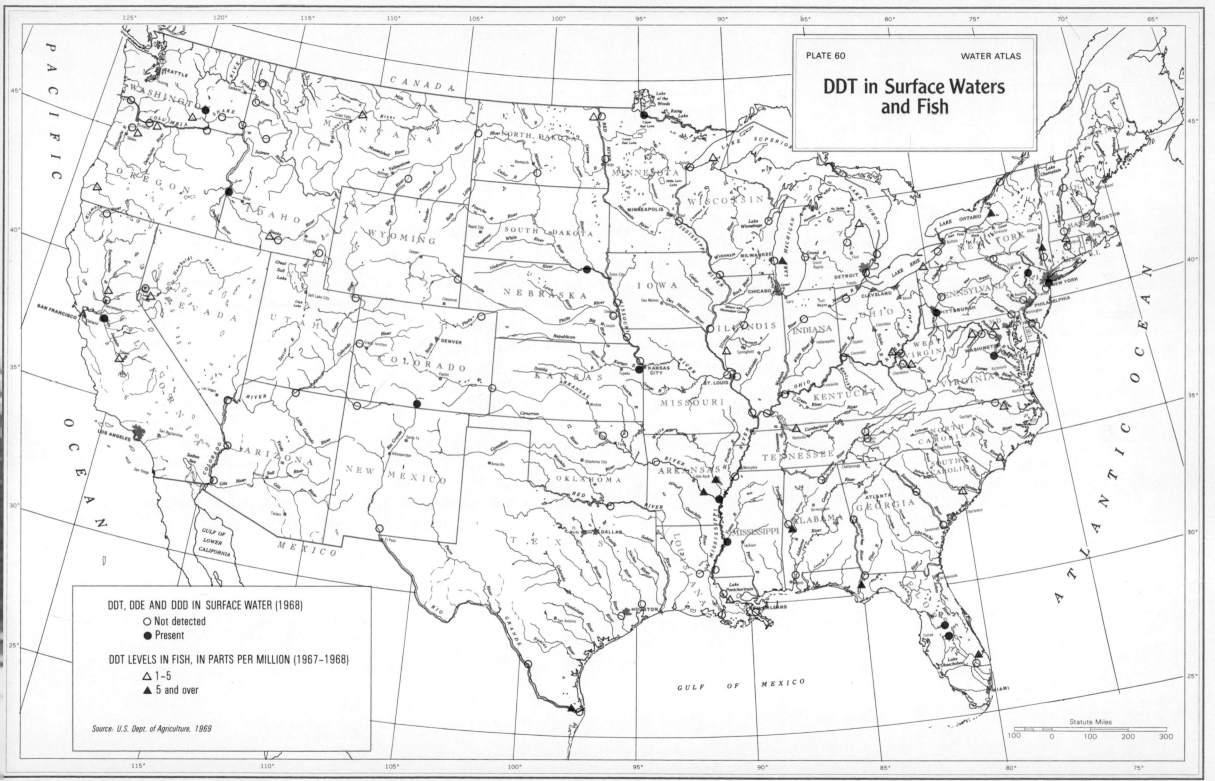

PLATE 60   WATER ATLAS

DDT in Surface Waters and Fish

DDT, DDE AND DDD IN SURFACE WATER (1968)
○ Not detected
● Present

DDT LEVELS IN FISH, IN PARTS PER MILLION (1967–1968)
△ 1-5
▲ 5 and over

Source: U.S. Dept. of Agriculture, 1969

Statute Miles
100   0   100   200   300

© WATER INFORMATION CENTER, INC.

PLATE 61 — DIELDRIN, LINDANE, AND BHC IN SURFACE WATERS

Dieldrin, lindane, and BHC, together with DDT (see Plates 59 and 60) are synthetic organics and members of the chlorinated hydrocarbon pesticide family. BHC and lindane are very similar chemically. Crops grown in soils containing lindane absorb the compound into their tissues, which may result in the crops becoming tainted with a characteristic taste and odor. Dieldrin is an insecticide similar to but more powerful than BHC or DDT. It is very dangerous in water even in very small quantities.

U.S. Government surveys made during the period 1964-68 have provided information on present levels and trends of pesticides in water. Dieldrin was found to dominate the pesticide occurrences in all rivers, with 199 positive results in 529 samples taken.

Dieldrin, lindane, and BHC were found mainly in the Mississippi River drainage basin and in many eastern states, with almost no occurrences in the western part of the country. One river where dieldrin has been detected in every survey is the Savannah River in South Carolina and Georgia. BHC has been found consistently in the main stem of the Ohio River since 1966. The sources of these pesticides have not yet been determined.

Dieldrin residues were reported present in approximately 75 percent of all fish samples collected during the Federal pesticide monitoring program of 1967-68. Concentrations in individual composite samples ranged upward to a maximum of 1.94 ppm (parts per million). Mean values of above 0.1 ppm were reported from the Connecticut River, the Delaware River, the Illinois River, and the Missouri River during three of the four sampling periods. Some lindane residues were found in 16 percent of the samples, but at levels usually less than 0.1 ppm.

PLATE 61   WATER ATLAS

Dieldrin, Lindane and BHC in Surface Waters

■ Dieldrin present
▲ Lindane present
○ Not detected
(Survey of June, 1968)

Source: U.S. Dept. of Transportation, 1970

Statute Miles

© WATER INFORMATION CENTER, INC.

PLATE 62 – POTENTIAL WATER POLLUTION FROM PIPELINE SPILLS

Although oil spills from tankers often earn the biggest newspaper headlines, there are other less spectacular forms of oil spills that are quite significant from the viewpoint of water pollution. In fact, the Corps of Engineers estimates that 40 percent of all oil-pollution cases involve non-waterborne discharges. These include waste oil from gasoline service stations, accidental spillage during industrial transfer and storage, discharges from offshore drilling operations, and leaks from pipelines and related systems. The map shows the nationwide network of major crude-oil and oil-products pipelines 10 inches or more in diameter, and gives a statewide breakdown of oil spills in 1969 related to these pipelines. The total quantity of petroleum products spilled through pipeline breaks in 1969 was 343,691 barrels. The oil spills often result in pollution of water, especially if they occur in places where the pipelines pass close to or under open water bodies.

Pipeline accidents were detected in 30 states in 1969. By far, the most spills occurred in Texas, which had 139 of the national total of 410 reported accidents. Twelve of the 30 states had ten or more such accidents. The major causes of pipeline spills are external corrosion, defective pipeline materials, and damage by construction equipment. Oil-pipeline companies are now required by Federal regulations to submit reports on oil spills when more than 50 barrels of liquid are lost.

Oil in raw-water supplies creates a number of problems at treatment plants, complicating coagulation, flocculation, and sedimentation processes. When free or emulsified oil reaches sand filters or ion-exchange beds, it coats the grains, thereby decreasing the effectiveness of filtration and interfering with backwashing. Because some petroleum compounds can be tasted in water in concentrations as low as one part in five million, greater use of activated carbon and/or heavy chlorination becomes necessary to remove the taste of oil from the water.

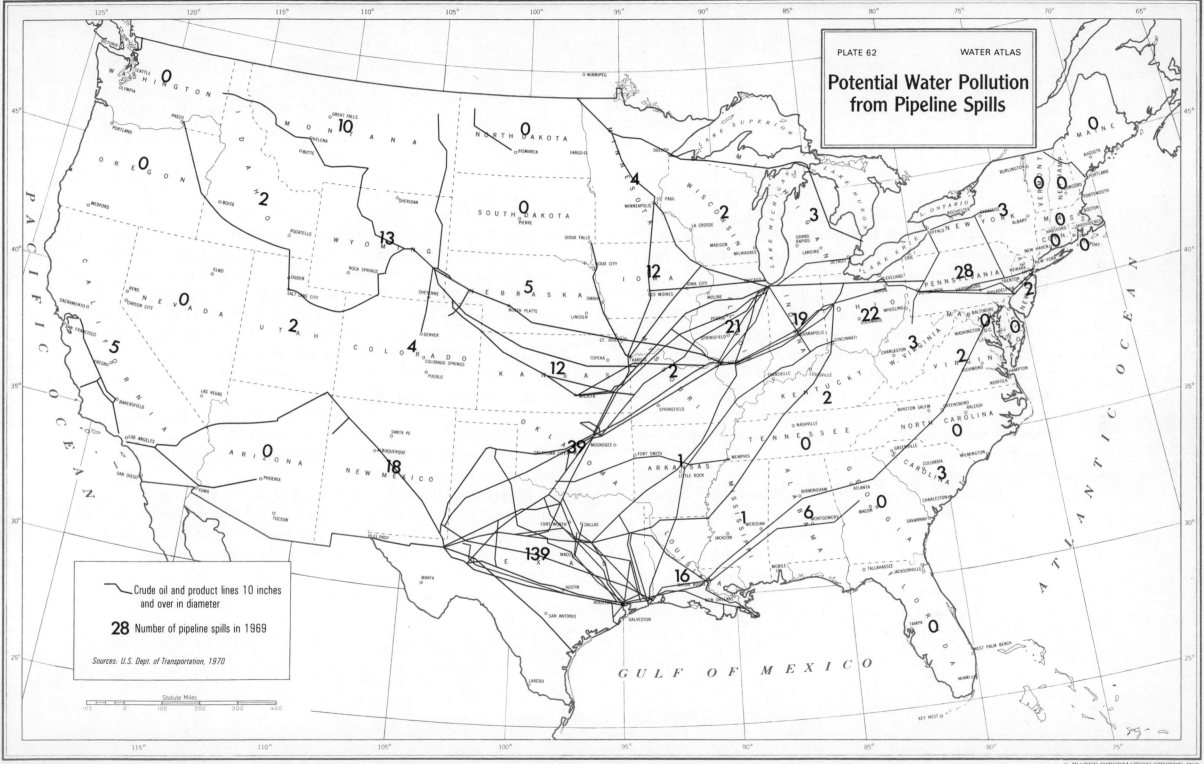

PLATE 62   WATER ATLAS

Potential Water Pollution from Pipeline Spills

Crude oil and product lines 10 inches
and over in diameter

28 Number of pipeline spills in 1969

Sources: U.S. Dept. of Transportation, 1970

Statute Miles

Base Map by U.S.C.&G.S.   © WATER INFORMATION CENTER, INC.

PLATE 63 — ARSENIC AND LEAD IN SURFACE WATERS

Arsenic and lead, which are dangerous to man when their concentrations exceed certain limits, are fortunately not present to any large extent so far in the nation's water resources. The map portrays the results of a nation-wide reconnaissance survey of these two elements conducted by the U.S. Geological Survey during the fall of 1970.

Arsenic is notorious for its toxicity to humans. Ingestion of 100 mg (milligrams) usually results in severe poisoning, and as little as 130 mg can prove fatal (when measuring concentrations of constituents in water, one mg/1 — milligrams per liter — is essentially equivalent to one part per million). Arsenic accumulates in the body, so that a series of small doses may become fatal in time. Arsenic is generally recovered as a by-product from the processing of copper, lead, zinc, and tin. Although it is used in metallurgy and chemical industries, its major use has been for pesticides and as a wood preservative. It is also encountered as a contaminant of phosphate fertilizers. Arsenic compounds occur naturally in some waters in the western part of the country.

The maximum arsenic concentration considered safe for drinking water is 0.05 mg/1. Of 727 samples examined during the 1970 survey, 21 percent had arsenic concentrations greater than 0.01 mg/1 and 2 percent had more than 0.05 mg/1. The highest arsenic content (1.1 mg/1) was found downstream from an industrial complex in North Carolina (Sugar Creek).

Lead occurs in nature principally as a sulfide ore (galena) in Missouri, Idaho, and Utah. Some natural waters in these regions contain amounts of dissolved lead in the range of 0.4 to 0.8 mg/1. Lead may be introduced into water as a constituent of various industrial and mining effluents, as a result of the action of water on lead in pipes, or, especially important, as a precipitate from leaded gasoline engine fumes. In 1968 alone, 180,000 tons of lead were emitted from leaded gasoline combustion — 14 percent of all lead consumed in the United States that year. Lead tends to be deposited in bone as a cumulative poison. The U.S. Public Health Service's limit for lead in drinking water is 0.05 mg/1. Lead poisoning in humans is reported to have been caused by drinking of water containing lead in concentrations varying from 0.042 to 1.0 mg/1 or more. According to a 1953 study, lead concentrations in surface and ground waters used for domestic supplies in the nation ranged from traces to 0.04 mg/1, averaging about 0.01 mg/1.

The results of the 1970 study found lead present in 63 percent of the samples in concentrations ranging from 0.001 to 0.05 mg/1. At 76 sites, lead was detected in concentrations between 0.01 and 0.05 mg/1, and in four places was detected in amounts in excess of 0.05 mg/1.

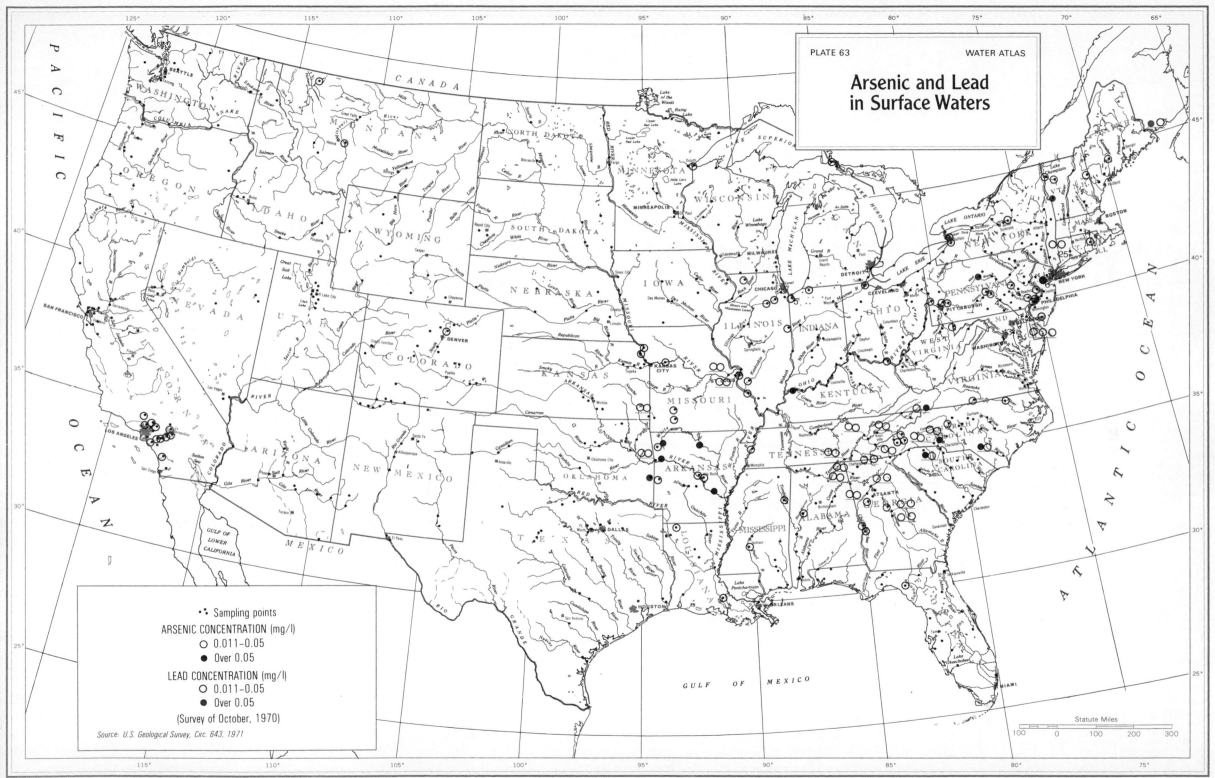

PLATE 63   WATER ATLAS

Arsenic and Lead in Surface Waters

• Sampling points

ARSENIC CONCENTRATION (mg/l)
○ 0.011–0.05
● Over 0.05

LEAD CONCENTRATION (mg/l)
○ 0.011–0.05
● Over 0.05

(Survey of October, 1970)

Source: U.S. Geological Survey, Circ. 643, 1971

Statute Miles
100   0   100   200   300

PLATE 64 — CADMIUM AND CHROMIUM IN SURFACE WATERS

Cadmium is a metal that occurs in nature in the mineral greenockite and often as an impurity in zinc-lead ores. Cadmium is employed in metallurgy to alloy with copper, lead, silver, aluminum, and nickel. It is used in electroplating, ceramics, pigmentation, photography, and nuclear reactors. Cadmium is found in concentrations of 50 to 170 ppm (parts per million) in super-phosphate fertilizers, and it is also used in some pesticides (when measuring concentrations of constituents in water, one ppm is essentially equivalent to one milligram per liter). The metal generally represents a minor element in surface waters. However, high concentrations of cadmium have been reported in Missouri mine waters, and one spring in that state is reported to yield water containing 1000 ppm of cadmium.

Cadmium is a highly toxic element, and foods containing excessive concentrations of this metal have caused a number of human deaths. It tends to concentrate in the liver, kidneys, pancreas, and the thyroid glands of humans and animals. Once it enters the body it is likely to remain. The mandatory limit set for cadmium in drinking water by the U.S. Public Health Service in 1962 is 0.01 mg/l (milligrams per liter).

A nationwide reconnaissance of selected minor elements in surface-water sources was made by the U.S. Geological Survey during the autumn of 1970. Cadmium was detected in 42 percent of the 720 samples collected, in concentrations ranging from 0.001 to 0.01 mg/l. About 4 percent of the river samples had cadmium in excess of the 0.01 mg/l upper limit. The maximum concentration found was 0.13 mg/l in Mineral Creek (Arizona). Forty-six percent of the samples contained measurable amounts of cadmium, with the high concentrations generally occurring in rivers and streams near areas of high population density.

Chromium is another natural metal used extensively in metal pickling and plating operations, in the leather industry as a tanning agent, and in the manufacture of paints, dyes, explosives, and paper. Chromium compounds may be present in wastes from such industries or may be discharged in chromium-treated cooling waters. When taken orally, chromium salts are not retained in the body but are rapidly eliminated; however, large doses of chromates lead to corrosive effects in the intestinal tract.

The U.S. Public Health Service's recommended upper limit for chromium in drinking water is 0.05 mg/l. The results of the 1970 survey showed no concentrations in excess of 0.05 mg/l; only 11 of more than 700 samples had concentrations in the range of 0.006 to 0.05 mg/l.

PLATE 64   WATER ATLAS

Cadmium and Chromium in Surface Waters

•∵• Sampling points

CADMIUM CONCENTRATION (mg/l)
○ 0.005–0.01
● Over 0.01

CHROMIUM CONCENTRATION (mg/l)
◍ 0.006–0.05

(Survey of October, 1970)

Source: U.S. Geological Survey, Circ. 643, 1971

Statute Miles
100   0   100   200   300

© WATER INFORMATION CENTER, INC.

PLATE 65 — MERCURY IN SURFACE WATERS

Mercury, in its elemental state, is a silvery liquid metal, approximately 13½ times as heavy as water, and is the only metal that occurs in liquid form at ordinary earth surface temperatures. Like other metallic elements, mercury reacts with inorganic and organic compounds to form simple and complex molecules ranging from cinnabar, a mercury sulfide and the most common ore mineral, to metalloorganic complexes which are now receiving world-wide attention as potential water pollutants and biologic toxins.

One form of mercury, methyl mercury, is particularly harmful. It is soluble in water and can be ingested by algae, plants, and lower forms of animal life, passing on along the food chain to fish and then to man. It becomes concentrated when higher forms of life such as fish eat the smaller organisms. When man eats the fish, he concentrates the mercury dosage further.

The toxic effects of waterborne mercury were emphasized during the early 1950's when about fifty persons in Japan died from consuming mercury-contaminated fish and shellfish. The fish originated in a bay that received large amounts of methyl mercury compounds in the waste effluent from a plastics factory.

To date, no mercury standards for drinking water in the United States have been set, although a limit of 0.005 ppm (parts per million) has been proposed (when measuring concentrations of constituents in water, one ppm is essentially equivalent to one milligram per liter). The Food and Drug Administration has set a limit of 0.5 ppm for fish consumed by humans. As a result of this limit, commercial fishing has been banned in many areas, particularly in the Great Lakes region, by both the United States and Canada. Fishermen have been advised to be especially careful in taking fish high on the food chain, such as pike, walleye, and yellow perch, that feed on other fish. Mercury contamination is not restricted to fresh water fish, but has also been found in tuna, swordfish, and even Arctic seals.

Over the years, industrial plants have discharged large quantities of mercury to the nation's rivers and waterways. Prior to the recent Federal investigation, industries dumped some 100,000 pounds of mercury in the nation's waterways every year. During the fall of 1970, this discharge was reduced to some 15,000 pounds. Major industrial centers identified with serious mercury pollution are shown on the map.

The map also shows the results of a reconnaissance sampling carried out by the U.S. Geological Survey during the autumn of 1970. More than 720 samples from lakes and rivers were taken during the period October 1-15, when rivers were at medium or low-flow stages in many parts of the country. A few results from samples collected in June 1970 also were incorporated.

The data shown represent total mercury or the amount in the water-sediment mixture. Dissolved mercury, which might occur in a filtered or treated water supply, was found in only seven percent of the samples. In none of them did it exceed the U.S. Public Health Service's suggested upper limit of 0.005 ppm for drinking water. Total mercury was found in excess of 0.005 ppm in some samples in California, Colorado, Idaho, and Ohio.

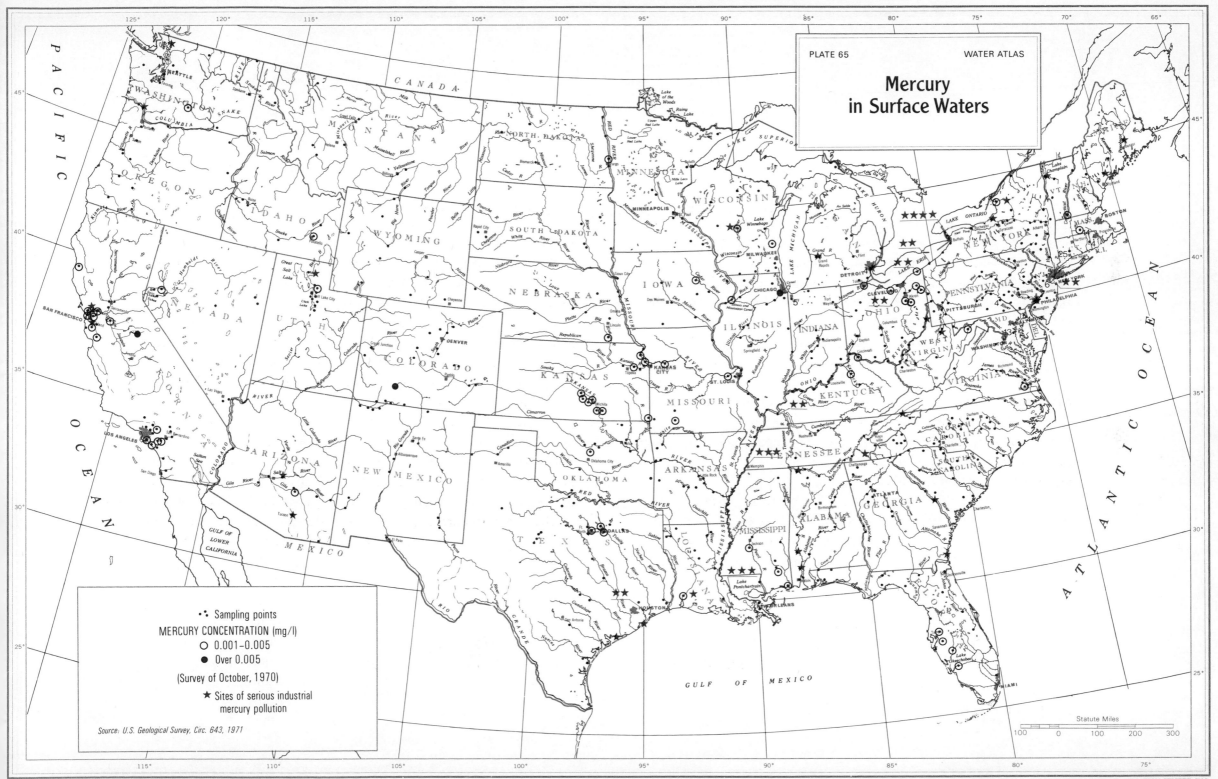

PLATE 65   WATER ATLAS

Mercury in Surface Waters

Legend

∴ Sampling points

MERCURY CONCENTRATION (mg/l)

○ 0.001–0.005

● Over 0.005

(Survey of October, 1970)

★ Sites of serious industrial
mercury pollution

Source: U.S. Geological Survey, Circ. 643, 1971

Statute Miles

100   0   100   200   300

© WATER INFORMATION CENTER, INC.

PLATE 66 — WATER POLLUTION FROM DEICING SALTS

Each winter many highway departments in the colder parts of the country apply salts (sodium chloride and calcium chloride) to their road networks to eliminate or control ice and snow. Problems stemming from this practice have now begun to show up, and there is an increasing concern about the environmental dangers caused by salt to vegetation, soil, and water supplies. Deicing salts contaminate surface runoff, ponds, streams, and ground water, principally near roadside areas. Substances added to deicing salts to prevent caking or to inhibit corrosion, such as sodium ferrocyanide and phosphorous compounds, can be extremely toxic to human, animal, and fish life. Deicing salts are potentially more harmful in arid regions where less precipitation and less dilution take place.

The use of salts on the nation's highways amounted to more than two million tons during the winter of 1965-66, and is steadily increasing with the expanding road network and increased traffic. Seventy percent of the deicing salts was applied in the northeastern region and 22 percent in the north-central area. During the 1965-66 winter, Massachusetts, the District of Columbia, Pennsylvania, and Illinois applied 20 to 37 tons of salts per lane-mile. Connecticut, Maine, New Hampshire, New Jersey, New York, and Vermont used 9 to 20 tons of salt per lane-mile on some highways. At such rates, more than one pound of salt is applied per square foot of pavement. If one pound of salt is dissolved in a normal winter's precipitation (25 to 30 inches of water in the north-eastern states), the resulting solution would have about 7,000 ppm (parts per million) of salt. Thus, the composition of runoff water from highways treated with salts may be significantly affected. For instance, in Wisconsin, some samples of runoff contained up to 10,250 ppm of chloride during the winter, as compared with only 16 ppm during the summer. Twelve states reported instances of water pollution as a result of deicing salt applications during the period 1961-66.

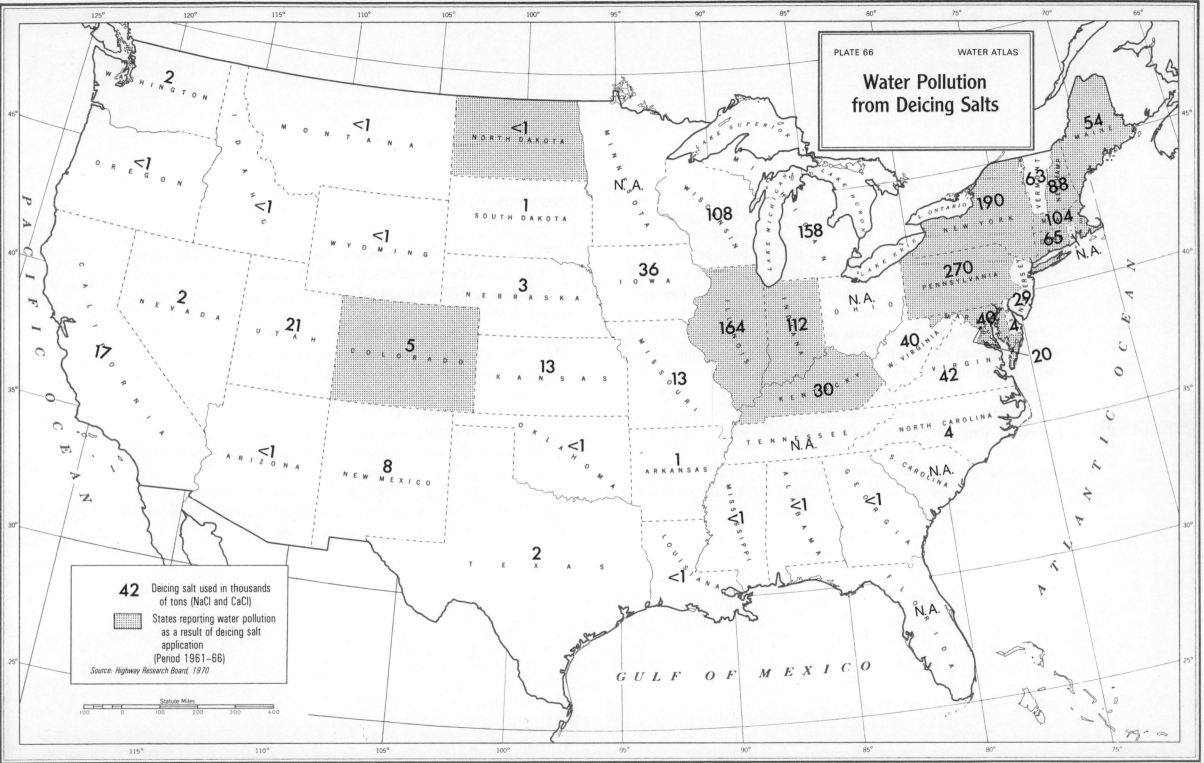

PLATE 66   WATER ATLAS

Water Pollution from Deicing Salts

42 Deicing salt used in thousands of tons (NaCl and CaCl)

States reporting water pollution as a result of deicing salt application
(Period 1961–66)

Source: Highway Research Board, 1970

Statute Miles

Base Map by U.S.C.&G.S.

© WATER INFORMATION CENTER, INC.

PLATE 67 – OFFSHORE DISPOSAL OF WASTES

Every year, large quantities of all sorts of waste materials are dumped in coastal waters. In 1968, excluding the Great Lakes, 48 million tons of dredge spoils, industrial wastes, sewage sludge, construction and demolition debris, solid waste, explosives, chemicals, and radioactive wastes was dumped at sea. Of this, 24 million tons was deposited in the Atlantic Ocean, 16 million tons in the Gulf of Mexico, and 8 million tons in the Pacific Ocean.

As of 1968, there were 246 offshore disposal sites in use in the country. One hundred and twenty-two of them were located off the Atlantic Coast, 68 off the Pacific Coast, and 56 in the Gulf of Mexico.

Dredge spoils account for 80 percent by weight of all ocean dumping. An estimated 34 percent of this material is polluted. Contamination occurs from deposition of pollutants from industrial, municipal, agricultural, and other wastes on the bottoms of water bodies. Polluted oxygen-demanding materials can reduce the oxygen in the receiving waters to levels at which certain fish and aquatic populations cannot survive. Toxic heavy metals present in the spoils deleteriously affect marine life.

Industrial wastes are commonly transported to sea in barges. Highly toxic materials, including refinery wastes that can include cyanides, heavy metals, and chlorinated hydrocarbons, are sometimes placed in drums and jettisoned from ships or disposal vessels at least three hundred miles from shore.

In the Great Lakes area, the U.S. Army Corps of Engineers removes sediment, mud, and sludge from approximately one hundred harbors and deposits this material at numerous sites in the lakes. On the average, 10.8 million cubic yards of material are dumped in the Great Lakes each year, of which 6.7 million cubic yards go into Lake Erie and 1.9 million into Lake Michigan.

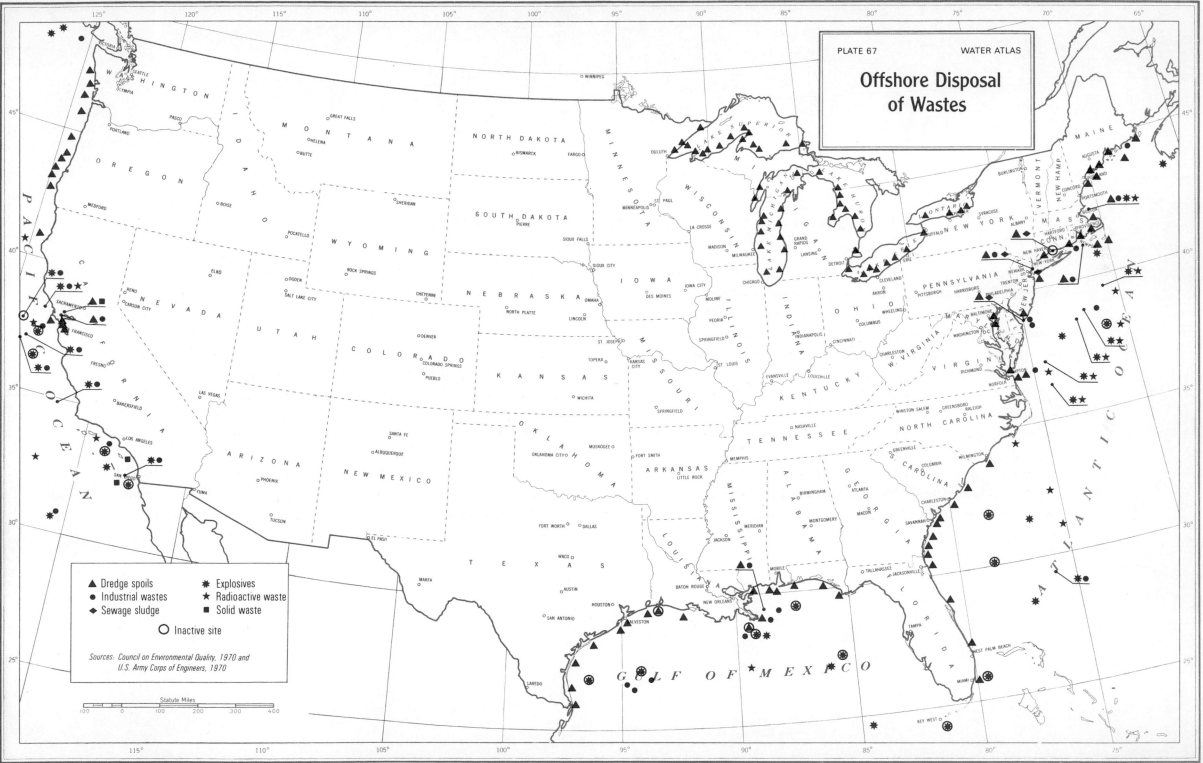

PLATE 67   WATER ATLAS

Offshore Disposal of Wastes

Legend:
- ▲ Dredge spoils
- ● Industrial wastes
- ◆ Sewage sludge
- ✳ Explosives
- ★ Radioactive waste
- ■ Solid waste
- ◉ Inactive site

Sources: Council on Environmental Quality, 1970 and U.S. Army Corps of Engineers, 1970

Statute Miles
100   0   100   200   300   400

PLATE 68 — SUBSURFACE DISPOSAL OF WASTES THROUGH WELLS

Disposal of liquid wastes through wells into porous and permeable rock formations is a comparatively new practice in the United States. Industries in particular have been looking into schemes of this kind as an alternative to expensive waste-treatment processes. Also, a few communities discharge treated municipal sewage into disposal wells.

The map shows that many parts of the country are suitable for underground injection of wastes. Some of the best regions from this viewpoint, are underlain by thick sequences of salt-water bearing sedimentary rocks, which can accept and store the waste liquids without creating any pollution hazards. Other regions are marginal, either because the rocks have low permeabilities or because contamination of freshwater resources is a possible outcome of the disposal method.

Chemical, petrochemical and pharmaceutical companies account for more than half of the 110 injection wells drilled prior to 1967 in the country. Well depths range from a few hundred feet to more than two miles, but most of the wells are less than 4,000 feet deep. The injection rates vary widely, from a few gpm (gallons per minute) to more than 900 gpm. About three-quarters of the wells operate at rates less than 400 gpm. Pumping under pressure is required in most cases to force the waste liquid out into the geologic formations, and only a small percentage of the wells accept the wastes by gravity.

State and Federal regulating agencies have mixed views on the whole subject of underground waste disposal. Some states favor the approach, but most have a guarded attitude about it or else forbid it entirely (see Plate 36).

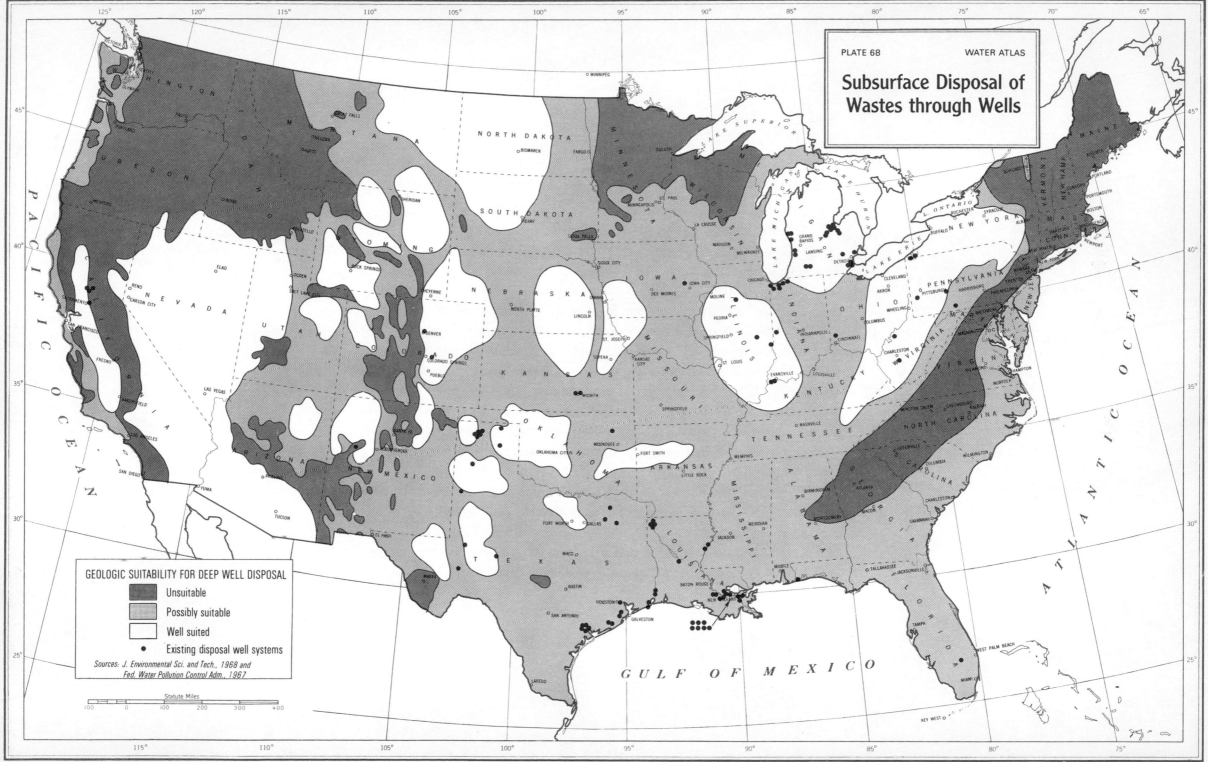

PLATE 68   WATER ATLAS

Subsurface Disposal of Wastes through Wells

GEOLOGIC SUITABILITY FOR DEEP WELL DISPOSAL

- Unsuitable
- Possibly suitable
- Well suited
- • Existing disposal well systems

Sources: *J. Environmental Sci. and Tech., 1968 and Fed. Water Pollution Control Adm., 1967*

Statute Miles

Base Map by U.S.C.&G.S.

© WATER INFORMATION CENTER, INC.

PLATE 69 – FISH KILLS CAUSED BY POLLUTION IN 1969

An annual U.S. Government census of fish kills was begun in June 1960, and by 1969, a total of over 140 million fish had been reported killed in 4,200 separate incidents. In 1969 alone, an estimated 41 million fish were reported killed in 45 states by identifiable pollution sources. This was an increase of 26 million over 1968 when some 15 million fish died.

In 1969, industrial wastes accounted for 199 incidents that killed 29 million fish. Agricultural use of insecticides and herbicides was responsible for 6 million fish killed, and transportation accidents such as pipeline breaks and oil spills killed 2 million fish. Malfunctioning municipal sewers and treatment plants killed some 1 million fish. Of the 465 fish kill incidents reported in 1969, 356 took place in rivers, affecting some 2,358 miles of waterways; 98 occurred in lakes, damaging 6,068 acres of water, and 11 took place in bays, affecting 113 miles of bay shore.

The largest fish kill ever recorded took place in 1969 in Lake Thonotosassa at Plant City, Florida, when more than 26 million fish died over a period of nine days as a result of the dumping of food products in the lake. The accumulation of untreated organic wastes reduced the dissolved oxygen level in the lake below that necessary to sustain all forms of fish life.

PLATE 69 WATER ATLAS

Fish Kills Caused by Pollution in 1969

• Pollution-caused fish kills

Source: Fed. Water Quality Adm., 1970

Statute Miles

© WATER INFORMATION CENTER, INC.

PLATE 70 – DISTRIBUTION OF POPULATION

The map shows, by means of dots and circles, the general distribution of population in the conterminous United States. Each dot represents 10,000 persons residing outside cities or other communities. The circles show concentrations of population, as explained in the diagram in the lower left-hand corner of the map.

There is obviously a strong relationship between population and the availability of water, because water is both a domestic necessity and an essential ingredient in such activities as agriculture, industry, and commerce. The population of the eastern half of the country is denser and more evenly distributed than in the western half, which is partly explained by the surplus of water in the East.

The western half of the country, beginning at the 20-inch rainfall zone in central Texas and running north through the Dakota plains, is much more sparsely settled than the East. Lack of moisture in that part of the country restricts most agriculture to irrigated valleys, which appear on the map as long belts or chains of dots. Large cities are not as numerous and generally are located in the irrigated belts. With the possible exception of the Pacific Northwest, the metropolitan centers of the West must reach out great distances to develop adequate water supplies for their growing populations.

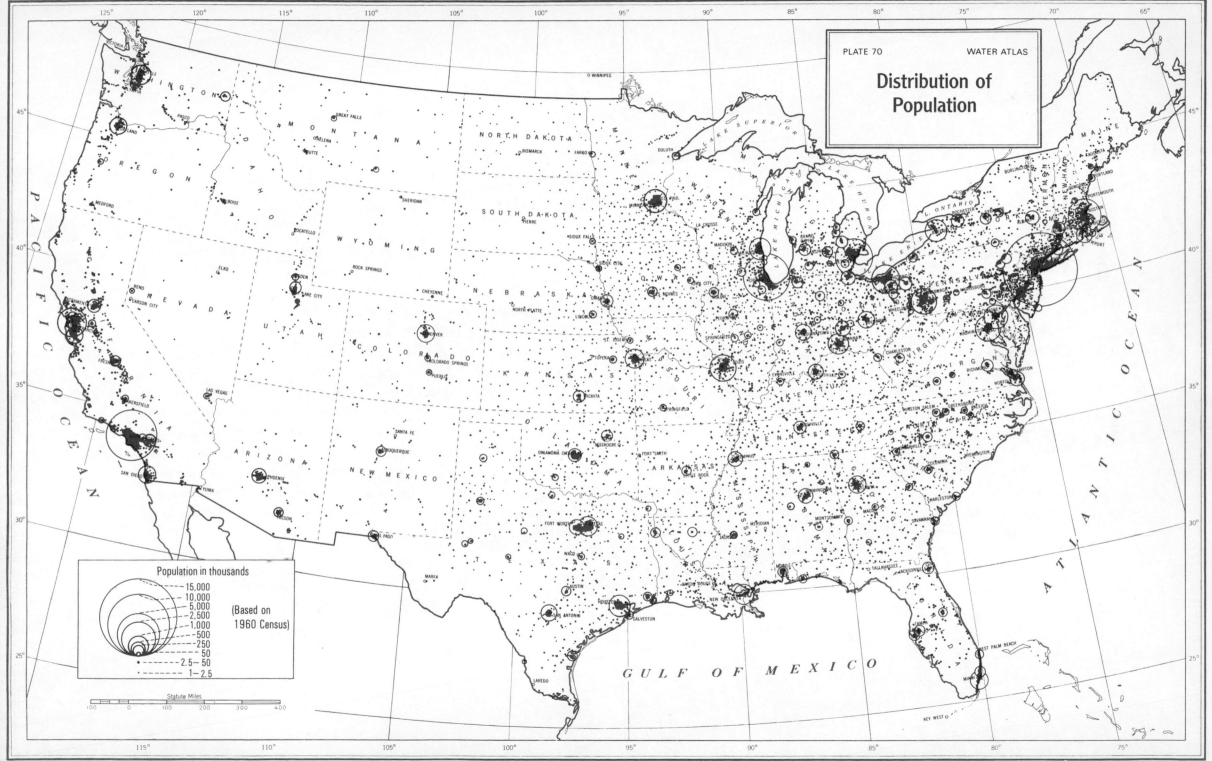

PLATE 70   WATER ATLAS

Distribution of Population

Population in thousands

- 15,000
- 10,000
- 5,000
- 2,500
- 1,000
- 500
- 250
- 50
- 2.5 – 50
- 1 – 2.5

(Based on 1960 Census)

Statute Miles

Base Map by U.S.C.&G.S.   © WATER INFORMATION CENTER, INC.

PLATE 71 — PER CAPITA INLAND WATER SURFACE

Approximately one-fourth of the nation's leisure activity is centered around water and water-based sports. In 1965, the general public spent 2.8 billion activity-days participating in swimming, fishing, boating, water skiing, and ice skating.

Water-based recreation also generates an extremely large amount of activity in the economic sense. The existence of more than 8 million pleasure boats in the country underlines this fact. It is estimated that there will be 30 million pleasure craft plying the nation's waters 50 years from now. An over-all increase of 60 percent in the use of water-based recreational facilities is expected by 1980.

Because most of the people in the country do not have easy access to the oceans or the Gulf of Mexico, they must turn to inland water bodies to satisfy their needs for water recreation. Inland surface waters are abundant in some regions and almost non-existent in others, and if a comparison is made between populations and the areas of available surface waters, it can be seen that some parts of the country are notably deficient in this respect. The map shows the areas of inland surface water available to residents in different regions of the country, and indicates, for example, that the relatively wet Middle Atlantic States and the East North Central States are already pressed, on a per-capita basis, to supply water-based recreation to their populations. By contrast, the relatively arid western states have a good supply on a per-capita basis. This imbalance in terms of population is expected to become more severe in the future, especially when one considers that in 30 years, 60 percent of the population will live on only 7 percent of the land, packed into three mega-cities. These huge urban centers will be located in areas that are already below the national average in terms of availability of inland surface water for recreational purposes.

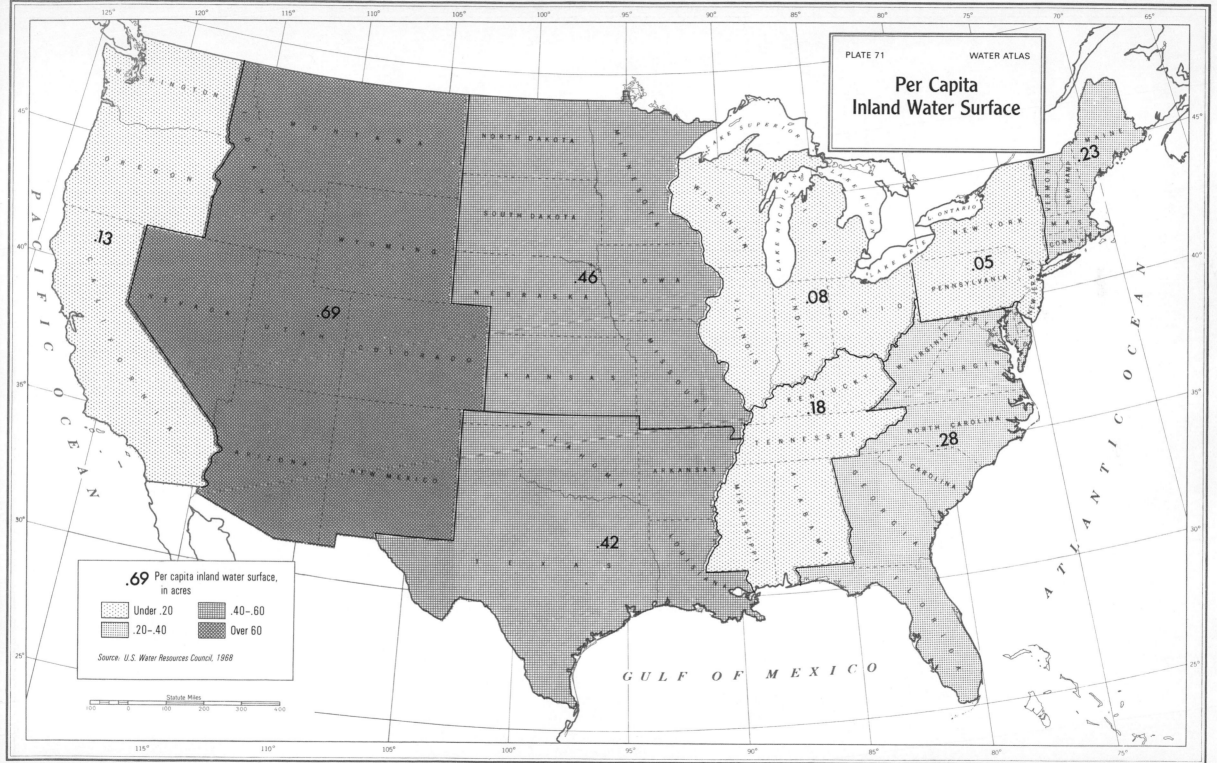

PLATE 71   WATER ATLAS

Per Capita Inland Water Surface

.69 Per capita inland water surface, in acres

Under .20
.20–.40
.40–.60
Over 60

Source: U.S. Water Resources Council, 1968

Statute Miles
100   0   100   200   300   400

.23
.13
.05
.08
.46
.69
.18
.28
.42

PACIFIC OCEAN

ATLANTIC OCEAN

GULF OF MEXICO

PLATE 72 – PER CAPITA SHORELINE LENGTH

Unfortunately, not all shorelines or waterfronts are available for recreation. In fact, in the places where shorelines are needed most, namely the urbanized localities, most of the waterfront has been taken over by industrial, commercial, and residential users, and often suffers from pollution (see Plates 51 and 67). On the other hand, as populations in these urban areas build up and as socio-economic forces work in favor of recreational use of shorelines, many industries, commercial establishments, and private residents are yielding to the pressure, thus making it possible to convert more waterfronts for recreational purposes.

The conflict of interests over available shorelines is compounded in the Middle Atlantic States, where a rather low ratio of shoreline to population is aggravated by the lowest area of inland water surface per capita (Plate 71) and a rather high personal income level, the latter a factor that encourages recreational use of leisure time.

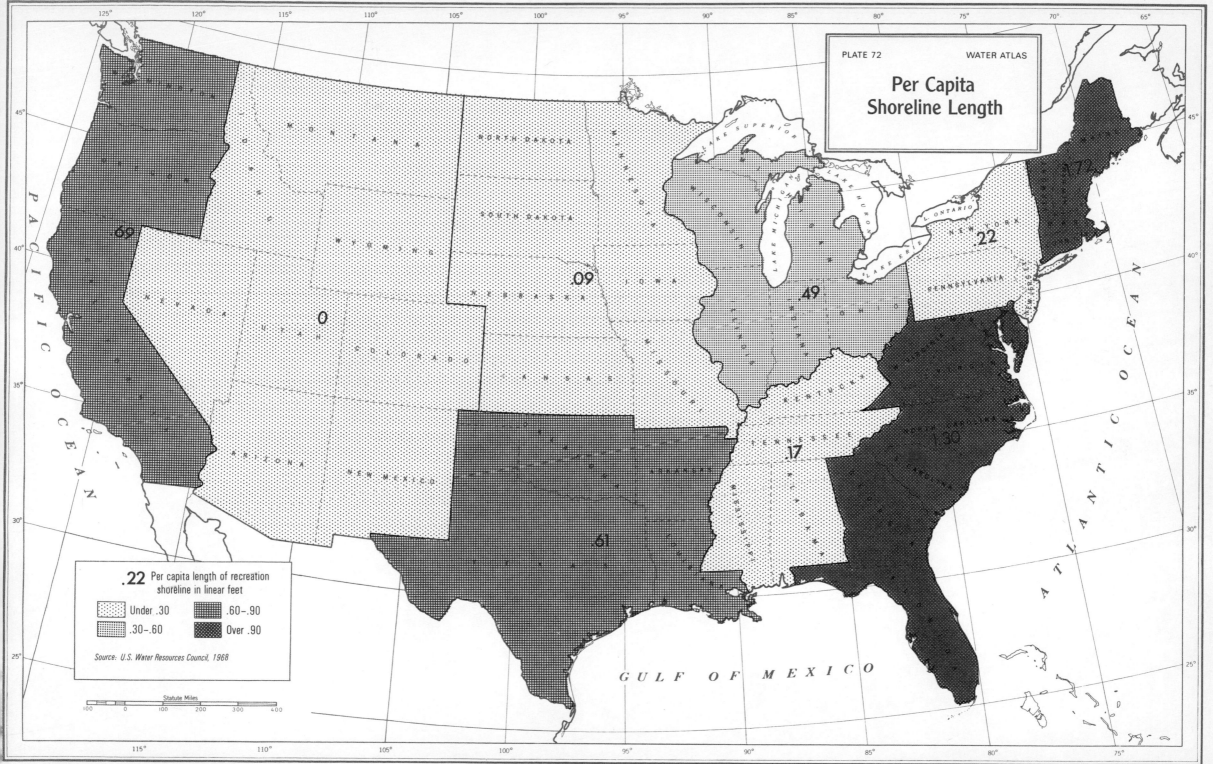

PLATE 72   WATER ATLAS

Per Capita Shoreline Length

.22 Per capita length of recreation
shoreline in linear feet

Under .30   .60–.90

.30–.60   Over .90

Source: U.S. Water Resources Council, 1968

Statute Miles
100   0   100   200   300   400

PACIFIC OCEAN

ATLANTIC OCEAN

GULF OF MEXICO

LAKE SUPERIOR

LAKE MICHIGAN

LAKE HURON

LAKE ERIE

L. ONTARIO

.69

0

.09

.49

.22

1.72

1.30

.17

.61

Base Map by U.S.C.&G.S.

© WATER INFORMATION CENTER, INC.

PLATE 73 – FISHABLE FRESH-WATER AREAS

Fish and wildlife resources presently provide outdoor recreation for about forty percent of the nation's population. In 1965, people in the United States spent 575 million activity-days pursuing recreational fishing activities, in both fresh and salt-water bodies. The value of the total 1965 commercial fresh-water related catch in the conterminous United States came to $265 million. The map shows the acreage of fishable fresh-water areas for each major drainage basin in the country.

In large urban areas, access to fresh-water fishing is becoming increasingly more difficult. A long exhausting trip to a crowded, partially polluted stream or lake is not an uncommon experience. The construction or expansion of large reservoirs near these population centers could be a solution. Such large alterations of the natural environment, however, do not always work to benefit fish and wildlife. In fact, some poorly planned impoundments, while increasing the area of fresh water, can at the same time destroy the wildlife habitat and reduce the quality of fishing.

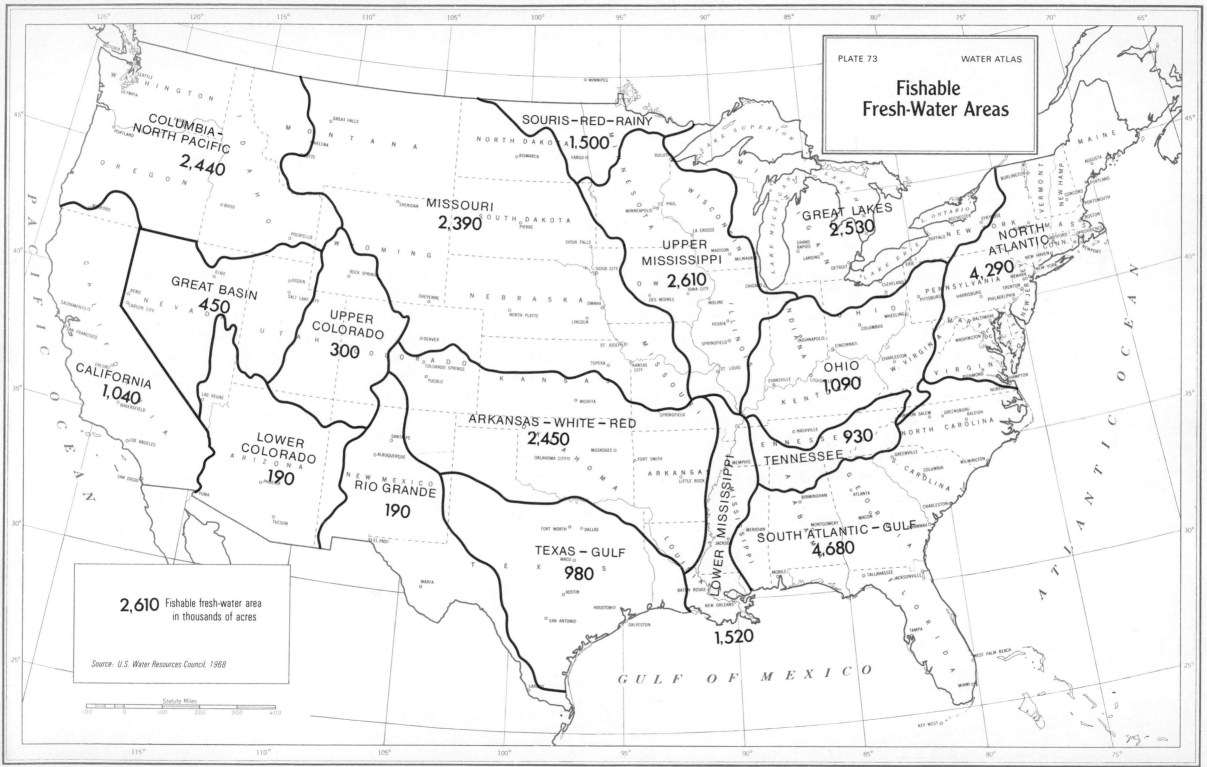

PLATE 73   WATER ATLAS

Fishable Fresh-Water Areas

COLUMBIA–NORTH PACIFIC **2,440**

SOURIS–RED–RAINY **1,500**

MISSOURI **2,390**

GREAT LAKES **2,530**

UPPER MISSISSIPPI **2,610**

NORTH ATLANTIC **4,290**

GREAT BASIN **450**

UPPER COLORADO **300**

CALIFORNIA **1,040**

OHIO **1,090**

LOWER COLORADO **190**

RIO GRANDE **190**

ARKANSAS–WHITE–RED **2,450**

TENNESSEE **930**

TEXAS–GULF **980**

LOWER MISSISSIPPI **1,520**

SOUTH ATLANTIC–GULF **4,680**

2,610 Fishable fresh-water area in thousands of acres

Source: U.S. Water Resources Council, 1968

Statute Miles

Base Map by U.S.C.&G.S.   © WATER INFORMATION CENTER, INC.

PLATE 74 — NATURAL WETLANDS

Wetlands include swamps, marshes, bogs, and other places where the land surface is almost always covered to some degree by water. They are, acre for acre, the most productive fish and wildlife habitats in the country. However, the responsibility of managing most wetlands does not fall under the control of conservationists, scientists, or enlightened governmental officials. For the most part, these lands are under private ownership, and historically have been used and destroyed without any regard for their importance.

It is the very nature of the wetlands that accounts for the general lack of appreciation of this resource. Often, wetlands are located between a desirable open body of water and the people who want access to this body. The wetlands are then filled in or cut away. The farmer may see his wetlands as only an awkward part of his property to be eventually drained and farmed. Many urban-centered people have never seen an unpolluted wetland. The word "swamp" conjures up thoughts of foul-smelling, garbage-strewn mud flats, choked with oil slime and wastes. The low areas around urban centers have traditionally been used as dumps, and it is difficult indeed to convince a developer or a homeowner that the local wetlands are desirable parts of the community and the environment.

It is hoped, however, that with continuing purchases by State and Federal conservation agencies and with constant educational pressure on the public, enough of the wetlands will be preserved to maintain sufficient quantities of fish and wildlife. The map shows the total acreage of such wetlands still available in the country's major drainage basins.

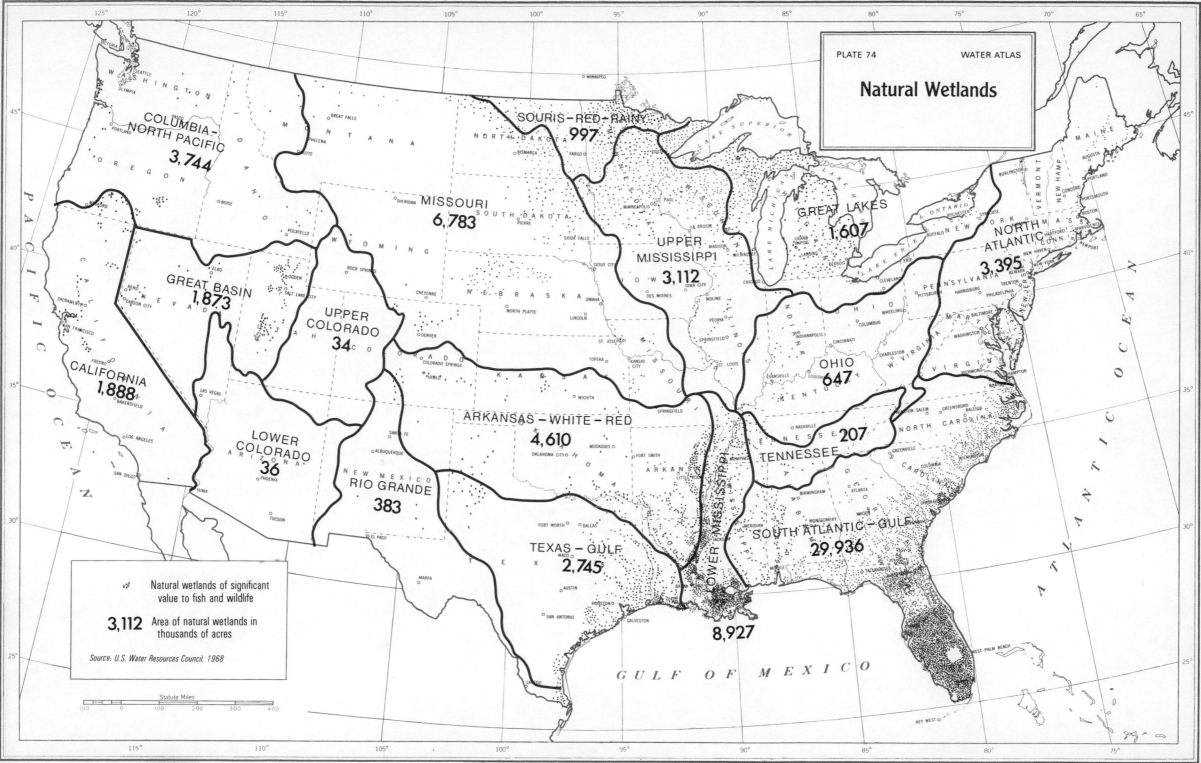

PLATE 74 — WATER ATLAS

Natural Wetlands

COLUMBIA–NORTH PACIFIC 3,744

SOURIS–RED–RAINY 997

MISSOURI 6,783

GREAT LAKES 1,607

NORTH ATLANTIC 3,395

UPPER MISSISSIPPI 3,112

GREAT BASIN 1,873

UPPER COLORADO 34

CALIFORNIA 1,888

OHIO 647

ARKANSAS–WHITE–RED 4,610

TENNESSEE 207

LOWER COLORADO 36

NEW MEXICO RIO GRANDE 383

TEXAS–GULF 2,745

LOWER MISSISSIPPI 8,927

SOUTH ATLANTIC–GULF 29,936

PACIFIC OCEAN

ATLANTIC OCEAN

GULF OF MEXICO

Natural wetlands of significant value to fish and wildlife

3,112 Area of natural wetlands in thousands of acres

Source: U.S. Water Resources Council, 1968

Statute Miles

Base Map by U.S.C.&G.S.

© WATER INFORMATION CENTER, INC.

PLATE 75 – TOTAL WITHDRAWAL OF WATER EXCLUDING HYDROELECTRIC POWER – 1970

The map shows the amounts of water used in the conterminous United States in 1970 for all purposes except the generation of hydroelectric power. The figures shown on the map represent the amounts withdrawn from rivers, lakes, reservoirs, wells, and other water sources in each state. It should be noted that each time water was withdrawn, the amount was included in the accumulated total, even though the same water may have been used over and over again by various consumers. However, if the water was recirculated several times in the same system (as for instance within a factory) before being discharged into a stream or on the ground, it was counted only once.

The estimated total withdrawal of water in the nation (including Alaska and Hawaii) amounted to about 370 billion gallons daily during 1970, exclusive of water used for hydroelectric power. This represents an increase of 19 percent over the estimated 1965 withdrawal. Industry took the largest part of this total, or 210 billion gallons daily. Irrigation took 130 billion gallons daily. Public water supply systems took 27 billion gallons per day, and rural, domestic and stock use was the least with 4.5 billion gallons daily. The greatest withdrawal was in the eastern industrial areas and in California and Texas where irrigation is practiced extensively. Withdrawals in the mid-continent region and in the northern New England states were the smallest.

Only about one-fourth of the fresh water withdrawn was actually consumed, in the sense that it was no longer available for possible reuse. The 17 western states consumed 86 percent of this water, whereas only 14 percent was consumed by the 31 eastern states.

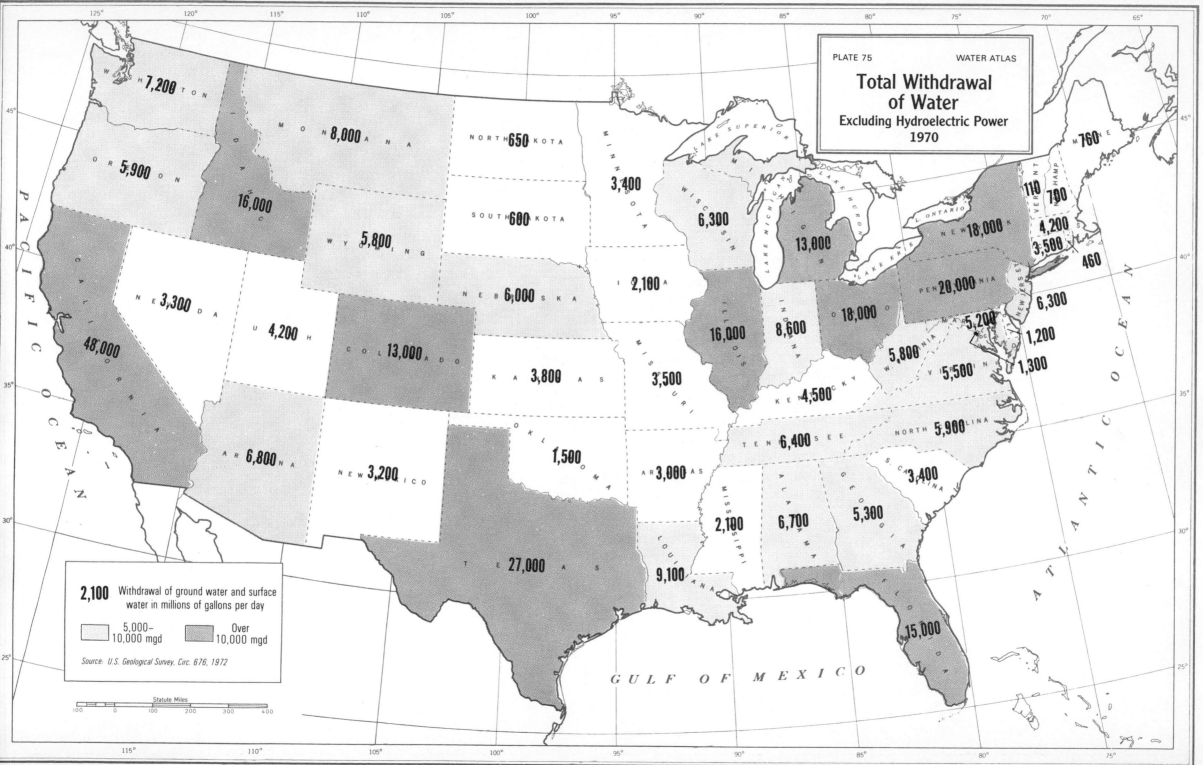

PLATE 75   WATER ATLAS

Total Withdrawal of Water
Excluding Hydroelectric Power
1970

2,100 Withdrawal of ground water and surface water in millions of gallons per day

5,000–10,000 mgd

Over 10,000 mgd

Source: U.S. Geological Survey, Circ. 676, 1972

Statute Miles

PACIFIC OCEAN

ATLANTIC OCEAN

GULF OF MEXICO

WASHINGTON **7,200**
OREGON **5,900**
MONTANA **8,000**
IDAHO **16,000**
NORTH DAKOTA **650**
SOUTH DAKOTA **600**
WYOMING **5,800**
MINNESOTA **3,400**
WISCONSIN **6,300**
MICHIGAN **13,000**
MAINE **760**
VERMONT **110**
NEW HAMPSHIRE **790**
NEW YORK **18,000**
4,200
3,500
460
NEVADA **3,300**
UTAH **4,200**
COLORADO **13,000**
NEBRASKA **6,000**
IOWA **2,100**
ILLINOIS **16,000**
INDIANA **8,600**
OHIO **18,000**
PENNSYLVANIA **20,000**
NEW JERSEY **6,300**
5,200
1,200
1,300
CALIFORNIA **48,000**
KANSAS **3,800**
MISSOURI **3,500**
KENTUCKY **4,500**
WEST VIRGINIA **5,800**
VIRGINIA **5,500**
ARIZONA **6,800**
OKLAHOMA **1,500**
ARKANSAS **3,000**
TENNESSEE **6,400**
NORTH CAROLINA **5,900**
NEW MEXICO **3,200**
MISSISSIPPI **2,100**
ALABAMA **6,700**
GEORGIA **5,300**
SOUTH CAROLINA **3,400**
TEXAS **27,000**
LOUISIANA **9,100**
FLORIDA **15,000**

LAKE SUPERIOR
LAKE MICHIGAN
LAKE HURON
LAKE ERIE
L. ONTARIO

se Map by U.S.C.&G.S.

© WATER INFORMATION CENTER, INC.

PLATE 76 – WITHDRAWAL OF WATER FOR
PUBLIC SUPPLIES – 1970

The figures on the map represent the total withdrawal of water by public water-supply systems in towns and communities during 1970 in each state. The national total (including Alaska and Hawaii) was 27 billion gallons daily and was used by an estimated 161 million people representing 80 percent of the total population.

Water used for public supplies includes all water pumped into the community systems. Because the water is measured at the source, it includes leakage from water mains, water supplied for public services such as fire-fighting, street washing, parks and municipal swimming pools. Such losses and public uses accounted for about 30 percent of the withdrawal. In general, the amount of withdrawal for public supplies depends on the size of the population in the particular state and the per-capita water use. On a national basis, municipal water use averages 164 gallons per person per day, but this varies from region to region, from less than 100 gallons per person per day in Kentucky to as much as 317 gallons in the State of Washington.

Commerce and industry received 8.7 billion gallons daily, a third of the total withdrawn by public supplies. Approximately 10 percent of the water used by commerce and industry was for air conditioning. About 22 percent of the total withdrawal for public supply is estimated to have been consumed. One-third of the water withdrawn for public supplies came from wells and springs, and two-thirds from surface-water sources.

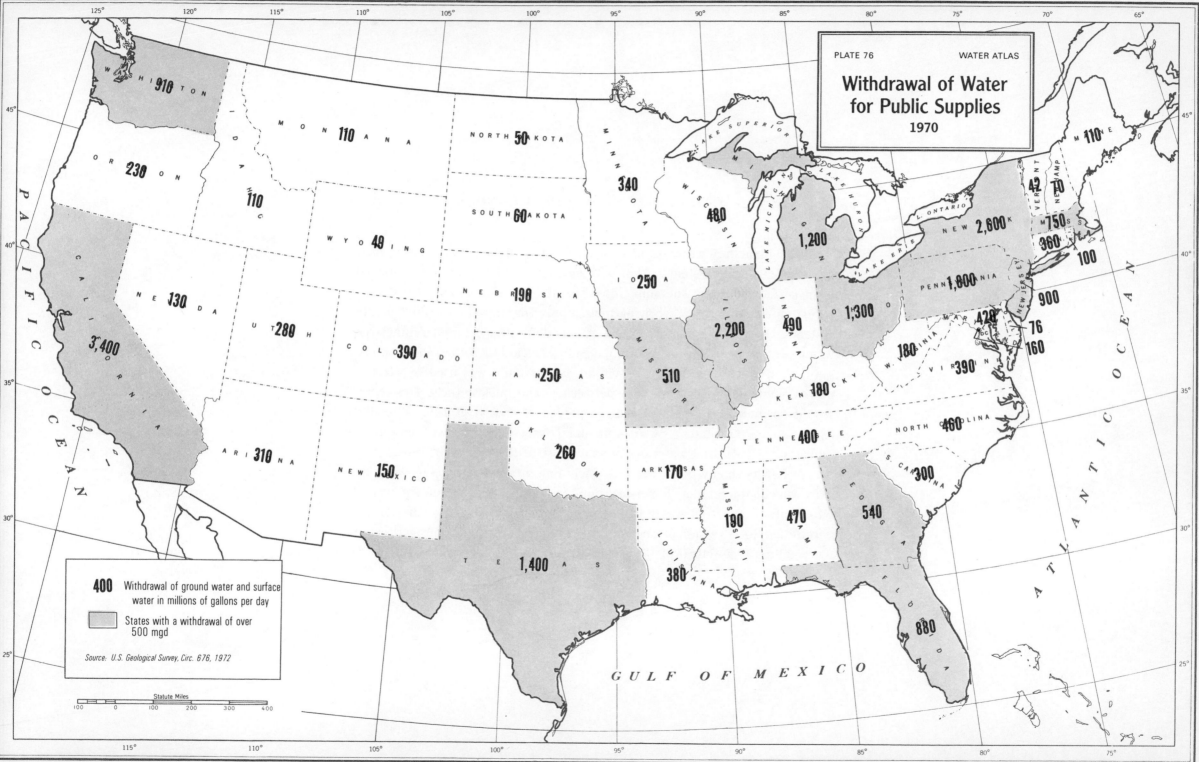

PLATE 76   WATER ATLAS

Withdrawal of Water for Public Supplies
1970

400 Withdrawal of ground water and surface water in millions of gallons per day

States with a withdrawal of over 500 mgd

Source: U.S. Geological Survey, Circ. 676, 1972

Statute Miles

100   0   100   200   300   400

WASHINGTON 910
OREGON 230
MONTANA 110
NORTH DAKOTA 50
SOUTH DAKOTA 60
WYOMING 49
IDAHO 110
MINNESOTA 340
WISCONSIN 480
MICHIGAN 1,200
NEW YORK 2,600
VERMONT 42
NEW HAMPSHIRE 70
MAINE 110
MASS 750
360
100
NEVADA 130
UTAH 280
COLORADO 390
NEBRASKA 190
IOWA 250
ILLINOIS 2,200
INDIANA 490
OHIO 1,300
PENNSYLVANIA 1,800
900
NEW JERSEY 428
76
160
CALIFORNIA 3,400
KANSAS 250
MISSOURI 510
KENTUCKY 180
W. VIRGINIA 180
VIRGINIA 390
ARIZONA 310
NEW MEXICO 150
OKLAHOMA 260
ARKANSAS 170
TENNESSEE 400
NORTH CAROLINA 460
S. CAROLINA 300
TEXAS 1,400
LOUISIANA 380
MISSISSIPPI 190
ALABAMA 470
GEORGIA 540
FLORIDA 880

PACIFIC OCEAN

ATLANTIC OCEAN

GULF OF MEXICO

LAKE SUPERIOR
LAKE MICHIGAN
LAKE HURON
LAKE ERIE
L. ONTARIO

Base Map by U.S.C.&G.S.

© WATER INFORMATION CENTER, INC.

PLATE 77 – WITHDRAWAL OF WATER FOR INDUSTRY – 1970

The map shows the withdrawal of water by industries operating their own water-supply systems. About 95 percent of this water was obtained from surface sources. The state totals do not include the use of water by industrial establishments receiving their supply from municipal water-supply systems. Of the total of 210 billion gallons daily of self-supplied industrial water used during 1970 in the United States (including Alaska and Hawaii), more than three-fourths or 170 billion gallons daily was used by electric power plants using fossil (coal or petroleum) and nuclear fuels. This represented an increase in water use of 23 percent over that of 1965. With the exception of the States of California and Texas, the largest withdrawals of self-supplied industrial water are in states east of the Mississippi River.

Water has many industrial uses, including processing, cooling, washing, conveyance of material, boiler-feed and sanitation. Ninety percent of the self-supplied industrial water is used for cooling. Most used cooling water is returned to a stream or an aquifer unchanged except for an increase in temperature. One-fourth of the water withdrawn by industry was saline.

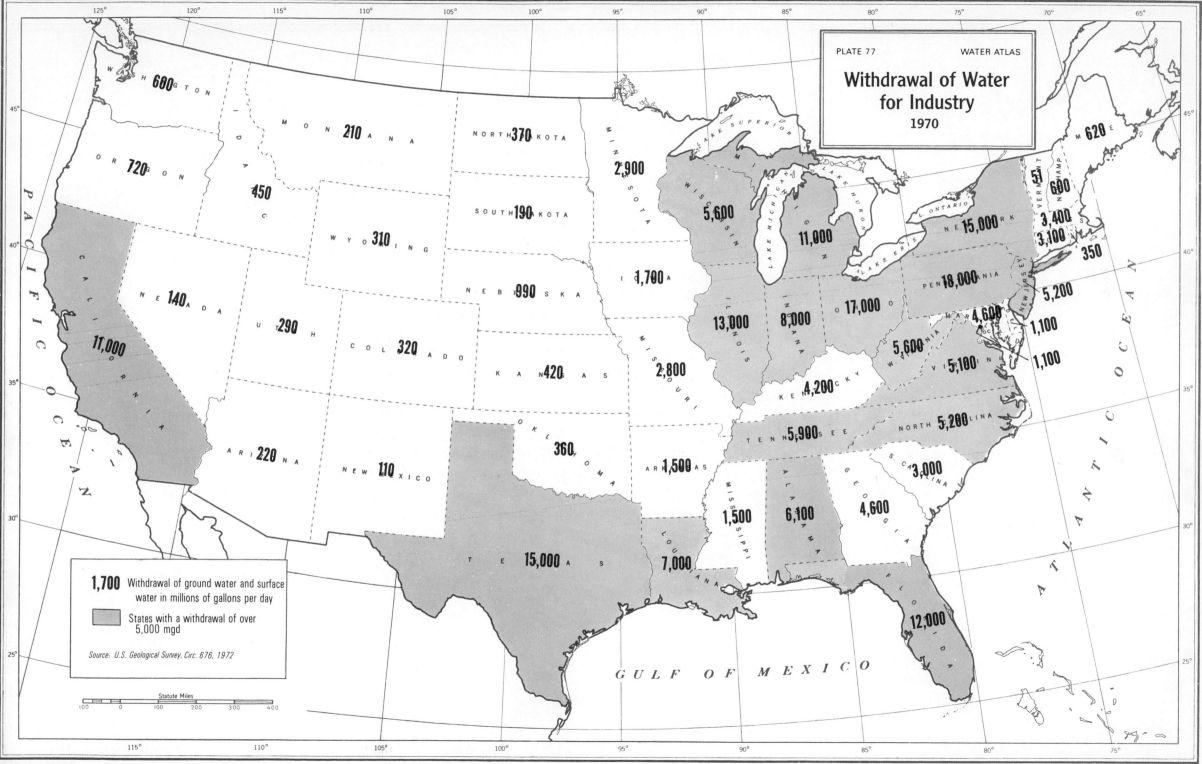

Withdrawal of Water for Industry
1970

1,700 Withdrawal of ground water and surface water in millions of gallons per day

States with a withdrawal of over 5,000 mgd

Source: U.S. Geological Survey, Circ. 676, 1972

Statute Miles

PACIFIC OCEAN

ATLANTIC OCEAN

GULF OF MEXICO

WASHINGTON **600**
OREGON **720**
MONTANA **210**
NORTH DAKOTA **370**
MINNESOTA **2,900**
IDAHO **450**
SOUTH DAKOTA **190**
WYOMING **310**
NEBRASKA **990**
IOWA **1,700**
WISCONSIN **5,600**
MICHIGAN **11,000**
NEW YORK **15,000**
VERMONT **51**
NEW HAMPSHIRE **600**
MAINE **620**
MASS **3,400**
3,100
350
NEVADA **140**
UTAH **290**
COLORADO **320**
KANSAS **420**
MISSOURI **2,800**
ILLINOIS **13,000**
INDIANA **8,000**
OHIO **17,000**
PENNSYLVANIA **18,000**
NEW JERSEY **5,200**
4,600
1,100
1,100
WEST VIRGINIA **5,600**
VIRGINIA **5,100**
KENTUCKY **4,200**
CALIFORNIA **11,000**
ARIZONA **220**
NEW MEXICO **110**
OKLAHOMA **360**
ARKANSAS **1,500**
TENNESSEE **5,900**
NORTH CAROLINA **5,200**
SOUTH CAROLINA **3,000**
MISSISSIPPI **1,500**
ALABAMA **6,100**
GEORGIA **4,600**
TEXAS **15,000**
LOUISIANA **7,000**
FLORIDA **12,000**

PLATE 78 – WITHDRAWAL OF WATER FOR RURAL USE – 1970

Rural homes are defined as those not served by central public water-supply systems. Of the total of 4.5 billion gallons daily withdrawn for rural use in the United States (including Alaska and Hawaii) in 1970, 1.9 billion gallons daily was used for livestock and 2.6 billion gallons daily for domestic purposes within the home. The per capita rate for rural domestic water use was 63 gallons per day.

About 3.6 billion gallons daily was obtained from wells and springs, and only 0.9 billion gallons daily was obtained from lakes, streams, and ponds. Of the 203 million people living in the nation in 1970, 41 million supplied their own water. The relatively heavy rural water use in the North-Central States and in Florida reflects a large number of small-sized farms and a high density of self-supplied suburban residences surrounding cities and towns.

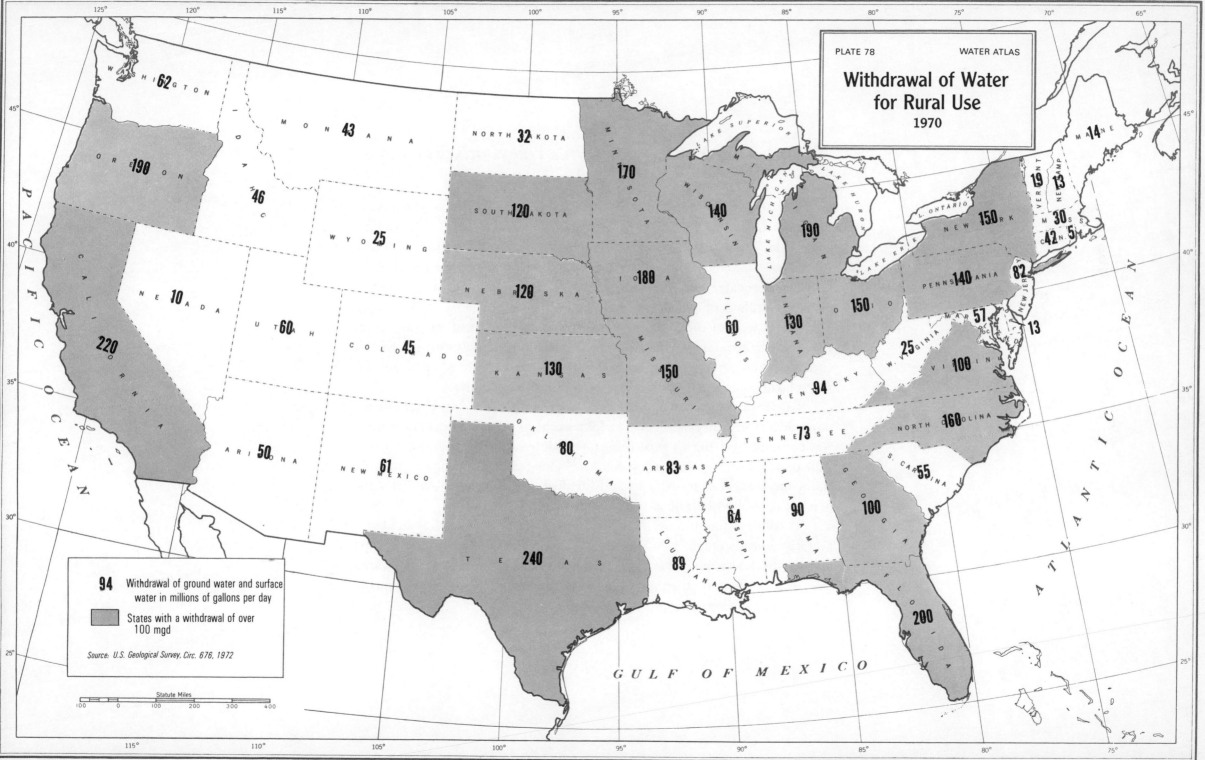

PLATE 78   WATER ATLAS

Withdrawal of Water for Rural Use
1970

94   Withdrawal of ground water and surface water in millions of gallons per day

    States with a withdrawal of over 100 mgd

Source: U.S. Geological Survey, Circ. 676, 1972

Statute Miles
100   0   100   200   300   400

Base Map by U.S.C.&G.S.

© WATER INFORMATION CENTER, INC.

PACIFIC OCEAN

ATLANTIC OCEAN

GULF OF MEXICO

WASHINGTON 62
OREGON 190
IDAHO 46
MONTANA 43
NORTH DAKOTA 32
SOUTH DAKOTA 120
MINNESOTA 170
WISCONSIN 140
MICHIGAN 190
NEW YORK 150
MAINE 14
VERMONT 19
NEW HAMPSHIRE 13
MASS 30
42
5
WYOMING 25
NEVADA 10
UTAH 60
COLORADO 45
NEBRASKA 120
IOWA 180
ILLINOIS 60
INDIANA 130
OHIO 150
PENNSYLVANIA 140
NEW JERSEY 82
MARYLAND 57
13
CALIFORNIA 220
ARIZONA 50
NEW MEXICO 61
KANSAS 130
MISSOURI 150
KENTUCKY 94
W. VIRGINIA 25
VIRGINIA 100
OKLAHOMA 80
ARKANSAS 83
TENNESSEE 73
NORTH CAROLINA 160
S. CAROLINA 55
TEXAS 240
LOUISIANA 89
MISSISSIPPI 64
ALABAMA 90
GEORGIA 100
FLORIDA 200

PLATE 79 – WITHDRAWAL OF WATER FOR IRRIGATION – 1970

The map illustrates strikingly the intensive concentration of irrigation in the western part of the United States. During 1970, a total of 130 billion gallons daily was used to irrigate 50 million acres in the nation (including Alaska and Hawaii) (see Plate 80 for the amount of irrigated acreage). Two-thirds of the water was obtained from lakes, reservoirs, and streams; the remaining third was obtained from wells and springs.

States west of the Mississippi River used 95 percent of the water withdrawn for irrigation. Irrigation water is usually applied only during a part of each year and at variable rates; therefore, the actual rate of application is much greater than the average daily rate shown on the map.

Of the total irrigation withdrawal, an estimated 22 billion gallons per day was lost in conveyance. About 59 percent or 73 billion gallons per day was consumed (in the sense of being unavailable for further use) by evaporation or taken up by growing vegetation. This percentage is more than 25 times the percent consumed by self-supplied industry, and four times the percent consumed by public water-supply systems.

It is interesting to note that the State of Florida, which has an above-average annual rainfall, uses more water for irrigation than any other state east of the Mississippi River. The explanation lies in the fact that Florida's rainfall is concentrated within a few months of the year, whereas its climate permits the growing of crops practically all year long.

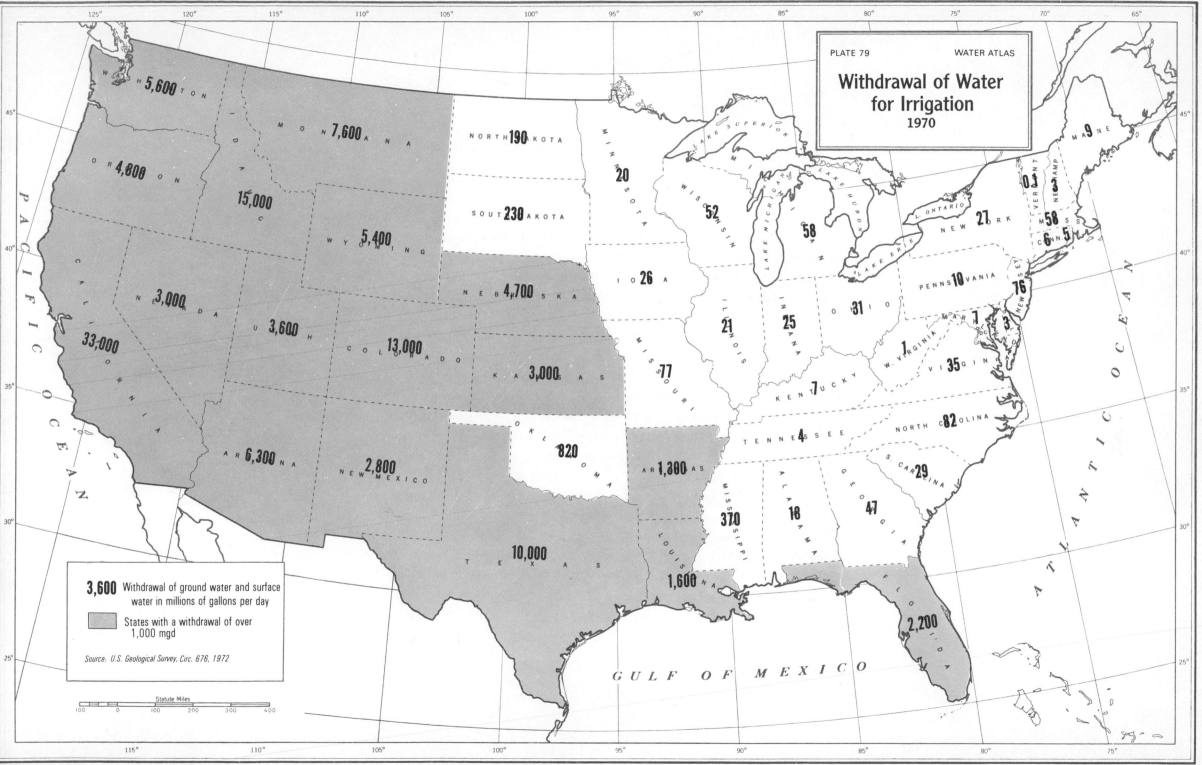

PLATE 79

WATER ATLAS

Withdrawal of Water
for Irrigation
1970

3,600 Withdrawal of ground water and surface
water in millions of gallons per day

States with a withdrawal of over
1,000 mgd

Source: U.S. Geological Survey, Circ. 676, 1972

Statute Miles

WASHINGTON 5,600

MONTANA 7,600

NORTH DAKOTA 190

20

OREGON 4,800

IDAHO 15,000

WYOMING 5,400

SOUTH DAKOTA 230

WISCONSIN 52

58

27 NEW YORK

9 MA NE

0 1

3

58 MASS

6 1 CONN 5

NEVADA 3,000

NEBRASKA 4,700

IOWA 26

PENNSYLVANIA 10

76 NEW JERSEY

CALIFORNIA 33,000

UTAH 3,600

COLORADO 13,000

ILLINOIS 21

INDIANA 25

OHIO 31

MARYLAND 1

3 DEL

1 W. VIRGINIA

KANSAS 3,000

MISSOURI 77

KENTUCKY 7

VIRGINIA 35

ARIZONA 6,300

NEW MEXICO 2,800

OKLAHOMA 820

ARKANSAS 1,300

TENNESSEE 4

NORTH CAROLINA 82

S. CAROLINA 29

MISSISSIPPI 370

ALABAMA 18

GEORGIA 47

TEXAS 10,000

LOUISIANA 1,600

FLORIDA 2,200

PACIFIC OCEAN

ATLANTIC OCEAN

GULF OF MEXICO

LAKE SUPERIOR

LAKE MICHIGAN

LAKE HURON

LAKE ONTARIO

LAKE ERIE

PLATE 80 – IRRIGATED ACREAGE

The U.S. Department of Agriculture estimates that irrigated pastures may produce as much as ten times as many pounds of forage per acre as non-irrigated land. As for other crops, yields may be increased two or three times through irrigation. In 1970, irrigation accounted for 35 percent of the total volume of water withdrawn for all purposes from ground and surface sources. Irrigation was used on 50 million acres to supplement or take the place of precipitation. The map shows the total irrigated acreage in each state of the conterminous United States (see Plate 79 for data on the amounts of water used for irrigation).

Irrigation plays a significant role in the overall national water picture. When looked at as a consumptive use, that is, where the water is not returned to the supply source, irrigation accounts for 84 percent of the total consumption in the nation. Ninety percent of all irrigation takes place in the 17 western states, which receive only 30 percent of the nation's precipitation.

Surface water taken from man-made and natural bodies of water furnished about 65 percent of the irrigation water. Except for a small fraction of one percent that was reclaimed sewage, ground water furnished the remainder. It should be noted that in the Southwestern States, where water needs are greatest, many ground-water reservoirs have been seriously depleted by pumping for irrigation.

PLATE 80   WATER ATLAS

Irrigated Acreage

· Each dot represents 20,000 acres under irrigation

1,200 Total land under irrigation in thousands of acres

Sources: U.S. Bureau of the Census, 1964 and U.S. Geological Survey, Circ. 676, 1972

Statute Miles

Base Map by U.S.C.&G.S.

© WATER INFORMATION CENTER, INC.

PLATE 81 – WITHDRAWAL OF WATER FOR
HYDROELECTRIC POWER GENERATION – 1970

Use of water for generation of electric power is by far the major withdrawal in the nation. In the conterminous United States, 2,800 billion gallons daily of water was used during 1970 for this purpose, an increase of 28 percent since 1965. This enormous quantity of water is more than twice the average annual runoff in the nation. It is, however, a non-consumptive use in the sense that nearly all the water passing through hydroelectric power plants is returned to the source; however, evaporation loss from storage reservoirs which are used to provide hydraulic head at the plants decreases the amount of water available for diversion. An indication of the magnitude of this loss is given by the fact that estimated losses from principal reservoirs and regulated lakes in the 17 western states, irrespective of purpose, is 11 billion gallons per day, or enough to satisfy 40 percent of the entire nation's withdrawals of water for public water supplies.

Large plants for generating electric power by means of falling water are usually restricted to those areas where hills or mountains are present and where streams carry substantial amounts of water. For that reason, states such as Washington, Oregon, New York, and Tennessee show rather large withdrawals of water for water power. Louisiana and Mississippi, by contrast, generate absolutely no water power because those states are essentially flat and their streams move sluggishly across the face of the land.

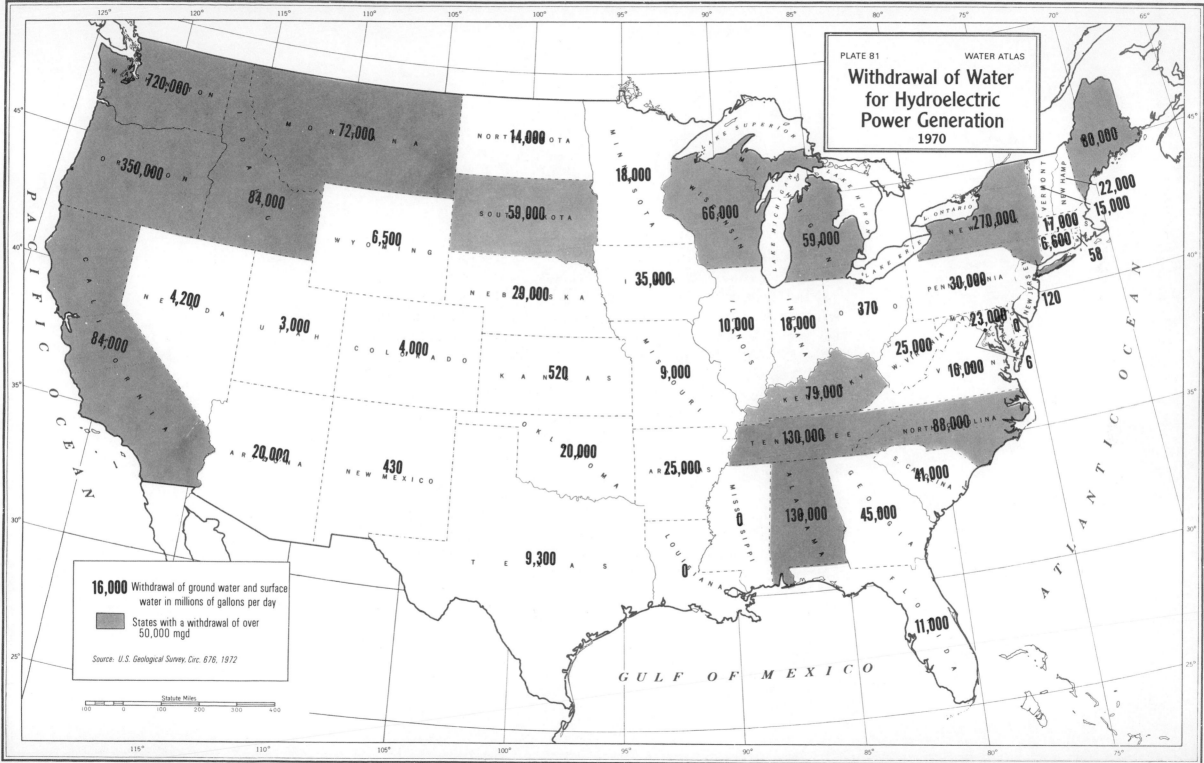

PLATE 81   WATER ATLAS

Withdrawal of Water
for Hydroelectric
Power Generation
1970

720,000 WASHINGTON

72,000 MONTANA

NORTH 14,000 DAKOTA

80,000 MAINE

350,000 OREGON

84,000 IDAHO

18,000 MINNESOTA

66,000 WISCONSIN

270,000 NEW YORK

22,000 NEW HAMP.

59,000 SOUTH DAKOTA

59,000 MICHIGAN

17,000 VERMONT

15,000 MASS.

6,600

6,500 WYOMING

35,000 IOWA

30,000 PENNSYLVANIA

58

4,200 NEVADA

3,000 UTAH

4,000 COLORADO

29,000 NEBRASKA

10,000 ILLINOIS

18,000 INDIANA

370 OHIO

23,000 MARYLAND

120 NEW JERSEY

0

84,000 CALIFORNIA

520 KANSAS

9,000 MISSOURI

79,000 KENTUCKY

25,000 W. VIRGINIA

16,000 VIRGINIA

6 D.C.

20,000 ARIZONA

430 NEW MEXICO

20,000 OKLAHOMA

25,000 ARKANSAS

130,000 TENNESSEE

88,000 NORTH CAROLINA

9,300 TEXAS

0 MISSISSIPPI

130,000 ALABAMA

45,000 GEORGIA

41,000 SOUTH CAROLINA

0 LOUISIANA

11,000 FLORIDA

LAKE SUPERIOR

LAKE MICHIGAN

LAKE HURON

L. ONTARIO

LAKE ERIE

PACIFIC OCEAN

ATLANTIC OCEAN

GULF OF MEXICO

16,000 Withdrawal of ground water and surface
water in millions of gallons per day

States with a withdrawal of over
50,000 mgd

Source: U.S. Geological Survey, Circ. 676, 1972

Statute Miles
100 0 100 200 300 400

Base Map by U.S.C.&G.S.

© WATER INFORMATION CENTER, INC.

PLATE 82 – WITHDRAWAL OF WATER – AIR CONDITIONING

Data on the quantity of water used for air conditioning are incomplete. Available information indicates that the use of water for air conditioning represents a very small withdrawal in the nation. In 1965, the total quantity used for this purpose in the United States (including Alaska and Hawaii) was estimated at 1.7 billion gallons per day. Of this, 760 mgd (million gallons per day) was derived from public water supplies and the remaining 1,000 mgd came from privately operated industrial water-supply systems. Many air conditioning systems use ground water in preference to surface-water supplies owing to the stability of the temperature of ground water the year around. Ground-water temperature generally is 10 to 20 degrees F. lower than that of surface water during the summer season.

The length of the air-conditioning season varies with latitude. In the Northern States a high summer demand for air conditioning, combined with other seasonal demands such as lawn watering, frequently causes large peak loads in public-supply systems. By contrast, demand for air conditioning exists through a greater part of the year in the Southern States. The map shows that the use of water for air conditioning is especially large in California, Texas, New York, New Jersey, and Pennsylvania.

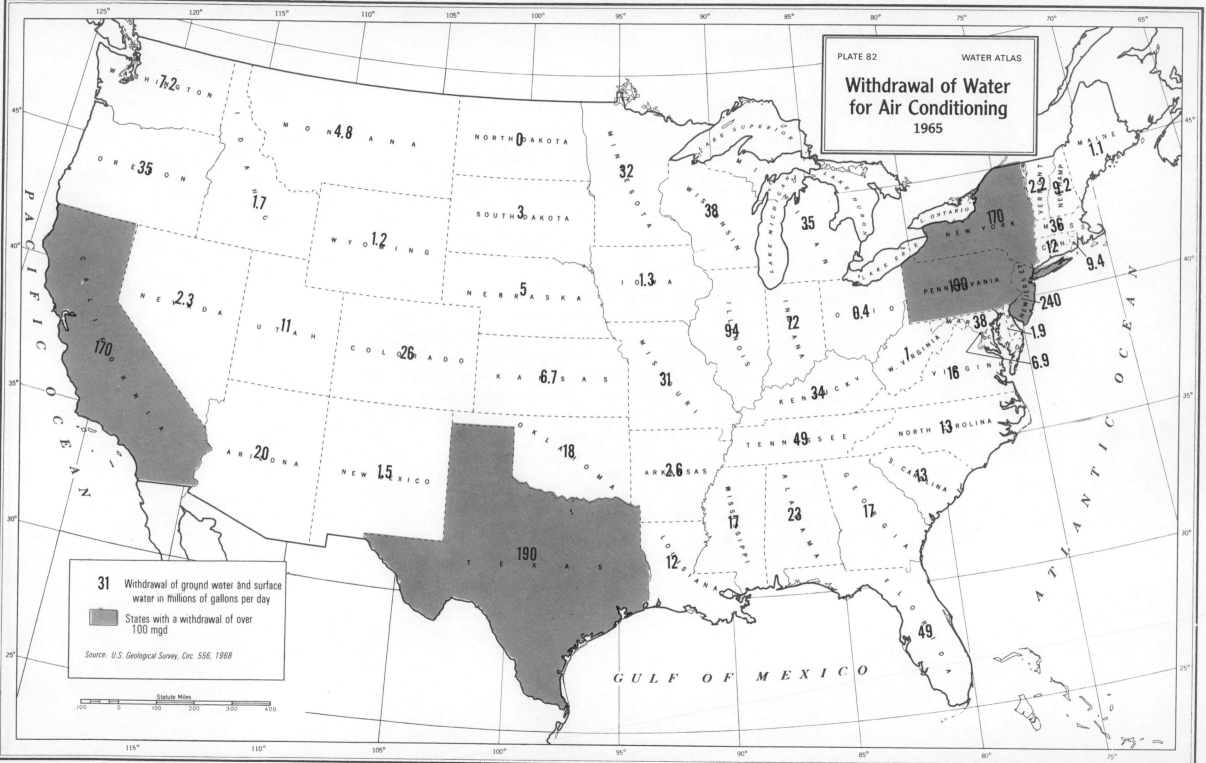

PLATE 82   WATER ATLAS

Withdrawal of Water
for Air Conditioning
1965

31 Withdrawal of ground water and surface
    water in millions of gallons per day

▓ States with a withdrawal of over
   100 mgd

Source: U.S. Geological Survey, Circ. 556, 1968

Statute Miles

Base Map by U.S.C.&G.S.

© WATER INFORMATION CENTER, INC.

PLATE 83 – PER CAPITA RUNOFF – 1970

The map shows how much water would be available daily to each person within a given region if the total annual amount of streamflow in that region were to be apportioned equally among its inhabitants. Although precipitation is generally heavier in the eastern part of the country, the number of gallons of runoff per person in some of the western states is considerably greater than in the East, owing to the smaller populations in the West. In the Missouri region, for example, where precipitation is only half that in some eastern and northeastern regions, each person has available 6,400 gallons per day. In the Great Lakes region, by contrast, only slightly more than 2,600 gallons per day are available for each inhabitant. The least amount of water available per person in the nation is in the comparatively dry Lower Colorado region in the Southwest.

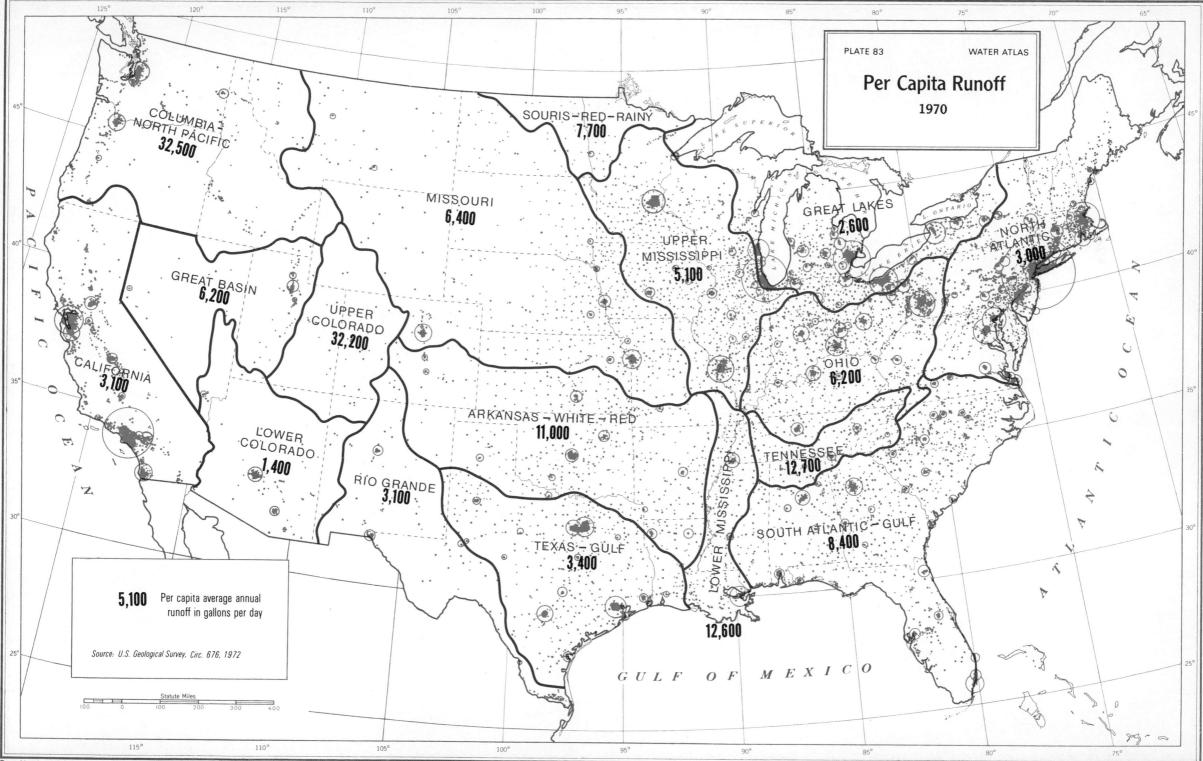

PLATE 83   WATER ATLAS

Per Capita Runoff
1970

COLUMBIA -
NORTH PACIFIC
32,500

SOURIS – RED – RAINY
7,700

GREAT LAKES
2,600

NORTH
ATLANTIC
3,000

MISSOURI
6,400

UPPER
MISSISSIPPI
5,100

GREAT BASIN
6,200

UPPER
COLORADO
32,200

OHIO
6,200

CALIFORNIA
3,100

ARKANSAS – WHITE – RED
11,000

TENNESSEE
12,700

LOWER
COLORADO
1,400

RÍO GRANDE
3,100

LOWER MISSISSIPPI

SOUTH ATLANTIC – GULF
8,400

TEXAS – GULF
3,400

12,600

PACIFIC OCEAN

ATLANTIC OCEAN

LAKE SUPERIOR

LAKE MICHIGAN

L. ONTARIO

L. ERIE

5,100 Per capita average annual
runoff in gallons per day

Source: U.S. Geological Survey, Circ. 676, 1972

Statute Miles
100   0   100   200   300   400

GULF OF MEXICO

Base Map by U.S.C.&G.S.

PLATE 84 – PER CAPITA WATER USE – 1970

The map shows the average amount of water used daily for all purposes within various regions of the United States, expressed in terms of gallons per day per inhabitant. When compared with the previous map on Plate 83, it gives some idea of how much undeveloped water still remains in various parts of the country.

In the North Atlantic region, for example, per-capita use in 1970 was 1,100 gallons per day, while average runoff per person was 3,000 gallons daily. In the Lower Colorado and Rio Grande regions, by contrast, per-capita use surpassed per-capita runoff, indicating that the withdrawal in these regions was greater than the average runoff. This is possible because of augmentation of the supply by inflow of water from the Upper Colorado region, importation of surface water, repeated withdrawals of the same surface water and mining of ground water. With the exception of these two regions, per-capita water use in the nation is everywhere substantially below the amount of runoff available per person.

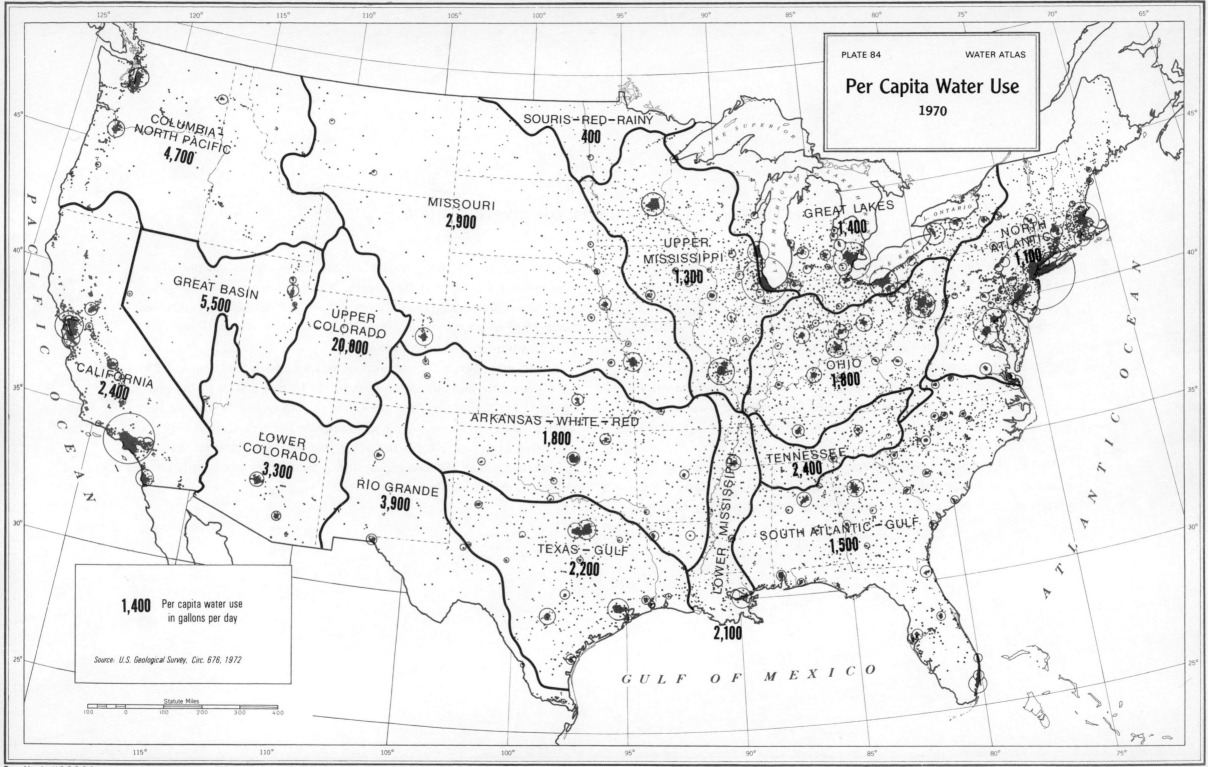

PLATE 84   WATER ATLAS

Per Capita Water Use
1970

COLUMBIA
NORTH PACIFIC
4,700

SOURIS–RED–RAINY
400

MISSOURI
2,900

GREAT LAKES
1,400

NORTH
ATLANTIC
1,100

UPPER
MISSISSIPPI
1,300

GREAT BASIN
5,500

UPPER
COLORADO
20,800

OHIO
1,800

CALIFORNIA
2,400

ARKANSAS – WHITE – RED
1,800

TENNESSEE
2,400

LOWER
COLORADO
3,300

RIO GRANDE
3,900

LOWER MISSISSIPPI

SOUTH ATLANTIC – GULF
1,500

TEXAS – GULF
2,200

2,100

GULF OF MEXICO

1,400   Per capita water use
in gallons per day

Source: U.S. Geological Survey, Circ. 676, 1972

Statute Miles
100   0   100   200   300   400

PACIFIC OCEAN

ATLANTIC OCEAN

PLATE 85 – PER CAPITA WATER CONSUMPTION – 1970

In evaluating the relation between water supply and water demand, it is important to determine how much water is actually consumed or lost from the natural water cycle and how much is simply borrowed temporarily and then returned so that it can be reused. The use of water for power generation, navigation, recreation, washing, cooling, or sanitation for example, is ordinarily a non-consumptive use, in the sense that little or none of the water is permanently removed from the natural water cycle. Consumptive uses include irrigation, production of steam, and the manufacture of products such as canned foods, in which water is incorporated.

An error made in many water-resource studies is to add up the quantities of water supplied to homes, industries, and farms in a particular area and then to compare this total with the estimated natural supply. In many instances, the use of water calculated in this manner far exceeds the supply, which is an obvious contradiction. The correct relation between supply and demand can only be established by classifying each particular use of water as to whether it is consumptive or non-consumptive.

The map shows the amounts of water actually consumed daily on a per-capita basis in each region of the United States. In the eastern part of the country, the amounts are comparatively low. In the western part, however, water consumption is very large owing to extensive irrigation. Except for one region in the Southwest (Lower Colorado), actual water consumption is well below the runoff on a per-capita basis (see Plate 83).

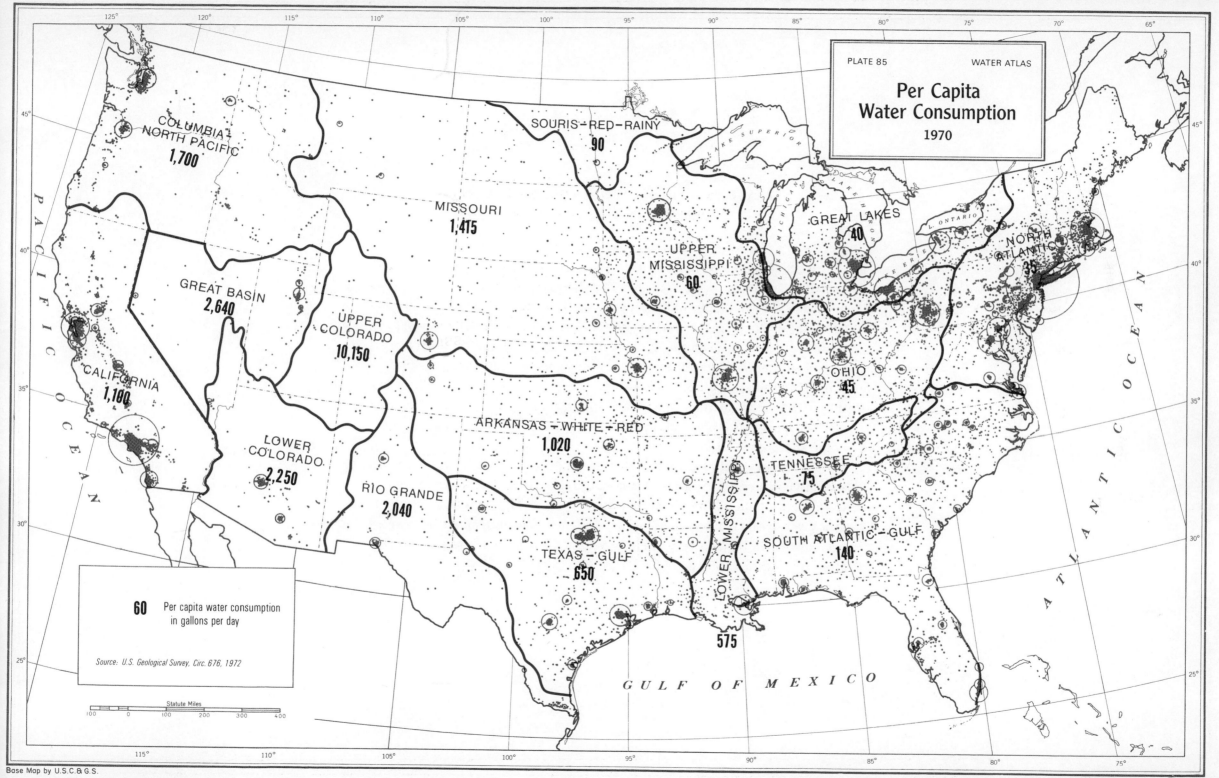

PLATE 85   WATER ATLAS

Per Capita Water Consumption
1970

COLUMBIA
NORTH PACIFIC
1,700

SOURIS—RED—RAINY
90

MISSOURI
1,415

GREAT LAKES
40

UPPER
MISSISSIPPI
60

NORTH
ATLANTIC
35

GREAT BASIN
2,640

UPPER
COLORADO
10,150

OHIO
45

CALIFORNIA
1,100

ARKANSAS—WHITE—RED
1,020

TENNESSEE
75

LOWER
COLORADO
2,250

RIO GRANDE
2,040

SOUTH ATLANTIC—GULF
140

TEXAS—GULF
650

LOWER MISSISSIPPI
575

60   Per capita water consumption
in gallons per day

Source: U.S. Geological Survey, Circ. 676, 1972

PACIFIC OCEAN

ATLANTIC OCEAN

GULF OF MEXICO

LAKE SUPERIOR

LAKE MICHIGAN

L. ONTARIO

Statute Miles
100   0   100   200   300   400

Base Map by U.S.C.&G.S.

© WATER INFORMATION CENTER, INC.

PLATE 86 – PROJECTED WATER SUPPLY AND
DEMAND IN THE YEAR 2000

In examining the figures on this map, it is important to recognize, as explained in the text for Plate 85, that demand for, or use of, water does not mean that all of the water is permanently removed from the total available supply. In fact, the portion of the water that is truly consumed (by being incorporated in products, lost through evaporation, or otherwise) is always substantially less than the total demand. In the North Atlantic region, for example, consumptive use of water in the year 2000 will be less than five percent of the demand, and only about three percent of the runoff. On the other hand, consumptive use and runoff will be almost equal in the Rio Grande region.

By the year 2000, total water demands will exceed total runoff in several regions in the Southwest and also in the Great Lakes region. In this connection, it should be noted that attempting to capture all of the runoff in a given basin is rarely feasible because most streams cannot be lowered beyond certain limits if they are to serve other uses such as navigation, recreation, and waste disposal.

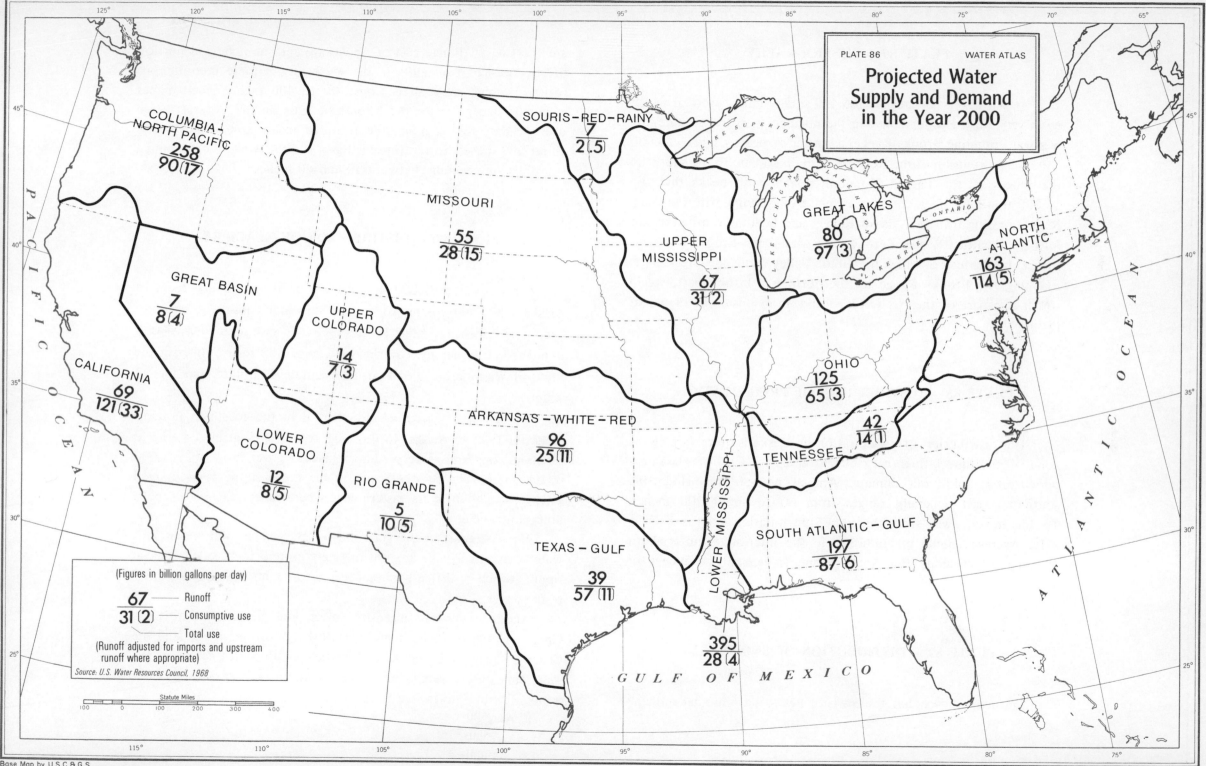

PLATE 86   WATER ATLAS

Projected Water Supply and Demand in the Year 2000

COLUMBIA-NORTH PACIFIC
$\frac{258}{90}$ (17)

SOURIS-RED-RAINY
$\frac{7}{2}$ (.5)

MISSOURI
$\frac{55}{28}$ (15)

GREAT LAKES
$\frac{80}{97}$ (3)

UPPER MISSISSIPPI
$\frac{67}{31}$ (2)

NORTH ATLANTIC
$\frac{163}{114}$ (5)

GREAT BASIN
$\frac{7}{8}$ (4)

UPPER COLORADO
$\frac{14}{7}$ (3)

CALIFORNIA
$\frac{69}{121}$ (33)

OHIO
$\frac{125}{65}$ (3)

ARKANSAS-WHITE-RED
$\frac{96}{25}$ (11)

TENNESSEE
$\frac{42}{14}$ (1)

LOWER COLORADO
$\frac{12}{8}$ (5)

RIO GRANDE
$\frac{5}{10}$ (5)

LOWER MISSISSIPPI

SOUTH ATLANTIC-GULF
$\frac{197}{87}$ (6)

TEXAS-GULF
$\frac{39}{57}$ (11)

$\frac{395}{28}$ (4)

PACIFIC OCEAN

ATLANTIC OCEAN

GULF OF MEXICO

LAKE SUPERIOR
LAKE MICHIGAN
LAKE HURON
LAKE ERIE
L. ONTARIO

(Figures in billion gallons per day)

$\frac{67}{31}$ (2)

— Runoff
— Consumptive use
— Total use

(Runoff adjusted for imports and upstream runoff where appropriate)

Source: U.S. Water Resources Council, 1968

Statute Miles
100 0 100 200 300 400

PLATE 87 – PHYSIOGRAPHY

Alaska covers an area of 566,432 square miles, most of which has a very rugged topography. In the northern part of the state, the westward-trending Brooks Range, a barrier of peaks rising to 10,000 feet, is an extension of the Rocky Mountain system. In the south are the ranges of the Pacific Mountain system with peaks that rise 15,000 to 18,000 feet, forming a great arc beginning with the Coast Range, passing into the Alaska Range, and bending southwestward into the Aleutian Range. Between the Alaska and Brooks Ranges is the Central Plateau of which the Yukon Valley forms the largest part. Flanking the Brooks Range on the north is a broad coastal plain which is a part of the Arctic Slope and an extension of the Great Plains.

PLATE 88 – DISTRIBUTION OF PRECIPITATION

The distribution of precipitation in Alaska is quite variable. A zone of maritime influence extending along the Gulf of Alaska experiences a mild, wet climate. Annual precipitation along the southern coast generally ranges from 60 to about 200 inches. To the north, away from this zone, precipitation decreases markedly. Average annual precipitation in the interior region is about 12 inches and along the Arctic Slope is generally 6 inches or less.

PLATE 89 – DISTRIBUTION OF SNOWFALL

The map shows that the areas of heavy mean annual snowfall are the Coastal Range east of Anchorage and the mainland portion of the Alaskan Panhandle in the southeast. In these mountainous regions, annual snowfall is from 200 to 400 inches. Even higher snowfalls occur locally. At Thompson Pass, in the Coastal Range near Valdez, for example, the recorded mean annual snowfall is about 600 inches. In the Interior Basin and the Arctic Slope, annual snowfalls are generally between 40 and 60 inches.

PLATE 90 – DISTRIBUTION OF GLACIERS

Glaciers cover 20,000 square miles or about three percent of Alaska. The total volume of ice and its water equivalent have not been determined, but must be enormous. To give some idea of what it might be, glacier ice covering only some 200 square miles in the State of Washington is estimated to contain 40 million acre-feet of water.

The greatest glacier development is in the coastal mountains along the Gulf of Alaska. In this area, some valley glaciers are up to 90 miles long and some piedmont glaciers cover more than 1,000 square miles. The Brooks Range in the north supports only small glaciers, except near its eastern edge where valley glaciers up to 10 miles long occur.

Many streams in the state are fed by glacial melt water. This water contains a large amount of finely ground rock called "glacial flour", which is difficult to remove and which impairs the usefulness of the water.

Alaska underwent intensive continental glaciation during the Great Ice Age of Pleistocene time. Both the Brooks Range and the Coastal Range were completely covered by thick ice sheets of the same type that covered Canada and northern regions of the conterminous United States (see Plate 8).

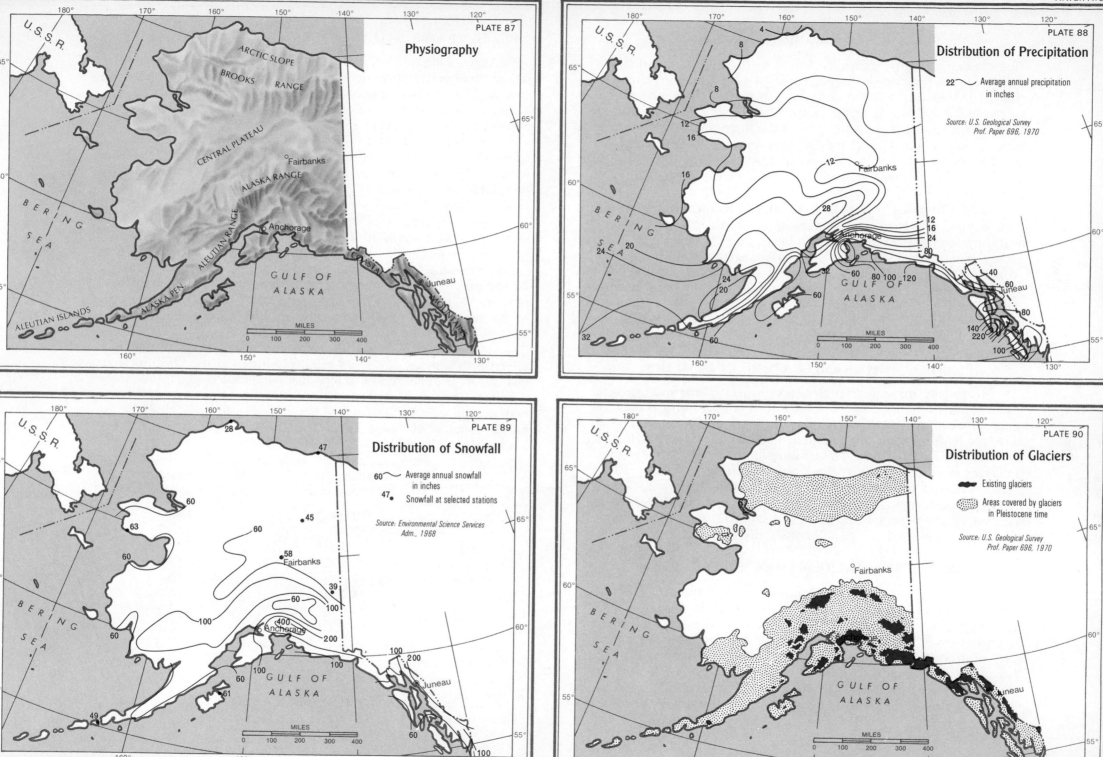

PLATE 87

Physiography

U.S.S.R.

ARCTIC SLOPE

BROOKS RANGE

CENTRAL PLATEAU

°Fairbanks

ALASKA RANGE

ALEUTIAN RANGE

ALASKA PEN.

ALEUTIAN ISLANDS

B E R I N G   S E A

GULF OF ALASKA

°Anchorage

COASTAL

°Juneau

MOUNTAINS

MILES
0   100   200   300   400

PLATE 88

Distribution of Precipitation

22 —— Average annual precipitation in inches

Source: U.S. Geological Survey Prof. Paper 696, 1970

U.S.S.R.

4

8

8

12

16

16

12   Fairbanks

28

12
16
24
80

B E R I N G   S E A

20
24

20

24
20

32

60   80   100   120

Anchorage

40
60

Juneau

80

GULF OF ALASKA

32

60

140
220
100

60

MILES
0   100   200   300   400

PLATE 89

Distribution of Snowfall

60 —— Average annual snowfall in inches

47 • Snowfall at selected stations

Source: Environmental Science Services Adm., 1968

U.S.S.R.

28

47

60

60

63

45

60

60

58
Fairbanks

60

39

60   100

60

400

200

Anchorage

100

100   200

60

100

B E R I N G   S E A

60

100

GULF OF ALASKA

61

49

Juneau

60

100

MILES
0   100   200   300   400

PLATE 90

Distribution of Glaciers

Existing glaciers

Areas covered by glaciers in Pleistocene time

Source: U.S. Geological Survey Prof. Paper 696, 1970

U.S.S.R.

°Fairbanks

B E R I N G   S E A

Anchorage

GULF OF ALASKA

Juneau

MILES
0   100   200   300   400

PLATE 91 — PERMAFROST REGIONS

Permafrost, or permanently frozen surficial earth materials, underlies the land surface in 85 percent of Alaska. The permafrost region is divided into (1) the continuous-permafrost zone, which occupies the area draining to the Arctic Ocean (permafrost present to depths of as much as 1,330 feet); (2) the discontinuous-permafrost zone, which occupies much of the area draining to the Bering Sea and the Pacific Ocean (permafrost at least 600 feet thick locally, but broken by unfrozen zones); and (3) a sporadic permafrost zone farther southward.

Local variations in thickness, extent, and temperature of permafrost depend on thermal properties of the earth materials, rate of heat flow from within the earth, climate, topography, vegetation, geology, and hydrology. Knowledge of permafrost conditions is important in locating ground-water sources and in understanding local hydrology. Frozen ground is an impermeable layer that restricts recharge, discharge, and movement of water. It also acts as a confining layer and reduces the volume in which liquid water may be stored in unconsolidated deposits and bedrock.

PLATE 92 — AIR TEMPERATURE IN JANUARY

Mean daily minimum temperatures in winter are quite variable in the state. Along the Gulf of Alaska, such temperatures at sea level range between 16 and 20 degrees F. The Southern Panhandle experiences somewhat higher temperatures of 20 to 32 degrees F. Inland, beyond the Coastal Ranges, temperatures drop sharply and are below 0 degrees F. In the Yukon Valley, temperatures are −16 to −20 degrees F., and on the Arctic Slope, they average −20 to −22 degrees F. The coldest area is the Fort Yukon and Porcupine River region with minimum temperatures of −28 degrees F., but with recorded extremes in the minus 50's and occasionally even lower.

PLATE 93 — AIR TEMPERATURE IN JULY

Mean daily maximum temperatures in the summer generally range from 50 to 70 degrees F. in the state. Along the Gulf of Alaska, temperatures are 60 degrees F. Temperatures on the Arctic Slope are somewhat lower and range from 46 to 52 degrees F. Mean temperatures of 76 degrees F. are recorded in the Interior Basin in the Fort Yukon area, with peaks in the 90's. This region experiences the greatest annual temperature variation, with a temperature difference of 100 degrees F. or more between winter and summer (See Plate 92).

PLATE 94 — PRINCIPAL RIVERS AND DRAINAGE BASINS

Alaska's largest river is the Yukon, which ranks among the five largest river systems of the North American continent. It drains an area of 330,000 square miles, one-third of which is in Canada. The Alaskan portion of the Yukon drainage basin constitutes roughly 40 percent of the state's land area.

The twelve largest river basins in Alaska, three of which are tributaries of the Yukon River, are listed in the table below, together with their estimated average runoff. These major rivers drain roughly two-thirds of the state. The remainder is drained by thousands of smaller stream systems.

Low-lying areas that drain into the Gulf of Alaska have high unit runoff with relatively little seasonal variation. Annual unit runoff from the mountains adjacent to the Gulf is unusually high — generally exceeding 100 inches, and in some areas exceeding 300 inches. At the other extreme, low runoff rates and short summer runoff seasons are characteristic of the northern areas. From 80 to 95 percent of the annual runoff in the latter areas occurs during the period from May to September.

Along the Gulf of Alaska, streams fed by glaciers exhibit sustained high summer flows and relatively little variation in flow from year to year. The Alaska Range has numerous glaciers, and these dominate the runoff characteristics of the Copper and Susitna River systems and of many Yukon and Kuskokwim tributaries draining the north slopes of the mountains. The glacier-fed streams carry large amounts of sediment.

River	Drainage Area in square miles	Average Annual Runoff in billion gallons per day
Yukon	330,000*	139.5
(Koyukuk)	(32,600)	(20.7)
(Tanana)	(44,500)	(22.0)
(Porcupine)	(46,500)	(12.3)
Kuskokwim	43,600	40.1
Copper	24,400*	34.0
Colville	24,000	7.8
Stikine	19,700*	40.1
Susitna	19,400	27.8
Nushagak	14,100	12.9
Noatak	12,600	6.5
Kobuk	12,000	8.4

*Partly in Canada

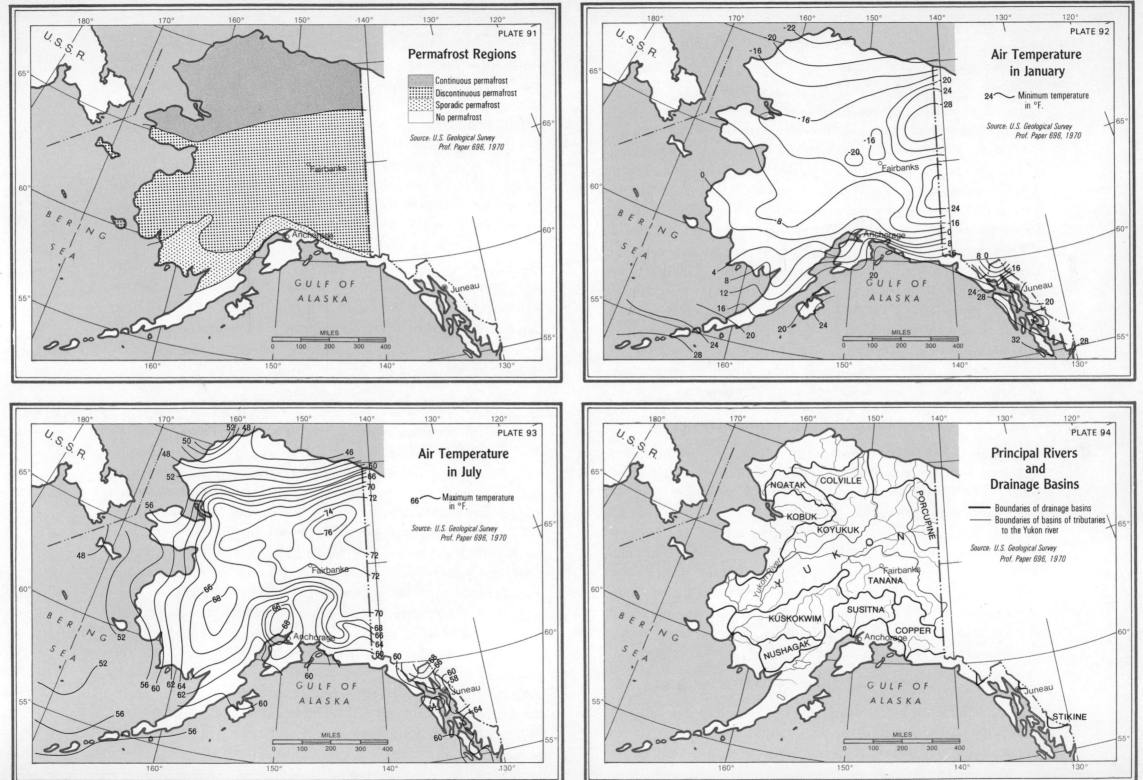

PLATE 91

Permafrost Regions

Continuous permafrost
Discontinuous permafrost
Sporadic permafrost
No permafrost

Source: U.S. Geological Survey
Prof. Paper 696, 1970

U.S.S.R.

BERING SEA

Fairbanks

Anchorage

GULF OF ALASKA

Juneau

MILES
0 100 200 300 400

PLATE 92

Air Temperature in January

24 — Minimum temperature in °F.

Source: U.S. Geological Survey
Prof. Paper 696, 1970

U.S.S.R.

BERING SEA

Fairbanks

Anchorage

GULF OF ALASKA

Juneau

MILES
0 100 200 300 400

PLATE 93

Air Temperature in July

66 — Maximum temperature in °F.

Source: U.S. Geological Survey
Prof. Paper 696, 1970

U.S.S.R.

BERING SEA

Fairbanks

Anchorage

GULF OF ALASKA

Juneau

MILES
0 100 200 300 400

PLATE 94

Principal Rivers and Drainage Basins

— Boundaries of drainage basins
— Boundaries of basins of tributaries to the Yukon river

Source: U.S. Geological Survey
Prof. Paper 696, 1970

U.S.S.R.

NOATAK   COLVILLE
KOBUK
KOYUKUK   PORCUPINE
Y U K O N
Yukon River
Fairbanks
TANANA
KUSKOKWIM   SUSITNA
COPPER
NUSHAGAK   Anchorage

BERING SEA

GULF OF ALASKA

Juneau

STIKINE

MILES
0 100 200 300 400

PLATE 95 — FLOWS OF LARGE RIVERS

The average annual runoff in Alaska is estimated to be 580 bgd (billions of gallons daily), exclusive of an additional 130 billions of gallons daily entering Alaska from Canada. The 580 bgd is equivalent to almost 50 percent of the runoff of the conterminous United States.

Although the stream-gaging network of Alaska is nowhere near as extensive as that of the conterminous United States, runoff from 270,000 square miles, or almost half the area of Alaska, is gaged. The Yukon River, one of the major rivers of North America, is by far the largest in the state, with a discharge of more than four times that of the next largest Alaskan river. At its entrance into the state along the Canadian border, the Yukon has an average flow of 79,000 cfs (a cfs is a cubic foot of water per second, or 7.48 gallons per second) with recorded peak flows of 561,000 cfs. At Kaltag, some 400 miles from its mouth, the average flow of the Yukon is 220,000 cfs with measured peak flows of 1,030,000 cfs. Its average discharge into the Bering Sea is estimated to be 259,000 cfs. Other large rivers are the Copper River, the Kuskokwim River, and the Stikine River.

PLATE 96 — NAVIGABLE INLAND WATERWAYS

The large rivers of Alaska provide excellent navigable waterways to the interior. The map shows the navigable portions of the inland waterways where the controlling depth of water is nine feet.

An estimated 2,000 miles of waterways in the state are navigable, with the Yukon River being the principal route. The rivers provide access to many parts of Alaska where there are no roads or railways. However, owing to the small population and the relatively low level of industrial development, the intensity of use of inland waterways is small. In 1969, for example, total inland waterway commerce was less than 2 million tons. Practically all inland waterway traffic took place in the panhandle region.

PLATE 97 — THERMAL SPRINGS AND VOLCANOES

Hot springs are widely distributed in Alaska. Approximately 80 known springs yield water with temperatures varying from 100 to 212 degrees F., and numerous others yield water with somewhat lower temperatures. Large concentrations of springs are present in the southeastern panhandle area, the Aleutian Islands, the Alaska Peninsula, and the Yukon River valley. The thermal springs in the southeastern part of the state are generally associated with shear zones in granitic rocks. Few hot springs are known in the Alaska Range, although the rocks of that region are intensely folded and faulted. Nearly all hot springs in the Alaska Peninsula and the Aleutian Islands are associated with volcanic rocks, and most of them are near volcanoes that are still active. Thermal springs in the Yukon River basin and on the Seward Peninsula are associated with areas of intrusive rocks of Mesozoic or Tertiary age.

Geothermal resources are largely unexplored, although several areas, especially on the Alaska Peninsula, are of interest. Numerous natural steam jets in the "Valley of Ten Thousand Smokes" near Katmai are indicators of intense thermal activity in this region. Hot springs are of local economic importance in supplying heat for buildings and in providing warm water for irrigation of gardens.

PLATE 98 — GROUND-WATER AREAS

Ground-water conditions are highly variable in Alaska. The principal aquifers are bodies of sand and gravel within the glacial drift that covers the uplands, and in the glacial outwash and alluvial deposits that extend from the uplands into the lowlands. The most productive aquifers are those in the vast Central Plateau where the Yukon and its tributaries have deposited sediments hundreds of feet thick, and in valleys and plains in the Alaska Range. Deposits on the Arctic Slope that would be considered permeable in warmer climates are permanently frozen, and ground water is available only locally beneath or near large bodies of surface water. Productive alluvial deposits are scarce in the southeastern coastal area. The sedimentary and crystalline rocks of the uplands are much less permeable, but are capable of small yields in most places. The presence of permafrost (see Plate 91) complicates ground-water conditions. Unfrozen zones are difficult to locate and often too deep for economical drilling. Once located, completed wells often must be operated continuously so as to prevent freezing.

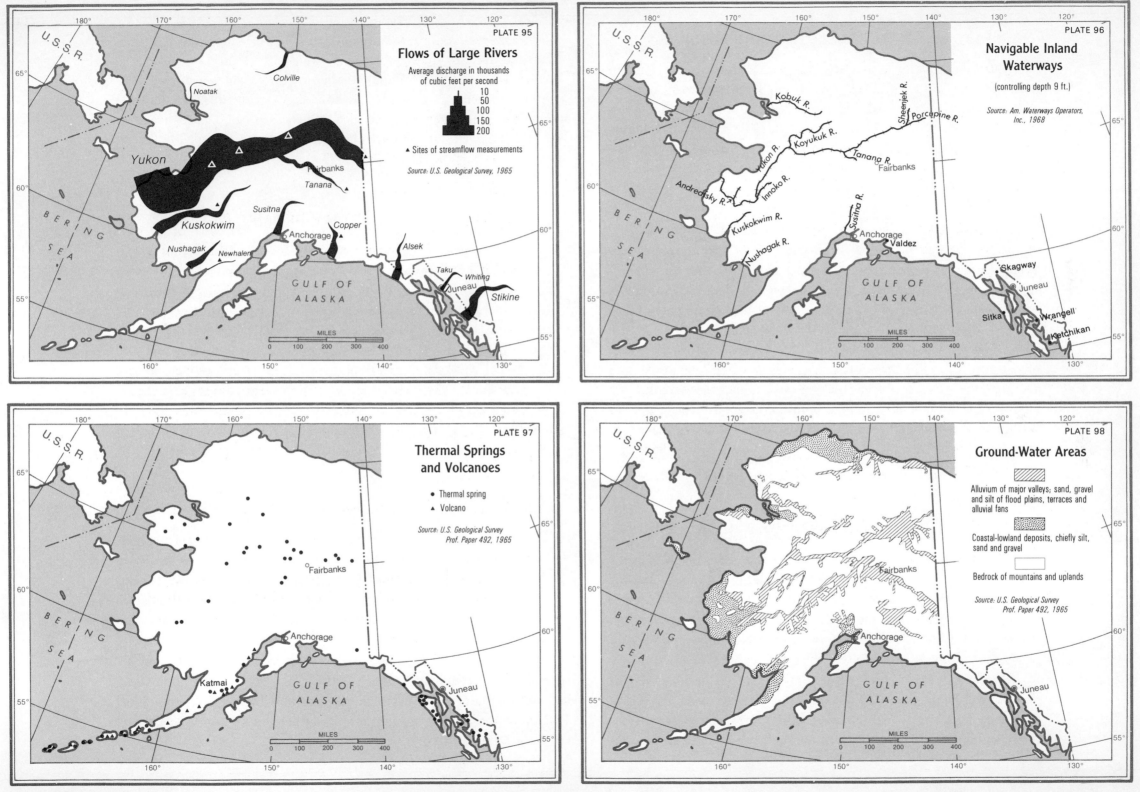

PLATE 95

Flows of Large Rivers

Average discharge in thousands
of cubic feet per second

10
50
100
150
200

▲ Sites of streamflow measurements

Source: U.S. Geological Survey, 1965

PLATE 96

Navigable Inland Waterways

(controlling depth 9 ft.)

*Source: Am. Waterways Operators,
Inc., 1968*

PLATE 97

Thermal Springs and Volcanoes

● Thermal spring
▲ Volcano

*Source: U.S. Geological Survey
Prof. Paper 492, 1965*

PLATE 98

Ground-Water Areas

Alluvium of major valleys; sand, gravel
and silt of flood plains, terraces and
alluvial fans

Coastal-lowland deposits, chiefly silt,
sand and gravel

Bedrock of mountains and uplands

*Source: U.S. Geological Survey
Prof. Paper 492, 1965*

PLATE 99 – WATER POLLUTION AND FISH KILLS

Little information is available on the occurrence of pollution in the waters of Alaska. Pesticides are presumably present in some rivers and streams. Numerous fish samples collected during 1967 and 1968 from the Chena River at Fairbanks and the Kenai River at Soldatna consistently showed the presence of DDT. None of the fish samples, however, exceeded the five ppm (parts per million) interim guideline limit set by the Food and Drug Administration in April, 1969. The probable source of these pesticides is agricultural runoff.

In 1969, fish kills resulting from water pollution were reported in the Swanson River (Kenai Peninsula), in the Sitka area, and in Belkofski Bay at the tip of the Alaska Peninsula. These fish kills destroyed aquatic life along 16 miles of river and 2 miles of shoreline. Fish kills in the Sitka area were caused by effluent from paper mills.

Although Alaska's waters are now predominantly pure, there are several local pollution problems. It is known, for instance, that raw sewage in the greater Anchorage area has polluted Cook Inlet and that the City of Juneau discharges its municipal waste directly into Gastineau Channel. Potential pollution is great in such areas as the Kenai Peninsula, where industrial expansion is taking place rapidly. Very few of the cities and major military installations have adequate treatment plants.

PLATE 100 – PRINCIPAL AREAS OF WATERFOWL AND FISH

The rivers, lakes, and flood plains of Alaska provide habitats for important waterfowl and other game populations. Prime zones for waterfowl are the Arctic Slope, the deltas of the Yukon and Copper Rivers, and the valleys of the Stikine, Koyukuk, Tanana, and Susitna Rivers. The Copper River area supports the largest known population of nesting trumpeter swans in North America.

Alaska has 7.4 million acres of lakes that are productive fish habitats and more than 365,000 miles of streams providing migration, spawning, and growth habitats. Salmon production constitutes the most important instream use of the state's waters. All five species of Pacific salmon are anadromous, that is, they migrate from the sea up the rivers to spawn. Salmon are widely distributed all over the region. In 1966, over 64 million salmon were caught, producing $119 million worth of canned fish. Salmon have narrow tolerance limits in their spawning habitats, and such influences as bed disturbance, oxygen deficiency, temperature changes, and other water-quality factors may cause high mortality.

PLATE 101 – FRESH-WATER DEMAND 1965 – 2000

Projected water demands in Alaska for industry, electric power, and public water supply, based upon anticipated growth, are shown on the adjacent graph. Water requirements for rural, domestic, and irrigation uses were only 18 mgd (millions of gallons daily) in 1965 and are not shown. The increase in industrial water demand reflects projected expansion of industry, mainly in the extraction and processing of Alaska's natural resources (such as fishery, timber, oil, gas, and minerals). The increase in use of public supplies reflects the anticipated growth of population. Hydroelectric power water use (748 mgd in 1965), not shown because it is a nonconsumptive use of water, will increase sharply to some 89,000 mgd by the year 2000.

PLATE 102 – MAJOR POPULATION CENTERS – 1970

Although Alaska covers an area more than double that of Texas, only a small percentage of the United States population resides in the state. According to the 1970 census, a total of 302,173 persons live in Alaska, an increase of 32.8 percent over the 1960 population count. The map shows, by means of shaded circles, the major population centers.

The cities of Fairbanks and Anchorage, together with their immediate surrounding areas, account for 50 percent of the population. Industrial development in the Kenai-Cook Inlet region caused the population in that area to double during the 1960 – 1970 period from 6,097 to 14,250.

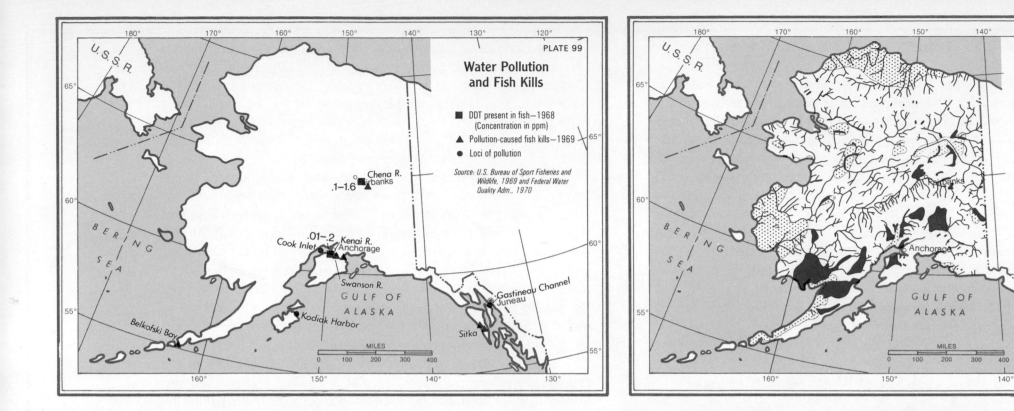

PLATE 99

Water Pollution and Fish Kills

■ DDT present in fish—1968
(Concentration in ppm)
▲ Pollution-caused fish kills—1969
● Loci of pollution

Source: U.S. Bureau of Sport Fisheries and Wildlife, 1969 and Federal Water Quality Adm., 1970

U.S.S.R.

Chena R.
Fairbanks
.1–1.6

B E R I N G S E A

.01–.2 Kenai R.
Cook Inlet Anchorage
Swanson R.
GULF OF ALASKA
Kodiak Harbor
Belkofski Bay
Gastineau Channel
Juneau
Sitka

MILES
0 100 200 300 400

PLATE 100

Principal Areas of Waterfowl and Fish

⬚ Waterfowl areas
◼ Cold water fish areas
✦ Anadromous fish areas

Source: R. A. Cooley, Alaska—a challenge in conservation, 1966

U.S.S.R.

Fairbanks
Anchorage

B E R I N G S E A

GULF OF ALASKA
Juneau

MILES
0 100 200 300 400

PLATE 101

Fresh Water Demand 1965–2000

Source: U.S. Water Resources Council, 1968

Million gallons per day

▤ Public
▥ Steam-electric power
▦ Industrial

1000
750
500
250

1965
32
20
102

1980
120
200
200

2000
230
250
400

PLATE 102

Major Population Centers 1970

Population

● ● ●
2,500 12,500 45,000

Source: Bureau of the Census, 1971

U.S.S.R.

Barrow
Kotzebue
Nome
FAIRBANKS
Bethel

B E R I N G S E A

ANCHORAGE
Kenai Valdez
Homer Cordova
Dillingham
Seward
Kodiak
GULF OF ALASKA
Skagway
Haines
JUNEAU
Sitka Petersburg
Wrangell
Ketchikan

MILES
0 100 200 300 400

PLATE 103 — TEMPERATURE OF SURFACE WATER

The range in the recorded temperatures of surface waters in Alaska is from 32 to 63 degrees F. The coldest waters are on the Arctic Slope, where maximum recorded temperatures are 37 degrees F. In the Yukon subregion, the maximum recorded summer temperature is 66 degrees F., measured on the Chena River near Fairbanks in June. The rivers in this subregion cool uniformly to about 32 degrees F. by October and usually remain at this temperature until late April. The Yukon River itself has a temperature range of 37 to 39 degrees F. during the summer. In the Anchorage area, the range of summer temperatures is from 41 to 54 degrees F. and averages 46 degrees F; the average winter temperature is 33 degrees F. In winter, the cold water is very close to its maximum density and viscosity, which retards physical processes and may affect mixing and sedimentation in water treatment plants.

PLATE 104 — TEMPERATURE OF GROUND WATER

The temperature of ground water in aquifers less than 50 feet below land surface is markedly affected by summertime rates of recharge of warm surface water and by the thickness of the zone of winter freezing. Seasonal variations in ground-water temperatures are out of phase with air temperatures. At Barrow, on the Arctic Slope, for example, the maximum ground-water temperature at a depth of 30 feet lags behind maximum air temperature by five months. In permafrost regions, the temperature of deeper ground water depends on proximity to permafrost zones and on the geothermal gradient of the rocks.

The temperature of water is an extremely important factor in designing water-supply systems in Alaska. Temperature data are needed to determine if continuous pumping or artificial heating is required to prevent freezing of water within wells and water mains.

PLATE 105 — DISSOLVED SOLIDS IN SURFACE WATER

Information on the chemical quality of Alaskan surface water is uneven. In some subregions, periodic sampling programs have been in effect over many years, but in others, only a few miscellaneous samples have been collected. Although the chemical characteristics of water in streams and lakes are variable, the ranges in concentrations are not as large as in the conterminous United States. Most Alaskan streams above tidal reaches contain water of a calcium bicarbonate type, generally containing less than 200 ppm (parts per million) of dissolved solids. The hardness varies with the dissolved-solids content; streams draining the lowlands and intermountain basins usually contain harder water than streams in the higher mountains.

The water in lakes in Alaska is more variable in mineral content than in the rivers. In some mountain lakes, the water is very low in dissolved solids and is similar to rainwater in content. Other lakes occupying lowlands near the sea, including many near the Arctic Slope, become mineralized periodically from salts brought in from the sea by overland flooding during storms or as ocean spray. The water in lakes in the lowlands remote from the seas is often very similar in chemical character to water in adjacent larger rivers.

The map shows the range of dissolved-solids content in the various subregions. Selected values at individual stations are also shown. Regions bordering the Pacific Ocean, especially the panhandle region, have waters with the lowest dissolved-solids concentration.

PLATE 106 — DISSOLVED SOLIDS IN GROUND WATER

Information about the chemical quality of ground water in Alaska is detailed for areas like Anchorage or Juneau but virtually non-existent for other large parts of the state. Analyses indicate that the dissolved solids content ranges from a low of 19 ppm (parts per million) to a high of 64,246 ppm. Most of the sampled ground water contains less than 250 ppm dissolved solids and is considered acceptable for general use. In inland areas, calcium bicarbonate type water or calcium magnesium bicarbonate type water is most common. Water of sodium bicarbonate or sodium chloride type is fairly common in coastal areas. Excessive amounts of iron are present in water from shallow wells. Water from below permafrost zones is variable in composition; some is highly mineralized and of the magnesium sulfide type. Mineralization generally increases with depth.

The map shows representative values or ranges of dissolved-solids content of ground water in the various subregions of the state.

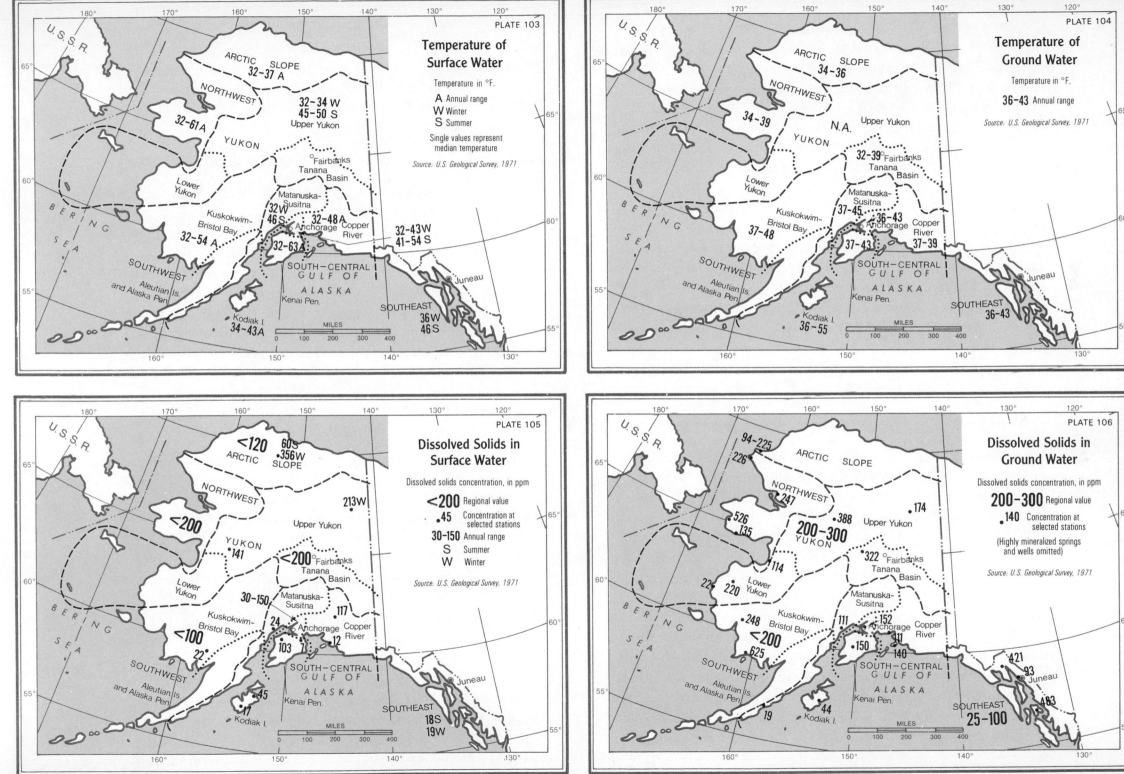

PLATE 103

Temperature of Surface Water

Temperature in °F.

A Annual range
W Winter
S Summer

Single values represent median temperature

Source: U.S. Geological Survey, 1971

U.S.S.R.

ARCTIC SLOPE 32-37 A

NORTHWEST

32-34 W
45-50 S
Upper Yukon

32-61 A

YUKON

Lower Yukon

°Fairbanks
Tanana Basin

Kuskokwim-Bristol Bay

Matanuska-Susitna
32 W
46 S

32-48 A
Anchorage Copper River

32-43 W
41-54 S

32-54 A

32-63 A

BERING SEA

SOUTHWEST
Aleutian Is. and Alaska Pen.

SOUTH-CENTRAL
GULF OF ALASKA
Kenai Pen.

Juneau

SOUTHEAST
36 W
46 S

Kodiak I.
34-43 A

MILES
0 100 200 300 400

PLATE 104

Temperature of Ground Water

Temperature in °F.

36-43 Annual range

Source: U.S. Geological Survey, 1971

U.S.S.R.

ARCTIC SLOPE 34-36

NORTHWEST

N.A.
Upper Yukon

34-39

YUKON

Lower Yukon

32-39 Fairbanks
Tanana Basin

Matanuska-Susitna
37-45

36-43
Anchorage Copper River

37-39

Kuskokwim-Bristol Bay
37-48

37-43

BERING SEA

SOUTHWEST
Aleutian Is. and Alaska Pen.

SOUTH-CENTRAL
GULF OF ALASKA
Kenai Pen.

Juneau

SOUTHEAST
36-43

Kodiak I.
36-55

MILES
0 100 200 300 400

PLATE 105

Dissolved Solids in Surface Water

Dissolved solids concentration, in ppm

<200 Regional value
•45 Concentration at selected stations
30-150 Annual range
S Summer
W Winter

Source: U.S. Geological Survey, 1971

U.S.S.R.

<120
60 S
•356 W
ARCTIC SLOPE

NORTHWEST

<200

213 W

Upper Yukon

YUKON
•141

<200 °Fairbanks
Tanana Basin

Lower Yukon

30-150
Matanuska-Susitna

Kuskokwim-Bristol Bay

24
•117
Anchorage Copper River

<100

22

103
71

12

BERING SEA

SOUTHWEST
Aleutian Is. and Alaska Pen.

SOUTH-CENTRAL
GULF OF ALASKA
Kenai Pen.

•45
17
Kodiak I.

Juneau

SOUTHEAST
18 S
19 W

MILES
0 100 200 300 400

PLATE 106

Dissolved Solids in Ground Water

Dissolved solids concentration, in ppm

200-300 Regional value
•140 Concentration at selected stations

(Highly mineralized springs and wells omitted)

Source: U.S. Geological Survey, 1971

U.S.S.R.

94-225
•226

ARCTIC SLOPE

NORTHWEST
•247

•174

526
•135

200-300
•388 Upper Yukon

YUKON

•114

322 °Fairbanks
Tanana Basin

22
•220
Lower Yukon

Matanuska-Susitna

•248
Kuskokwim-Bristol Bay

111
•152
Anchorage Copper River

311

<200

•150

140

625

•421
•93 Juneau

BERING SEA

SOUTHWEST
Aleutian Is. and Alaska Pen.

SOUTH-CENTRAL
GULF OF ALASKA
Kenai Pen.

44
19
Kodiak I.

SOUTHEAST
25-100

483

MILES
0 100 200 300 400

PLATE 107 — PHYSIOGRAPHY

The Hawaiian archipelago includes 122 islands and extends more than 2,000 miles across the Pacific Ocean. The eight principal islands of the State of Hawaii all lie within the southeast portion of the chain and together account for over 99 percent of the 6,450 square-mile land area of the archipelago. The islands represent the summits of a range of basaltic volcanic mountains that were built over a fissure in the ocean floor. The domes rise from the sea floor at a depth of 15,000 feet to altitudes ranging from as little as 1,280 feet above sea level in Niihau and 1,477 feet in Kahoolawe to 10,025 feet in Maui and 13,784 feet in Hawaii.

Rains and prevailing northeasterly tradewinds have been the dominant factors in weathering and eroding the mountain masses. Slopes on the windward sides are generally steep, with cliffs 2,000 to 3,000 feet high. Deep canyons are present in some places. The leeward sides, with less rainfall and wind, have longer and more gentle slopes. Oahu and Niihau have the only extensive coastal plains.

PLATE 108 — DISTRIBUTION OF PRECIPITATION

Compared with the rainfall regimes of the United States mainland, those of Hawaii are unique. Rainfall gradients are very steep, so that over a distance of three miles, for example, the mean annual rainfall may differ by an amount of 100 inches or more. Rainfall differences from year to year are very great, often exceeding 300 percent. Also, maximum rainfall intensities are very high, with falls of 12 inches or more in a day occurring at least once a year in one part or another of the islands. These highly distinctive rainfall characteristics pose many special problems of water management.

Mean annual rainfall ranges from 6.5 inches at Kawaihae, which is on the leeward side of Mauna Kea on the island of Hawaii, to 461 inches on Mt. Waialeale on Kauai. On each of the six major islands except Lanai, the range is from less than 18 inches to more than 250 inches. On Lanai, the range is from 10 to slightly less than 40 inches.

The median annual rainfall for the Hawaiian Islands is slightly less than 72 inches; in terms of water volume, this represents nearly eight trillion gallons. Median figures, rather than mean or average figures, give a more realistic picture of the precipitation in Hawaii because they are not influenced by infrequent values of very small or very large magnitude.

PLATE 109 — AIR TEMPERATURES — JANUARY AND JULY

The map shows normal daily average air temperatures in four cities during the months of January and July. In general, at elevations below 2,000 feet, the mean temperature for the period May to September is 73 to 78 degrees F., and the mean for October to April is 70 to 75 degrees F., with the higher temperatures being experienced in drier areas. It is very unusual to experience temperatures above 90 degrees F. except in the driest parts of the islands.

The extreme temperatures of record are 100 degrees F. at such dry localities as Kaanapali, Maui, and 18 degrees F. on Mount Haleakala on the same island.

PLATE 110 — SURFACE-WATER RUNOFF

Natural runoff on the islands amounts to 44 inches, or 60 percent of the annual median precipitation, which averages 72 inches. The runoff includes both surface and ground-water discharges, since most of the latter issue at springs near the shore. Approximately 28 percent of the discharge is surface water in streams; 72 percent is ground water, including tidal springs. The heavy rainfall in the mountainous areas of Hawaii produces high rates of runoff in many watersheds.

All of the islands have runoffs of more than 50 percent of precipitation, with both Molokai and Maui showing runoffs exceeding 70 percent. Average annual runoff is lowest on the island of Lanai, owing to the low rainfall there. Average runoff varies from a low of 0.08 bgd (billions of gallons daily) for the island of Lanai to a high of 8.48 bgd for the island of Hawaii. The total average runoff from all the islands is 13.3 bgd.

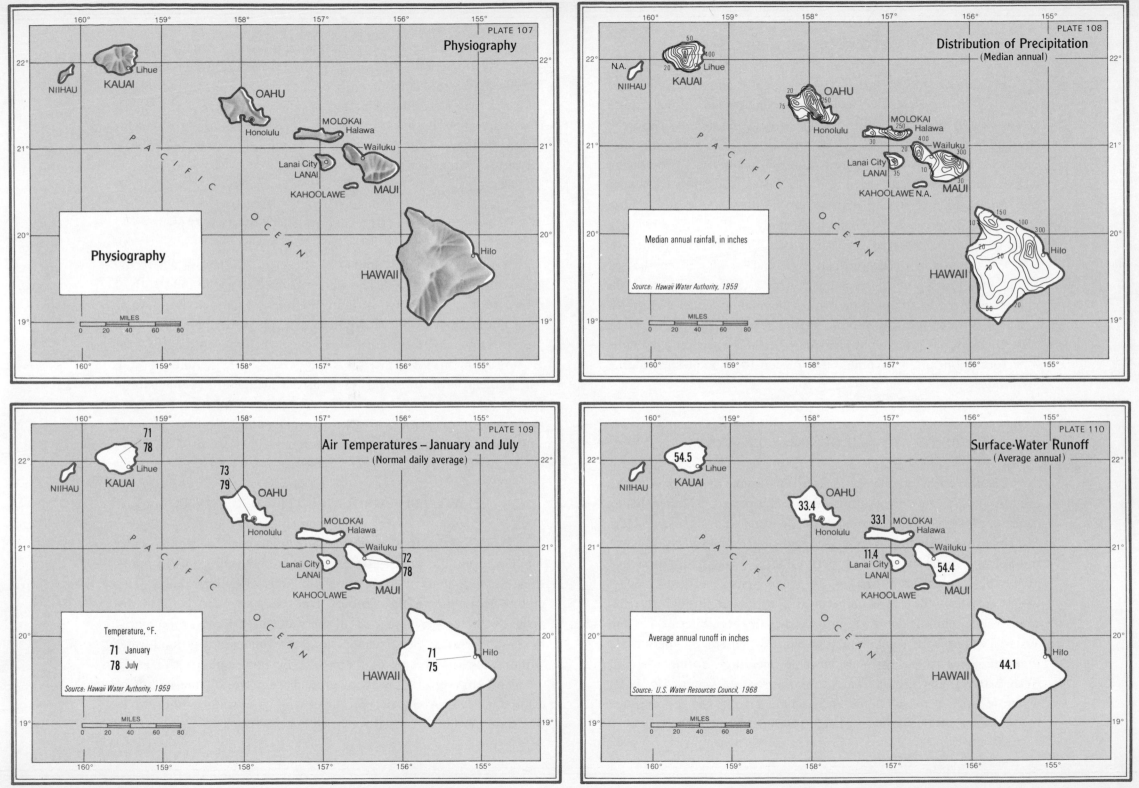

PLATE 107

Physiography

160° 159° 158° 157° 156° 155°

22°   22°

NIIHAU   KAUAI   Lihue

OAHU

Honolulu   MOLOKAI   Halawa

21°   Wailuku   21°

Lanai City   LANAI

KAHOOLAWE   MAUI

Physiography

Hilo

HAWAII

MILES
0 20 40 60 80

160° 159° 158° 157° 156° 155°

PLATE 108

Distribution of Precipitation
(Median annual)

160° 159° 158° 157° 156° 155°

22°   50   22°
N.A.   400
NIIHAU   20   Lihue
KAUAI   20

20   OAHU
75   250
Honolulu   MOLOKAI   250   Halawa
30   400
21°   20   Wailuku   21°
Lanai City   35   300
LANAI   10   30
KAHOOLAWE N.A.   MAUI

Median annual rainfall, in inches   150
100   100
20   300
20°   20   Hilo   20°
HAWAII   20
Source: Hawaii Water Authority, 1959   50
19°   50   20   19°

MILES
0 20 40 60 80

160° 159° 158° 157° 156° 155°

PLATE 109

Air Temperatures – January and July
(Normal daily average)

160° 159° 158° 157° 156° 155°

71
22°   78   22°
NIIHAU   Lihue
KAUAI
73
79
OAHU
Honolulu   MOLOKAI   Halawa
21°   Wailuku   72   21°
Lanai City   78
LANAI
KAHOOLAWE   MAUI

Temperature, °F.

71 January

78 July

71   Hilo
75
Source: Hawaii Water Authority, 1959
HAWAII

MILES
0 20 40 60 80

160° 159° 158° 157° 156° 155°

PLATE 110

Surface-Water Runoff
(Average annual)

160° 159° 158° 157° 156° 155°

22°   54.5   22°
NIIHAU   Lihue
KAUAI

33.4   OAHU
Honolulu   33.1   MOLOKAI   Halawa
21°   Wailuku   21°
11.4   LANAI
Lanai City   54.4
KAHOOLAWE   MAUI

Average annual runoff in inches

20°   44.1   Hilo   20°
HAWAII
Source: U.S. Water Resources Council, 1968
19°   19°

MILES
0 20 40 60 80

160° 159° 158° 157° 156° 155°

PLATE 111 — FLOWS OF PRINCIPAL STREAMS

Because of the mountainous topography and relatively small land areas of the Hawaiian Islands, numerous streams, usually quite steep, extend from the heavy rainfall belts in the mountains to the shoreline at the sea. Hawaii has no large watershed areas with complex stream systems comparable to those in many other parts of the world, but has relatively small drainage basins, consisting usually of only one principal stream with minor tributaries. As most of the streams have only a few branches, generally in their upper reaches, the water, unless diverted for use, quickly finds its way to the sea.

On the island of Hawaii, no perennial streams reach the sea along three-fourths of the coastline, or for a distance of about 225 miles. Water can be found in the stream channels at higher elevations, but it infiltrates into the ground before reaching the coastline. In general, the steep topography, narrow valleys, and generally pervious rock formations are unfavorable for the construction of impounding reservoirs.

PLATE 112 — GROUND-WATER AREAS

Basaltic rocks originating as lava flows make up the bulk of the islands, and are the only aquifers of any importance. Of lesser significance are local alluvial deposits, beach deposits, and some sand, clay, and limestone beds that overlie lava rocks in coastal valleys. Most of the volcanic rocks have a high permeability, owing to the presence of cavities, cracks, and fissures. In many places, vertical "dikes," which are sheets of dense, impermeable rock, cut through the volcanic rocks and divide them into compartments. Where dikes are absent, water from rainfall and streamflow enters the permeable rock, descends to the main water table, and there forms a lens of fresh water (basal ground water) floating on sea water. The basal water is subject to saltwater encroachment from the sea or from below whenever the freshwater head is lowered excessively.

High-level ground water collects in the compartments formed by intersecting dikes. When these reservoirs are full, water will overflow or leak into the next compartment, often in the form of springs visible at high elevations. This high-level ground water in the islands is a great asset because it can be developed economically by means of gravity flow. Many compartments are tapped by wells and tunnels for public water supply and irrigation.

PLATE 113 — THERMAL SPRINGS AND WELLS

Active volcanism is limited to the island of Hawaii, where the great volcanic craters of Kilauea and Mauna Loa are found. Both of these erupt occasionally, with outpourings of molten lava. Apart from the areas of high-level ground water, the water table is, in most places, only a few feet above sea level, so that conventional springs are not common. Eight thermal springs exist on the island of Hawaii. All of them have low yields and variable temperatures that are reported to range from "warm" to "hot". Springs near the craters issue as steam from crevices. Two thermal wells on the islands of Molokai and Maui yield water that ranges in temperature from 93 to 95°F.

PLATE 114 — GROUND-WATER USE — 1970

In 1970, the total ground-water withdrawal for public water supplies, domestic and livestock, irrigation, and self-supplied industrial establishments was 842 mgd (millions of gallons daily). This ground-water use in the various islands is shown on the map, together with the percentage of all the water used that is represented by ground water. Not included in these figures are ground-water withdrawals for cooling of thermoelectric power plants (82 mgd).

The largest withdrawals of ground water are on the islands of Oahu and Maui. About 65 percent of all ground water withdrawn in the State of Hawaii is used for irrigation.

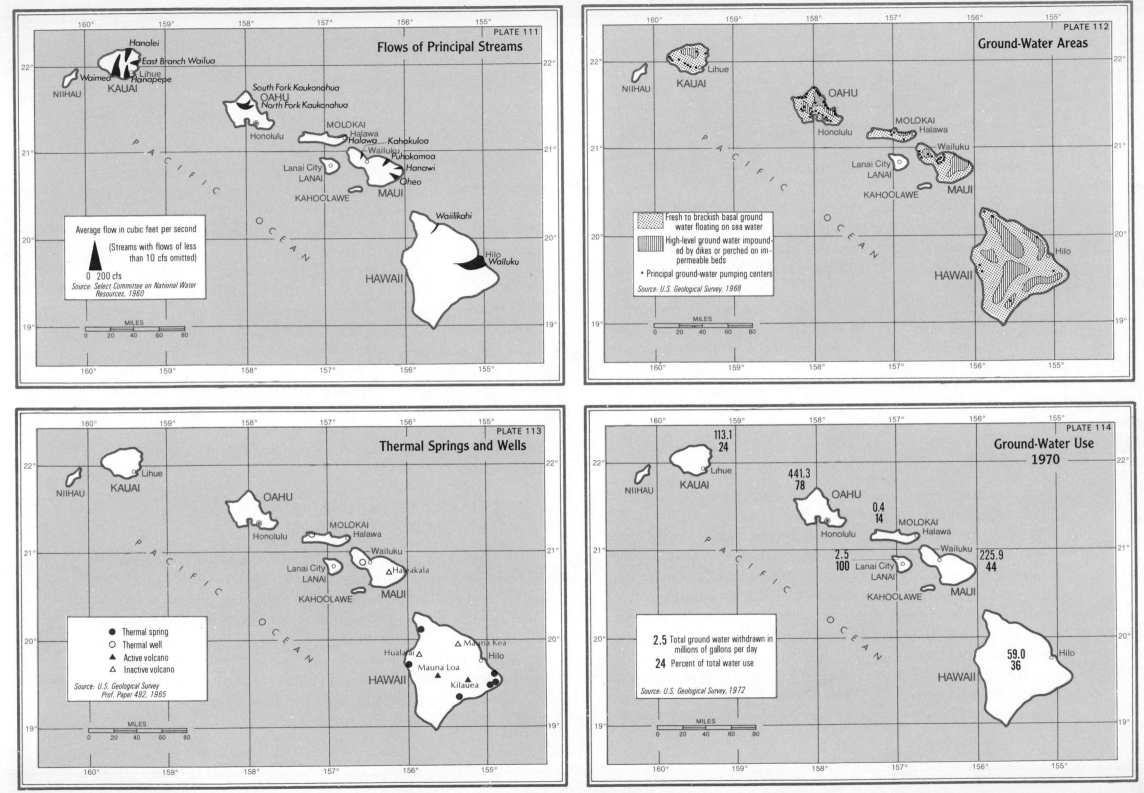

PLATE 111

Flows of Principal Streams

Hanalei
East Branch Wailua
Waimea • Lihue
Hanapepe
KAUAI
NIIHAU

South Fork Kaukonahua
OAHU
North Fork Kaukonahua
Honolulu

MOLOKAI
Halawa
Halawa Kahakuloa
Wailuku
Lanai City Puhokamoa
LANAI Hanawi
Oheo
KAHOOLAWE **MAUI**

Waiilikahi

Hilo
Wailuku

HAWAII

PACIFIC OCEAN

Average flow in cubic feet per second

(Streams with flows of less than 10 cfs omitted)

0   200 cfs

Source: Select Committee on National Water Resources, 1960

MILES
0 20 40 60 80

PLATE 112

Ground-Water Areas

KAUAI
Lihue
NIIHAU

OAHU
Honolulu

MOLOKAI
Halawa
Wailuku
Lanai City
LANAI
KAHOOLAWE **MAUI**

Hilo

HAWAII

PACIFIC OCEAN

Fresh to brackish basal ground water floating on sea water

High-level ground water impounded by dikes or perched on impermeable beds

• Principal ground-water pumping centers

Source: U.S. Geological Survey, 1968

MILES
0 20 40 60 80

PLATE 113

Thermal Springs and Wells

KAUAI
Lihue
NIIHAU

OAHU
Honolulu

MOLOKAI
Halawa
Wailuku
Lanai City
LANAI
△Haleakala
KAHOOLAWE **MAUI**

PACIFIC OCEAN

△ Mauna Kea
Hualalai △
Mauna Loa ▲ ○ Hilo
▲
Kilauea
HAWAII

● Thermal spring
○ Thermal well
▲ Active volcano
△ Inactive volcano

Source: U.S. Geological Survey Prof. Paper 492, 1965

MILES
0 20 40 60 80

PLATE 114

Ground-Water Use
1970

113.1
24
KAUAI
Lihue
NIIHAU

441.3
78
OAHU
0.4
14
Honolulu
MOLOKAI
Halawa
2.5   Wailuku   225.9
100 Lanai City   44
LANAI
KAHOOLAWE **MAUI**

HAWAII
59.0
36
Hilo

PACIFIC OCEAN

2.5 Total ground water withdrawn in millions of gallons per day
24 Percent of total water use

Source: U.S. Geological Survey, 1972

MILES
0 20 40 60 80

PLATE 115 — WASTE DISPOSAL INTO THE SEA

Millions of gallons of untreated or partially treated industrial and municipal wastes enter the coastal waters of the Hawaiian Islands every day. Oil refineries, pineapple canneries, and sugar mills discharge their wastes directly into lagoons connected with the ocean or directly into the ocean. The map shows major points of waste disposal into the sea.

Most of the waste is untreated and is discharged on the assumption that it will be adequately diluted by the surrounding ocean. However, unfavorable coastal and tidal currents have carried polluted water close to beaches, endangering recreational centers and fishing areas.

The Honolulu Division of Sewers alone, serving more than 290,000 people, discharges all sewage directly into the ocean without treatment. Based on the assumption that 50 percent of the per-capita water use of 190 gallons per day passes into sewers, the volume of sewage would amount to over 25 million gallons per day.

PLATE 116 — WITHDRAWAL OF WATER
FOR INDUSTRY — 1970

The map shows how much water is withdrawn by industries that operate their own private water-supply systems. Of a total of 283 mgd (millions of gallons daily) taken by such systems during the year, 170 mgd, or 60 percent, was obtained from ground-water sources. Water used by industries supplied by municipal water systems is not included in this tabulation nor is the water used by steam and hydroelectric power plants. Industrial use of water is primarily for milling sugar, processing pineapples and other food products, and manufacturing.

About 332 mgd was used for hydroelectric power generation at small-capacity plants; the locations of these plants are shown on the map. Most of these plants are operated by sugar plantations for their own use. Steam-electric power plants used 985 mgd of water for cooling purposes; practically all of this was sea water.

PLATE 117 — WITHDRAWAL OF WATER
FOR IRRIGATION — 1970

By far the largest withdrawal of water on the islands is for irrigation. In 1970, a total of 1,284 mgd (millions of gallons daily) of water was used, an amount equivalent to 75 percent of all the water withdrawn in the State of Hawaii for all purposes (except thermoelectric and hydroelectric power generation).

The map shows the areas and acreage irrigated on the islands as well as the total amounts of water withdrawn for irrigation. The rates of use differ considerably from island to island, due partly to variations in climate, soil conditions, and management, but mainly to differences in crop requirements. Sugar-cane irrigation requires from 2.6 to 3.3 millions of gallons per acre per year and truck crops require from about 0.5 to 1 million gallons per acre per year. By contrast, pineapples need only about 160,000 gallons per acre per year. Of the total amount of water withdrawn for irrigation, 47 percent originated as surface water and 53 percent was derived from ground-water sources.

PLATE 118 — WITHDRAWAL OF WATER
FOR PUBLIC SUPPLIES — 1970

In 1970, public water supply systems served 694,000 people in the State of Hawaii. The total water withdrawn by these systems was 137 mgd (millions of gallons daily). Ninety-two percent of this water, or 125 mgd, came from ground-water sources and the remainder from surface waters.

Per-capita water withdrawal on a statewide basis was 197 gallons per day, but this varied from island to island, from a high of 279 gallons per day on Kauai to a low of 142 gallons per day on the island of Hawaii.

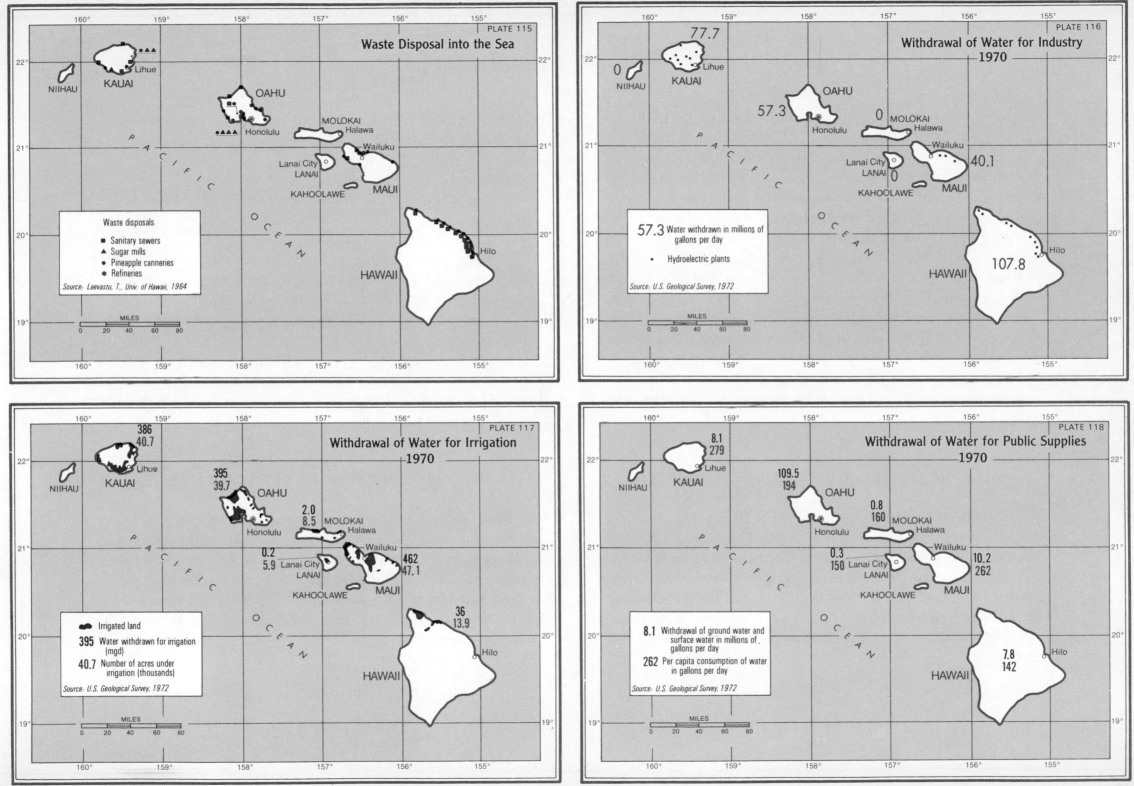

PLATE 115

Waste Disposal into the Sea

NIIHAU
KAUAI — Lihue
OAHU — Honolulu
MOLOKAI — Halawa
Wailuku
Lanai City — LANAI
KAHOOLAWE
MAUI
HAWAII — Hilo

PACIFIC OCEAN

Waste disposals
■ Sanitary sewers
▲ Sugar mills
● Pineapple canneries
✱ Refineries

Source: Laevastu, T., Univ. of Hawaii, 1964

MILES
0 20 40 60 80

PLATE 116

Withdrawal of Water for Industry
1970

77.7
0 NIIHAU
KAUAI — Lihue
57.3 OAHU — Honolulu
0 MOLOKAI — Halawa
Wailuku
Lanai City — LANAI 0
40.1
KAHOOLAWE MAUI
107.8 HAWAII — Hilo

PACIFIC OCEAN

57.3 Water withdrawn in millions of gallons per day
● Hydroelectric plants

Source: U.S. Geological Survey, 1972

MILES
0 20 40 60 80

PLATE 117

Withdrawal of Water for Irrigation
1970

386
40.7
NIIHAU
KAUAI — Lihue
395
39.7 OAHU — Honolulu
2.0
8.5 MOLOKAI — Halawa
Wailuku
0.2 462
5.9 Lanai City — LANAI 47.1
KAHOOLAWE MAUI
36
13.9
HAWAII — Hilo

PACIFIC OCEAN

🖤 Irrigated land
395 Water withdrawn for irrigation (mgd)
40.7 Number of acres under irrigation (thousands)

Source: U.S. Geological Survey, 1972

MILES
0 20 40 60 80

PLATE 118

Withdrawal of Water for Public Supplies
1970

8.1
279
NIIHAU
KAUAI — Lihue
109.5
194 OAHU — Honolulu
0.8
160 MOLOKAI — Halawa
Wailuku
0.3
150 Lanai City — LANAI
10.2
262
KAHOOLAWE MAUI
7.8
142
HAWAII — Hilo

PACIFIC OCEAN

8.1 Withdrawal of ground water and surface water in millions of gallons per day
262 Per capita consumption of water in gallons per day

Source: U.S. Geological Survey, 1972

MILES
0 20 40 60 80

PLATE 119 – FRESH-WATER DEMAND 1965-2000

Projections of future water demand on the islands are based on the assumption that present economic and population trends will continue. The projected water requirements for irrigation, public water supplies, and self-supplied industry are shown on the graph, and indicate that the total water use for these three sectors will increase from 1.4 bgd (billions of gallons per day) used in 1965 to 2.5 bgd in the year 2000.

Water requirements for hydroelectric (not available) and steam-electric power generation (mostly sea water) are not shown. Rural domestic requirements and livestock requirements are extremely small and also have been omitted. Actually, rural domestic water use will decrease as community water-supply systems are enlarged. Projected increases for irrigation are based primarily on expanding cultivation of sugar cane.

PLATE 120 – DISTRIBUTION OF POPULATION – 1970

In 1970, the population of the State of Hawaii (including military personnel) was 768,560. The populations of the individual islands and the densities of populations per square mile are shown on the map. Eighty-two percent of the total population was on the island of Oahu, which has a high density of over 1,000 persons per square mile. Nearly half of the Oahu population resided in the Honolulu metropolitan area, which had a population of 324,870 in 1970.

Projections indicate that the population of the state will increase to 1,086,000 in 1980 and 1,680,000 in the year 2000.

PLATE 121 – DISSOLVED SOLIDS IN PUBLIC WATER SUPPLIES

The map shows the range in dissolved-solids content of selected public water supplies. No distinction is made between surface-water and ground-water sources. Surface-water supplies would be characterized by lower amounts of dissolved solids than ground-water supplies.

In 1962, the well fields that supplied the Honolulu municipal system yielded water having a dissolved-solids content that ranged from 184 to 251 ppm (parts per million). Except for chlorination, this water was not treated.

PLATE 122 – HARDNESS OF PUBLIC WATER SUPPLIES

Most of the water distributed by municipal water-supply systems is soft or only moderately hard, and does not require softening. A discussion of the meaning of hardness of water is given in the text accompanying Plate 41. Surface-water supplies generally have a lower hardness than ground-water supplies. In 1962, the water distributed by the Honolulu municipal system had a hardness ranging from 42 to 70 ppm (parts per million).

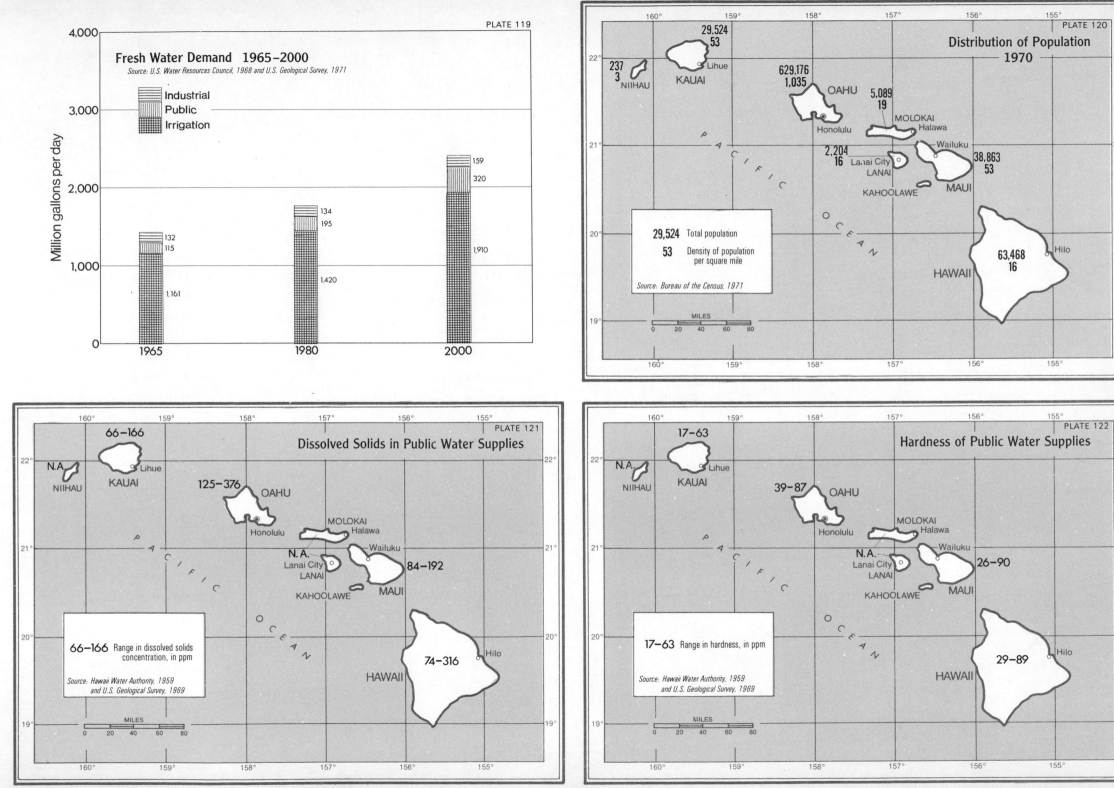

PLATE 119

Fresh Water Demand 1965–2000

Source: U.S. Water Resources Council, 1968 and U.S. Geological Survey, 1971

Industrial
Public
Irrigation

Million gallons per day

1965:
132
115
1,161

1980:
134
195
1,420

2000:
159
320
1,910

PLATE 120

Distribution of Population
1970

NIIHAU 237 3

KAUAI 29,524 53 Lihue

OAHU 629,176 1,035 Honolulu

MOLOKAI 5,089 19 Halawa

LANAI 2,204 16 Lanai City

MAUI 38,863 53 Wailuku

KAHOOLAWE

HAWAII 63,468 16 Hilo

29,524 Total population

53 Density of population per square mile

Source: Bureau of the Census, 1971

MILES 0 20 40 60 80

PLATE 121

Dissolved Solids in Public Water Supplies

NIIHAU N.A.

KAUAI 66–166 Lihue

OAHU 125–376 Honolulu

MOLOKAI Halawa

LANAI N.A. Lanai City

MAUI 84–192 Wailuku

KAHOOLAWE

HAWAII 74–316 Hilo

66–166 Range in dissolved solids concentration, in ppm

Source: Hawaii Water Authority, 1959 and U.S. Geological Survey, 1969

MILES 0 20 40 60 80

PLATE 122

Hardness of Public Water Supplies

NIIHAU N.A.

KAUAI 17–63 Lihue

OAHU 39–87 Honolulu

MOLOKAI Halawa

LANAI N.A. Lanai City

MAUI 26–90 Wailuku

KAHOOLAWE

HAWAII 29–89 Hilo

17–63 Range in hardness, in ppm

Source: Hawaii Water Authority, 1959 and U.S. Geological Survey, 1969

MILES 0 20 40 60 80